W9-CZT-873

UNIVERSITY OF WINNIPEG
LIBRARY
DISCARDED
515 Portage Avenue
Winnipeg, Manitoba R3B 2E9

RALPH WALDO
EMERSON

The GREAT AMERICAN THINKERS *Series*

GEORGE BANCROFT • *Russel B. Nye*
JOHN C. CALHOUN • *Richard N. Current*
JOHN DEWEY • *Richard J. Bernstein*
JONATHAN EDWARDS • *Alfred Owen Aldridge*
RALPH WALDO EMERSON • *Warren Staebler*
BENJAMIN FRANKLIN • *Ralph L. Ketcham*
ALEXANDER HAMILTON • *Stuart Gerry Brown*
WILLIAM JAMES • *Edward Carter Moore*
THOMAS JEFFERSON • *Stuart Gerry Brown*
JAMES MADISON • *Neal Riemer*
CHARLES PEIRCE • *Thomas S. Knight*
JOSIAH ROYCE • *Thomas F. Powell*
GEORGE SANTAYANA • *Willard E. Arnett*
HENRY DAVID THOREAU • *James G. Murray*
THORSTEIN VEBLEN • *Douglas Dowd*
JOHN WOOLMAN • *Edwin H. Cady*
CHAUNCEY WRIGHT • *Edward Madden*

IN PREPARATION

HENRY ADAMS • *James Murray*
JOHN ADAMS • *Edward Handler*
FELIX ADLER • *Robert S. Guttchen*
AMERICAN LIBERALISM • *William Gerber*
PERCY BRIDGMAN • *Harold Allen*
RUDOLPH CARNAP • *Albert Blumberg*
NOAM CHOMSKY • *Justin Leiber*
MORRIS COHEN • *Marvin Kohl*
J. K. GALBRAITH • *John Gambs*
HENRY GEORGE • *Jacob Oser*
JOHN F. KENNEDY • *Peter J. Schwab*
HORACE MANN • *Americo D. Lapati*
HERBERT MARCUSE • *Karsten and Paula Struhl*
C. WRIGHT MILLS • *Howard Press*
THEODORE PARKER • *Arthur W. Brown*
WILHELM REICH • *Robert Pasotti and John Bell*
THEODORE ROOSEVELT • *William Harbaugh*
GEORGE SANTAYANA • *Willard E. Arnett*
ISRAEL SCHEFFLER • *Bertram Bandman*
ROY WOOD SELLARS • *W. Preston Warren*
B. F. SKINNER • *John A. Weigel*
TRANSCENDENTALISM • *Donald Koster*
FREDERICK JACKSON TURNER • *Wilbur R. Jacobs*
ALFRED NORTH WHITEHEAD • *Nathaniel Lawrence*
WOODROW WILSON • *Milton S. Gurvitz*

PS
1631
.S48

RALPH WALDO EMERSON

Warren Staebler
Professor of English
Earlham College

✷

SERIES EDITORS

Arthur W. Brown, Ph.D.
President, Marygrove College; and

Thomas S. Knight, Ph.D.
Professor and Chairman of the
Department of Philosophy, Adelphi University

Twayne Publishers, Inc.   ::   New York

All Rights Reserved

Copyright © 1973 by Twayne Publishers, Inc.

Library of Congress Catalog Card Number: 79-161813

For Patricia, also a celebrant of life

MANUFACTURED IN THE UNITED STATES OF AMERICA

Contents

Foreword

This book is an introduction to Ralph Waldo Emerson, dealing critically with certain facts of his life and times, distinctive qualities of his character and style of living, and salient features of his thought in relation to various strains of thought which have influenced the growth of America. In his genius Emerson was as many-sided as he was brilliant—at once prose essayist and poet, preacher and metaphysician, child of the eighteenth century and of the nineteenth, Classicist and Romanticist, admirer of the ancients and prophet of moderns, eclectic quoter and original phrase-maker, in this world but not wholly of it. Reading life through the eye of a poet and the affections of a saint, he wedded the esthetic and the spiritual with a moral imagination possessed by few other American writers. Platonist, he invested the elements of experience of modern man with the right quality of otherworldly significance. Believer in ecstasy, he lifted the obscuring veil of familiarity from the homeliest of things in daily life and laid bare the beauty at their heart. Champion of individualism and self-reliance, he infused manhood into his readers with a prose whose music, like that of Satan's instruments in Milton's Hell, "instead of rage/Deliberate valour breathed." Mystic, he developed his religious views beyond the confines of ecclesiastical Christianity to reconcile the evolutionary principle of modern science with the idea of divinity. Nationalist thinker, he was led by his catholic sympathies embracing oriental studies straight to internationalism and opened, perhaps before any other American thinker, the vision of one world, with humanity standing above all nations.

I have adopted no particular point of view toward Emerson save one of admiration and have no new thesis to advance regarding him. Many attitudes toward him over the years have been expressed, and in many ways his "essence" has been revealed. I would be happy if my volume, at once wide-ranging and concentrated, attracted readers back to Emerson's writings. I say "wide-ranging," but I should add that although I want to cast the lance far, I am concerned that it be my lance and that its point be sharp: I want for my study both breadth and bite. I have drawn a profile of Emerson's character and mind, to disclose a figure of singular light, courage, and germinal potency, about whom I think there is popular misunderstanding today.

In this venture my indebtedness to other scholars is so enormous that I could never circumscribe it. I am indebted in some respect to everything about Emerson I have seen in print, to everything I have heard.

Earlham College
Richmond, Indiana

WARREN STAEBLER

Acknowledgments

I am grateful to my wife above all and to my friends and former colleagues, Professor Emeritus Robert Almy of Miami University and Professor Emeritus Frank Davidson of Indiana University, for their critical reading of the manuscript.

It pleases me to thank my colleagues of the Lilly Library of Earlham College and the administrators and staff workers of the Widener and Houghton Libraries at Harvard University for their many courtesies to me as I used their books.

I should also like to express my gratitude to the following publishers for permission to quote miscellaneous passages from the following works:

Beacon Press, Boston, Massachusetts, for phrases from Theodore Parker's "Emerson" in *The American Scholar,* 1907.

Columbia University Press, New York, N.Y., for lines from *Emerson on Race and History* by Philip L. Nicoloff, 1961. *The Letters of Ralph Waldo Emerson,* edited by Ralph L. Rusk, 1939. *The Life of Ralph Waldo Emerson* by Ralph L. Rusk, 1949. *The Correspondence of Emerson and Carlyle,* edited by Joseph Slater, 1964.

Dodd, Mead & Company for sentences from *On Emerson and Other Essays* by Maurice Maeterlinck, 1912.

Doubleday & Company for sentences from *The American Puritans* by Perry Miller, 1956.

Farrar, Straus & Cudahy for a paragraph from *On Poetry and Poets* by T. S. Eliot, 1957.

Harper & Row, Publishers, Incorporated for a phrase originally from Henry James's *The American Scene* but cited by Matthiessen in his *The James Family,* 1948.

Harvard University Press, Cambridge, Mass., for lines from *Emerson's Plutarch* by Edmund Berry, 1961. *Emerson and Asia* by Frederick Ives Carpenter, 1930. *Our First Love,* edited by Edith W. Gregg, 1962 (The Belknap Press of the Harvard University Press).

Holt, Rinehart and Winston, Inc., for sentences from *Characters and Events by John Dewey,* 1929.

Houghton Mifflin Company, Boston, Mass., for sections from *The Complete Works of Ralph Waldo Emerson,* 1903-4. *The Journals of Ralph Waldo Emerson,* 1909-14. *A Memoir of Ralph Waldo Emerson* by J. E. Cabot, 1887. *American Criticism* by Norman Foerster, 1928. *Correspondence Between Ralph Waldo Emerson and Herman Grimm* by F. V. Hollis, 1903. *Young Emerson Speaks* by A. M. McGiffert, 1938.

Oxford University Press, New York, N.Y., for phrases from *American Renaissance* by F. O. Matthiessen, 1941.

Prentice-Hall, Inc., Englewood Cliffs, N.J., for phrases from *Emerson: A Collection of Critical Essays,* edited by M. Konvitz and S. Whicher, 1962.

Random House, Inc., for sentences from *Utopian Essays and Practical Proposals* by Paul Goodman, 1962.

Charles Scribner's Sons, New York, N.Y., for phrases from *Emerson and Other Essays* by John Jay Chapman, 1898. *The Nature and Destiny of Man* by Reinhold Niebuhr, 1955.

University of California Press, Berkeley, Cal., for phrases from *Emerson and Greenough. Transcendental Pioneers of an American Aesthetic* by Charles R. Metzger, 1954.

By permission of the Trustees of the R. W. Emerson Memorial Association and the Harvard College Library, I am also able to quote various lines from certain Emerson manuscript materials.

The Princeton Alumni Weekly, Princeton, N.J., has generously given me permission to quote several sentences from its issue of May 16, 1967.

Legend for Footnote References
of Quotations

C   Cabot, James Elliot: *A Memoir of Ralph Waldo Emerson.*
Car   Carpenter, Frederic Ives: *Emerson and Asia.*
Cn   Cameron, Kenneth Walter: *Emerson The Essayist.*
D   Dewey, John: "Ralph Waldo Emerson" in *Characters and Events.*
EL   *The Early Lectures of Ralph Waldo Emerson.*
G   Gonnaud, Maurice: *Individu et Société dans l'Oeuvre de Ralph Waldo Emerson.*
H   Houghton Library Manuscript Material.
HJ   James, Henry: "Emerson" in *Partial Portraits.*
Ho   Holmes, Oliver Wendell: *Ralph Waldo Emerson.*
J   *The Journals of Ralph Waldo Emerson.*
KW   Konvitz, Milton and Whicher, Stephen (editors): *Emerson.*
L   *The Letters of Ralph Waldo Emerson.*
Mat   Matthiessen, F. O.: *The James Family.*
N   Nicoloff, Philip L.: *Emerson on Race and History.*
TUE   *Two Unpublished Essays.*
W   *The Complete Works of Ralph Waldo Emerson.*
Wo   Woodbury, George Edward: *Ralph Waldo Emerson.*

Works not listed in the Bibliography and only incidentally
quoted from in this Book yet figuring in the legend:

TSE   Eliot, T. S.: "Milton II" in *On Poetry and Poets,* Farrar, Straus & Cudahy, New York, N.Y., 1957.
PG   Goodman, Paul: *Utopian Essays and Practical Proposals,* Vintage Books, Alfred Knopf, N.Y., 1964.

PM   Miller, Perry: *The American Puritans: Their Prose and Poetry*, Doubleday, Garden City, N.Y., 1956.

RN   Niebuhr, Reinhold: *The Nature and Destiny of Man*, Charles Scribner's Sons, New York, N.Y., 1955.

PAL   *The Princeton Alumni Weekly*, Princeton, N.J., May 16, 1967.

CHAPTER 1

The Man and His Era

L IKE various other intellectuals of his time, Ralph Waldo Emerson, born in Boston on May 25, 1803, was one of many children in the family of a clergyman. His father, William Emerson, marked only one of a half dozen successive generations during which Emersons had been preachers of the Word. The William Emerson before him, Ralph Waldo's grandfather and builder of the famous Old Manse, occupied a pulpit in Concord near Boston at the time of the outbreak of the Revolutionary War. When the minutemen gathered to oppose the British redcoats at the rude bridge that arched the flood—his wife holding the children at an upstairs window to watch what was going on— it was he who steeled their nerves with fervent words before they fired the shot heard round the world. Later he enlisted in the army as chaplain but died of illness before the cause was won.

On his mother's side Emerson's forebears were said to have been more worldly, practical persons close to business and the workaday town. Yet although he inherited features of her strain it was his father whom he more resembled, a man of special personal attractiveness, given to liberal theological views, a lover of books and founder of libraries, a member of the Massachusetts Historical Society, an aspirant writer, an amateur maker of music, and not only a patron of the arts, but, eager to assist in the advancement of Boston, also a contributor to their vitality; for six years, in company with distinguished thinkers and literary figures, he edited *The Monthly Anthology,* whose brief flourishing marked an epoch in the early cultural life of the nation.

William Emerson, however, died prematurely in 1811, at the age of forty-two. His widow, left with a family of six children to support, compensated for the lack of a patrimony by taking in boarders and raising her boys with a frugal discipline. The family was poor but not destitute; all the children, as their age allowed, had regular tasks assigned at home. It was a classic example of plain living and high thinking. Mrs. Emerson being a woman of taste and standards, the house was never without books, drawn from subscription lending libraries, and her sons were educated not only at the Boston Latin School but at Harvard College in Cambridge as well, already far along toward its two hundredth year and no less a fixture in the history of the Emersons than the ministry which followed it. As the sons became young men they immediately, and proudly, assumed the responsibility of helping their mother meet her increasing expenses, earning the money not only to pay off the debts from their own schooling but also to make the way clearer for their brothers who followed.

Harvard College, which Emerson entered in 1817, was, in spite of occasional outbursts of student rowdyism and intermittent town-gown tensions, a moral community and with stern paternalism did not allow undergraduates to forget that fact. Each day started with prayers at six o'clock. No young man could take a meal in any eating establishment off the grounds without being accompanied by a parent or relative and without official permission; nor could he anywhere during the term take part in, have association with, or be a spectator at a theatrical performance of any kind. Yet the college aimed also to be an intellectual community and, in spite of what nowadays would seem very meager resources, provided an intellectual atmosphere of sorts. It offered the student at least the chance to be often by himself to read or think independently. Later in life Emerson considered a room of one's own the most precious feature of a college experience. Although he often said that a college education was valuable only in revealing that it had no value, he believed that unless a young man had the chance to serve an apprenticeship under a great master or go on an exploring expedition around the world, the right place for him, with his moderate abilities and average circumstance, was college, where he could encounter books and conversation.

Emerson's years at Harvard, 1817-21, were those of his middle teens, for he was only eighteen when he was graduated. The curriculum he followed was largely Classical and unchanged from that of the eighteenth century; at one point in his sophomore year he was dividing his time among Greek, Latin (Tacitus and Cicero), geometry, logic, and English rhetoric. To professors who were learned and eloquent he reacted with ardor. Although he was not a joiner, he had several happy undergraduate associations. With some friends he contributed to a small private fund for the purchase of subscriptions to various English journals and to the *North American Review* then new. In his sophomore year he met periodically with friends in their dormitory rooms to discuss such issues as whether poetry had been beneficial to morality, whether the conduct of the United States toward the Indians could be reconciled with the principles of justice and humanity, and whether love or ambition was the stronger passion.

Emerson was proud of his kin and of the claim to distinction of the family name. That he and his three brothers, tied to one another in strong affection, had all been born to do uncommon things, they each believed. Yet the fame they sought must be in pursuits of benefit to mankind. Emerson took himself to task again and again, however, for being "idle, vagrant, stupid, and hollow." Gratitude flooded him when he encountered eloquence such as that of the great Unitarian preacher Dr. William Ellery Channing, the swift contagion of whose mind, stimulating "the young to purposes of great and awful effort," revived his spirit.

Emerson's academic record at Harvard was not one of distinction. He ranked at graduation thirtieth in a class of fifty-nine. Slow in maturing, much inferior in performance to his brothers, he was more interested in literature than in any of his regular classroom studies. Of the various characters who influenced the world—conqueror, statesman, reformer, poet—the poet was to him greatest; and he spent much of his free time in the practice, begun several years before, of writing verses, often interlarding his letters with improvised rhymes. He read a good deal and was groping toward a taste. He loved Bacon for his concentration and sententiousness, Milton for his music and noble thought, and Shakespeare for his vitality and splendor, although he regretted that since what was painted by Shakespeare was nature not in the purity of its original state but in its subsequent depravity, the plays could only tend to deprave. The vogue for Scott and Byron the young man shared; in his senior year he was recommending the Third Canto of Byron's *Childe Harold* as the most beautiful poetry he had ever read. In fact, if he were situated

"like Lord Byron and some other British poets," he declared in
1818 with freshman affectation, "he would cultivate Poetry and
endeavor to propitiate the muses," but in the United States where
one was "obliged to study his profession for assistance in living"
and where so little encouragement was given to poets, it was
"a pretty poor trade." Nevertheless, he continued to write poetry,
making special efforts for several special collegiate occasions.
He was asked to be class poet, but since a half dozen others
had already said no to the same invitation, the honor was dubious.
His attention to the language of poetry grew steadily sharper;
he kept lists of "phrases poetical" for use and found stimulation
in Ben Jonson's vigorous lines and "quaint, peculiar words."

But his most substantial achievement at Harvard was not in
original verse. Nor was it in his part in the Commencement ex-
ercises, in which he spoke for John Knox in a "conference"
(termed by him "stupid") along with classmates who defended
other famous religious thinkers. It was in his contributions, as
both junior and senior, to the Bowdoin Prize Competition for
dissertations. Although neither of his efforts, "The Character of
Socrates" and "The Present State of Ethical Philosophy," won
first prize, they show that what he was capable of in the way of
intellectual effort when only seventeen and eighteen was com-
mendable.

The circumstances of Emerson's family upon his graduation
remained unchanged. Solicitous of his mother's state, for the next
several years he occupied various positions as schoolmaster. He
suffered under the tedium of his situations and was humiliated
by his immaturity and wrong temperament. Still harboring
"dream-like anticipations of greatness," he concluded that one
had "better tug at the oar, dig the mine, or saw wood; better
sow hemp, or hang with it, than sow the seeds of instruction"
(L, I, 105, 6). In winter he resented being the prisoner of a "hot,
steaming, stoved, stinking, dirty, A-B spelling-room" and was
grateful if at the end of the day he could find a field in which
to soar and mount the atmosphere.

Emerson in the early 1820's, looking in perplexity at his times,
was tempted to call them times of psychological war. "A thousand religions" were in arms, and systems of education were
contesting. Every thoughtful young man must be besieged by a
chaos of doubts. Should he read or think? The wise did not

know. Should he choose solitude or active life? The wise could give no answer. From the vast amount of matter what should he read—history (what has been) or morals (what ought to be)? No one could give the resolving word. Nor was there any to the questions whether a specialized was better than a generalized preparation, whether an adherence to rules was more profitable than originality, and whether reason made a richer life than fancy. What was needed, the young man exclaimed, was a reform in education. "Teach us no more arts, but how those which are already should be learned" (J, I, 344).

He had moments of disturbing doubt about himself. He was, he believed, ungenerous and selfish, cautious and cold, without even the kind affections of a pigeon, and he was still the victim of indolence. Yet he remained devoted to the pursuit of fame and greatness.

Emerson was not only a Christian; he was an American. At the disclosure of some small scandals in 1822 he renewed his hope that the experiment made by America, of men governing themselves, would not fail through "too much knowledge and too much liberty" making them mad. Thinking about such matters, appropriately on the eve of the Fourth of July, "our great national anniversary," he wished for some way in which the government could be in wholesome relation to the everyday life of citizens, for, as it was, it seemed to be real to them only on festivals, when it bore "the form of a kind of General Committee for popular amusements." He loved the freedom of opinion and action to be found in America, its equality of opportunity, and in terms strongly Jeffersonian, celebrated it as

the only [land] where freedom has not degenerated to licentiousness; in whose well-ordered districts education and intelligence dwell with good morals; whose rich estates peacefully descend from sire to son, without the shadow of an interference from private violence, or public tyranny; whose offices of trust and seats of science are filled by minds of republican strength and elegant accomplishments. (J, I, 161-62)

Xenophon and Thucydides would have thought this achievement worthier of their powers than Persia or Greece, and in the American Revolution Plutarch would have found a gallery of heroes. If the Constitution survived a century, it would be a

wonderful omen to the human race, for it would mean that
utopian dreams had been outdone by reality.

Emerson viewed with elation the contemporaneous struggles
for liberation in South America. In a few years the histories of
Greece and Rome would be forgotten, and the new empires of
the West would have their Caesars, Cleopatras, and Alexanders.
Yet the great idea of democracy was too often dangerously
travestied by brutish forms. The expansion of the frontier in
the United States was fraught with peril, for many pioneers were
the licentious "off-scouring of civilized society." Would the federal government have enough men of mind and character to
pass and enforce right laws on the frontier however far from
Washington it moved? It would be a disaster to history if "this
new storehouse of nations" should "pour out upon the world an
accursed tribe of barbarous robbers." Furthermore, the governments of the individual states-to-come would need to be strong:
"if the senates that shall meet hereafter in those wilds shall be
made to speak a voice of wisdom and virtue, the reformation
of the world would be to be expected from America" (J, I, 248).

Few inducements to young men of parts seeking a career could
exceed that of the opportunity in public life to insure that "the
oracles of moral law and intellectual wisdom" were never suffered
to "speak faintly and indistinctly" to barbarous roughnecks.

In the spring of 1824, however, when Emerson decided on his
own career, he cast his lot not for politics or philosophy or poetry,
but for theology. He could not stomach most of the preaching
he heard, he knew that historically the Church had been the butt
of ridicule of humanist critics, and he even had a strong suspicion
that something in the very nature of their profession prevented
ministers from being fully men. Yet the strength of his desire
to emulate his ancestors, his love of oratory, his desire to provide
a home for his mother as soon as possible, and his belief that by
nature he was better fitted for the ministry than for anything
else overcame his doubts and intellectual objections. Soon en-
rolled as a student in the recently established School of Divinity
at Harvard College, he was allowed to pursue his studies in a
loose arrangement allowing him to be part time in residence
and part time in absentia, doing much work independently.

During eight years, from 1824 until 1832, Emerson was asso-
ciated with the Church, for the first five as a probationer fitting

himself for a pulpit and in the last three as a minister in one of the most desirable posts in Boston. Until 1826, however, by necessity he continued to spend his vacations teaching. The ecclesiastical period was a very rich one, not only in the extent of his intellectual growth, but also in the widening of his emotional experience.

The Emerson youths, all by nature finely strung and rather delicate, were by early circumstance and continued habit prevented from developing in play that degree of robustness which most boys in rough-and-tumble acquire. Furthermore, intelligent and ambitious, they lived at an extremely high nervous pitch in driving themselves to attainments of distinction. This unrelenting effort consumed their energies and meant that they were dangerously near breaking their frail physiques and continuously vulnerable to tuberculosis, one of the chief scourges of the population at that time. In 1828, Edward, Emerson's brother next in age, exhausted by his study of the law and his teaching, suddenly broke down, mentally as well as physically. Emerson, who tried to help in nursing him, was horrified at the sight of his maniacal state. After a half year of confinement in an institution, Edward emerged again into society, but, requiring a mild and sunny climate, from then on lived in Puerto Rico.

In the meantime Emerson's own health came perilously close to destruction. Severe eyestrain in the middle of his twenty-second year prevented all work with books, and rheumatic pains developed in his leg and hip. In spite of short-lived alleviations, these symptoms persisted, and a painful stricture in the breast also set in. Alarmed, his physician and family sent him south for recovery, to St. Augustine, Florida, where he spent several months in fresh air and convalescent leisure. When he returned home in the spring of 1827, he was able to take up his studies and his preaching, but only with a careful restriction of activity.

Throughout this crisis, along with high idealism, Emerson exhibited singular objectivity. He saw very clearly that his was a case of life and death; if he wanted to live he must tread on eggs to conserve his wasting forces. He took life seriously enough to know that there are occasions when it cannot be taken seriously. He must relax and laugh. Playing the role of the detached observer, he strolled on the beach and drove an orange before him with a stick. He sat and watched the ocean.

Whoever is in St. Augustine, resembles what may be also seen in St. Augustine, the barnacles on a ledge of rocks which the tide has deserted; move they cannot; very uncomfortable they surely are—but they can hear from afar the roaring of the waters & imagine the joy of the barnacles that are bathed thereby. (L, I, 187)

Back in Divinity Hall in Cambridge, he continued to enjoy a "lounging capricious unfettered mode of life," reading a little, writing his family and friends, quietly and slowly multiplying sermons (at the rate of one a month), and hoping for a day of firmer health and solid power.

This is not to say that he experienced no despondency. In Saint Augustine in February, 1827, while drinking in sunshine, sure of his utter uselessness to others, he had been profoundly rueful: "What then, young pilot [would-be] . . . art not thyself a castaway?" (J, II, 166). Trying to face what he considered the decay of his hopes and the miscarriage of all his best efforts he had affirmed pregnantly, "He has seen but half the Universe who never has been shown the house of Pain" (J, II, 180). He had occasional deep misgivings about the nature of God, about His very existence, and about the order of the universe.

Ellen Tucker of Concord, New Hampshire, with whom Emerson fell in love in 1828, was admitted by everybody, he wrote, to be very lovely and to have feelings that were "exceedingly delicate and noble." Unfortunately, her health, ravaged by consumption, was exceedingly delicate also, which meant that she was a doomed creature at the time she consented to marry her suitor. Finally judged by her physician after nine months of engagement to be fit for marriage, Emerson had the bliss of uniting himself, in September, 1829, to the girl he called his Queen of Sheba, his noble flower, his Phoenix bird, "the fairest, virtuousest, discreetest, and best," although with her "angel's soul" and sweet, serene detachment, she seems to have been from the start under no illusion about the length of her life. She was stricken fatally in January, 1831, after less than a year and a half of matrimony.

Six months after the loss of his wife, Emerson's youngest brother Charles became suddenly sick, lapsing into deep despondency, listless in "great stupor and much weakness." "Who would have thot that Edward & Charles on whom we put so

much fond pride shd. be the first to fail whilst Ellen my rose is
gone" (L, I, 336). Fortunately, Charles rallied and, also in Puerto
Rico, regained his former condition.

Throughout these years of preparation and vicissitude Emerson
assiduously kept his *Journals.* He concurred with Samuel Johnson
that the great value of such an exercise comes from every man's
loving to review his own mind. He was convinced that a thing
was perfectly known only after it had been put into words; as
though no man could know what he thought until he saw what
he said he thought. As trenchant as he was fertile, with nothing
of his flooding vitality wasted, he strove to put things succinctly
and aptly, for writing was essentially finding the right word.
"The manner of using language," he recorded, "is surely the most
decisive test of intellectual power, and he who has intellectual
force of any kind will be sure to show it there" (J, II, 449). The
laws of composition were as strict as those of sculpture or architecture, in which there was only one line that should be drawn
and one attitude realized: "So in writing there is always a right
word, and every other word than that is wrong" (J, II, 401).

As conspicuous as the liveliness and illuminating point of the
Journals is their honesty. By temperament as well as intellectual
commitment, Emerson was drawn to show the two-facedness of
things. He had more awareness than most persons of the duali-
ties, or antitheses, of life and a stronger tendency to think in
terms of them. To this propensity he was referring when later
on he said that he was always insincere as always knowing there
were other modes. And it was this which led Whitman in his
wake to value him supremely, not as poet or essayist, but as
critic, and to complement his "A foolish consistency is the hob-
goblin of little minds" with "Do I contradict myself? Very well,
then, I contradict myself." Emerson was fond of repeating the
remark made by his grandfather Ripley, the sturdy, downright
Calvinist minister of Concord: "My children, you will never see
anything worse than yourselves." Whatever the worse features
of Emerson were, one feels them to be faced unblinkingly in his
pages. Recognizing the congenital human aversion to change,
he confessed that he would probably have helped the conservative monks belabor Galileo for saying that the earth moved.
"It is idle in us to wonder at the bigotry and violence of the
persecution of Galileo. Every man may read the history of it in

himself when he is contradicted and silenced in argument by a
person whom he had always reckoned his inferior," (J, II, 467).
He did not envy others in the sense of wishing their goods his,
but he admitted that he was capable of malevolence toward
those who had injured him or before whom he had "played the
fool."

In spite of discouragements Emerson retained his conviction
that his life must be spent for the betterment of mankind. He
looked on himself as at once discoverer and revealer, poet and
preacher—a bard of the pulpit. He longed to give an accurate
description of the great adventure of life, to show the color,
orbit, and composition of his particular star. Animated as one
imagines Lear to have been in calling himself one of God's spies,
he wanted to see all and know all. Coming always "eagerly into
the enjoyment to which we are invited, instead of skulking to a
mouthful in the dark," how better could he show his gratitude
than by having "a noble daring," an ambition to "grapple with
what is great, . . . follow what flies" and "risk something to
acquire a light on the nature" of our condition (J, II, 61-62).
In early 1830 he exclaimed, "I write the things that are, not
what appears." Like the critic-metaphysician Coleridge, whom
he described as "a restless human soul bursting the narrow
boundaries of antique speculation and mad to know the secrets
of that unknown world, on whose brink it is sure it is standing,"
he too aspired to be a citizen of the universe, a spectator of all,
a philosopher at the center "sending sovereign glances to the
circumference of things" (J, II, 277-78).

But to whom was he to communicate the magnificent vision
as he comprehended it? To his parishioners, to ordinary men
and women, to the "great body of society who make up nations
and conduct the business of the world." In the composition of
his book, therefore, he would be guided always by the knowledge
that it was the people he must reach. In order to make his mark
he must overcome his propensity to abstraction: "The only dis-
pensers of fame are the middle class of mankind, and they will
not value the far-sought abstraction, no matter how inaccessible
or sublime, more than the fowl on the dunghill regards the pearl"
(J, II, 167). The big minds intended by God throughout history
to influence men had never squeamishly avoided contact with
coarse, unlettered folk. Jesus had liberally used homely facts

got in low and familiar life from tax collectors, customs officers, and boys in the marketplace, and if he were alive in the nineteenth century, would use the printing press, the loom, steam and gas, or any of the features of our throbbing cities. What Emerson eventually came to prize, using Samuel Johnson's phrase for it, was a diction above grossness and below refinement.

Emerson's sermons, during his tenure in the pulpit of the Second Unitarian Church of Boston, once formidably occupied by Cotton Mather and Samuel Sewall, were, on the testimony of persons moved by them, singularly effective. The eloquence he had admired as an undergraduate years earlier in the orator Edward Everett, dependent on fervor and prone to floridity, he had outgrown, substituting for it restrained dignity and sweetness, flexible and natural. The sermons were the product of an unusual mind and the emanation of an extraordinary character. Most ministers were wrong not only in the orientation of their preaching—"If you won't be good you will be punished" rather than "Be good and you won't be punished"—but also in not providing in their lives an example for their parishioners to follow. Emerson aimed to be to his congregation not a severe critic but "the Herald of glad tidings of great joy" and a "mild and blameless friend," wearing "the light of God's presence with him always," so that good conversation, good manners, and good actions would proceed from him "as naturally as clean water from a pure spring."

But the same preaching which drew young idealistic intellectuals was of a kind to perplex ordinary, conventional minds. Twice he had to be informed of the dissatisfaction of members of his congregation over the frequency of "profane" illustrations in his sermons and the infrequency of "authority of scripture quotation," which suggested that he did not look to the Bible with the same respect as others. Tactfully, he explained that he had "affected generally a mode of illustration rather bolder than the usage of our preaching warrants, on the principle that our religion is nothing limited or partial, but of universal application, & is interested in all that interests man" (L, I, 257). As for his respect for the Scriptures, he revered the Bible as divine authority, as revelation which showed the "being and character of God," and which, along with natural history, established the immortality of the soul. But he chose not to be a preacher like too many he had seen, only putting together sermons that were "nothing but a patch-work of un-chosen texts."

This, however, was far from a full statement of his feelings on his situation. He had long before made up his mind that although Christianity had outstripped, it had not contradicted, the teachings of his beloved Greek, Plato, and that although he was willing to help diffuse the Christian revelation through the globe, it did not have for him "the same exclusive and extraordinary claims it has for many." Maintaining that the Creator would not abuse his children by addressing them in messages which were wild and unintelligible, he held "Reason to be a prior Revelation, and that they do not contradict each other." It was clear from this last that in cases where revelation happened to conflict with the discoveries of reason, it would be reason, antecedent to Revelation, to which he would assent (J, I, 386).

Within three years the strains of accommodating his own religious views to church doctrine, his personal life to the demands of a preacher's routine (visiting parishioners as well as marrying and baptizing them), and his poetic sensibilities to the restrictions of pulpit performance had become extreme and bred a feeling of futility. The ministry was a blind alley. It was the best part of a man, apparently, which rebelled against his being a minister; and in order to be a good one, a man had to leave the church. More and more restive at having to direct corporate prayer, in which he did not believe (a family of like mind and common habits might practice it, but a "promiscuous assemblage," never), and more and more repelled by the barbarousness of the Sacrament of Holy Communion, he reached the point where he could no longer continue in his post.

Early in June, 1832, Emerson sent a letter to the proprietors of the Second Church, stating a change in his opinions concerning the ordinance of the Lord's Supper and recommending some change in the mode of administering it. The note was passed for consideration to an appropriate committee, which decided that it was under no duty to assent to his request. Unable to acquiesce in that decision, Emerson decided to withdraw; and in September, after weeks of anguished brooding, in which he had to say, Luther-like, to various members of his family and friends who pleaded with him not to jeopardize his career, that what he had done was only what he could do, he preached a sermon explaining his beliefs to his parishioners. Charitably, his brother Edward observed, he refused to print the sermon because he did "not wish to do anything in hostility to the ordinance or shocking to good but weak vessels." Seven weeks later his connection with the church was officially severed.

The period following his farewell sermon found Emerson depleted by the long strain. Weak, thin, dispirited, and sick for days, he was recurrently up and down. What would he do next? Projects sprouted and bloomed in his head; he was alternately drawn to action, literature, and philosophy. His self-laceration was fortunately terminated by his abrupt decision, drawn by a "purpureal vision of Naples and Italy," to go abroad.

In a sense, Emerson went to Europe to prove to himself something he had known all along—that it was not necessary to travel the world in order to learn human nature, for each person at home had twenty or thirty companions and two or three hundred acquaintances who afforded a book of human character quite large enough. Later he was accustomed to saying that one went to Europe to become Americanized. In Italy it was the same humanity under a thousand different masks, speaking the same commandment, too, though in a strange tongue. The only good he could see in travel was that it shook a person out of his habits. "My greatest want is the very one I apprehended when at home, that I never meet with men that are great or interesting" (L, I, 371). The wise man was elusive on a worldwide scale.

Rome impressed him mightily and his respect for the inexhaustible city he summed up in calling it, Yankee fashion, "a venerable egg shell of nations, institutions, arts, religions." It was true that a man trained in a New England barnyard might measure with Scipio Africanus, but he admitted that the idea of Rome, only Rome could supply; she contained so much beauty and grandeur that it formed part of a man's education simply to have seen it. In Florence, in the Church of Santa Croce, suddenly finding himself before the tablet in the wall marking the burial place of Michelangelo Buonarotti, he was overcome by an ineffable agitation and awe which made his flesh creep.

But it was in Paris, to which he went after leaving Italy, that the supreme experience of his continental travel occurred. He visited a great exhibition of minerals and shells, of insects, reptiles, and fishes, and of birds and animals in the Jardin des

Plantes. The vast show, on a scale unprecedented, included also a "collection of comparative anatomy," with specimens that seemed to run the gamut from the skeleton of a whale to "the upright form and highly developed skull of the Caucasian race of man." At once Emerson was transported to a world of sensation and thought he had never before inhabited, removed as far from the second-hand bookishness and besetting practicalities of Harvard and Boston as from the slumbrous antiquity of Rome and Syracuse.

The limits of the possible are enlarged, and the real is stranger than the imaginary. The universe is a more amazing puzzle than ever, as you look along this bewildering series of animated forms, the hazy butterflies, the carved shells, the birds, beasts, insects, snakes, fish, and the upheaving principle of life every where incipient, in the very rock aping organized forms. Whilst I stand there I am impressed with a singular conviction that not a form so grotesque, so savage, or so beautiful, but is an expression of something in man the observer. We feel that there is an occult relation between the very worm, the crawl-ing scorpions, and man. I am moved by strange sympathies. I say I will listen to this invitation. I will be a naturalist. (EL, I, 10)

In England, Emerson made visits to Coleridge, Wordsworth and Carlyle, detailed accounts of which in *English Traits* he later offered to the public. Coleridge, whom he had come to venerate, and Wordsworth, whose "Intimations Ode" he con sidered the high-water mark of the century in English thought were profoundly disappointing. Carlyle, however, was anothe matter. This was a man still in his prime, the force of whos mind and pulse of whose heart Emerson had felt back home i reading his latest work as it issued from the press, almost befor the ink was dry. From the fleeting visit to the thought-torrente philosopher of *Sartor Resartus* flowered a friendship which foun its record in a rich and unique correspondence of almost ha a century, ended only by Emerson's death in 1882.

Upon his return, the resumption of his preaching on an invit tional basis, which brought him occasionally again into Bostc pulpits, did not altogether satisfy Emerson. The literary side of h nature was beginning to assert itself strongly, and he meditate "something more seriously than ever before, the adventure of periodical paper which shall speak truth without fear or favor all who desire to hear it, with such persuasion as shall compel them to speak it also" (L, I, 402). Yet, needing more money than came from invitational Sunday sermons, instead of embarking on such a project, he began a new career, lyceum lecturing. His audiences were some of the many Societies for the Diffusion of Useful Knowledge which had recently been founded by cities and towns eager to emerge, only a generation and a half after the winning of national independence, from their intellectual and cultural immaturity. Within a month of his arrival home he gave his first lecture before the Boston Natural History Society.

Having visited in Florence the establishment of Professor Amici, manufacturer of optical instruments, whose microscopes were the best in Europe, having seen the amazing natural-history exhibitions of the Jardin des Plantes in Paris, and having had the secrets of the power of the mighty new English locomotives explained to him in Liverpool by the man who made them, Emerson's eyes were opened to the significance of science. He saw that where the interests of the reading part of the populace were concerned, natural history was the new wave. He had himself said, after the revelation of the show in Paris, that he would be a naturalist. Now was his chance. Accordingly, his first address was to a "scientific" society on an appropriate subject, "The Uses of Natural History." This lecture was followed within the space of six months by three others, though not all to the same body—"On the Relation of Man to the Globe," on "Water," and on "The Naturalist." Although his addresses did not for long remain on specifically scientific topics, his thought continued increasingly to be colored by science, particularly by theories and discoveries relating to evolution. As for platform appearances, from the outset able to lecture "to a charm," he had fastened himself to an activity which was to claim his energies every winter from then on, with very few exceptions, for the next forty years, orbiting him farther and farther from home, eventually out of New England into New York, then down into Pennsylvania, and finally in the 1850's through Ohio out across the Mississippi. Many more people knew Ralph Waldo Emerson as lecturer than as writer.

On October 1, 1834, however, death struck his family again. Edward died in Puerto Rico of consumption. With sorrow and shock Emerson realized that he was bereaved of a part of him-

self in the loss of "one pile more of hope for this life" (C, I, 222).
At the end of 1834 he had to write to Charles, dispirited and
enervated through overdoing, to bolster his courage. "The world—
its Governor stand pledged that opportunity shall come home to
each man. And opportunity commensurate with his qualification.
. . . Blessed are the cold days in spring that keep the flower shut
till it is strong enough to open without danger to the plant. . . .
Nothing nothing is lost" (L, I, 426). A year later he was addressing a letter of reassurance to his older brother William in New
York, whose first child had died after only a few months of life.
Familiar as death is, he confessed, we shall never get used to it.
It will continue to astonish and wound and mangle us, but "to
great & good ends, however I hope & believe." (L, I, 457)

Emerson was now more nearly independent in what he said
than at any time in the past. He resolved to stake out his own
plot and cultivate it by himself. "Henceforth I design not to utter
any speech, poem, or book that is not entirely and peculiarly
my work. I will say at public lectures, and the like, those things
which I have meditated for their own sake, and not for the first
time with a view to that occasion" (J, III, 361). A lecturer, like
a minister, should remember that the people confronting him
were there for all sorts of reasons and did not care about him.
Fools they were, granted, but "potentially divine, every one of
them convertible," seeking a master and grateful to have one.
"Be to them a Plato; be to them a Christ, and they shall all be
Platos, and all be Christs" (J, III, 476). And the way to be a
Plato, a Christ, was not to ask "What ought to be said in a
Lyceum?" but "What discoveries or stimulating thoughts have
I to impart to a thousand persons?" One needed an authority
deriving from such an integrity as had led the Quaker George
Fox to declare, "What I am in words, I am the same in life."
Truth was forever new to the mind discovering it, and an audi-
ence knew immediately whether the things uttered by a man
had been discovered by him—and were being lived by him.
Every word from pulpit or platform should be not separate from
a speaker like a flower in a bouquet but "like a leaf or a flower
or a bud" joined to the stem and seed.

In 1835 Emerson was busy with two series of lyceum lectures,
on biography and on English literature; and in September of
that year he had the honor of delivering the major address, the

"Historical Discourse," at Concord on the occasion of the bi-centennial celebration of the founding of the town. In this he revealed not only his attachment to the beauty of the place of his ancestors, formed years before during summer vacation visits to the Old Manse, but as well the deep association he felt with various elements of its historical character. By this time, in fact, he was a citizen of Concord. He had bought late that very summer a big and substantial house on the Lexington Road at the edge of town, which he looked forward to occupying soon, once more in the status of family man, for he was about to wed a second time.

Off and on through the latter half of 1834 and during 1835 he had been preaching in Plymouth, and there Lydia Jackson, known locally to some for her love and good works as "the Abbess," had attracted him more and more with her high intelligence and exemplary character. He took delight in his "quite domestic position" with her, feeling "good understanding" in continual growth between them. That he acted "without one vehement word or one passionate sign," however, was not to be misconstrued: "Do not think me a metaphysical lover. I am a man & hate & suspect the over refiners, & do sympathize with the homeliest pleasures & attractions by which our good foster mother Nature draws her children together. Yet am I well pleased that between us the most permanent ties should be the first formed & thereon should grow whatever others human nature will" (L, I, 434). On September 14, having married Lydia Jackson, her name for euphony's sake now changed at his request to "Lydian," he moved with her into the spacious house prepared for her. There they stayed for the rest of their lives, the days and weeks in rich accumulation making a near half century in which Concord was the intellectual hearthstone of the nation.

Emerson's increasing independence showed itself in a desire to write as well as to speak. There was always for him the closest connection between the two activities, for he never gave a lecture or sermon that had not been written out beforehand, but he now meditated a literary work per se, a volume that would be published without ever having been platform-read beforehand. In his *Journal* at the time of his leaving England he had written simply and enigmatically that he liked his little book on nature very much, although it may then have been something only in prospect. In the summer of 1835, however, it was a little volume well advanced in the writing, which it gave him pleasure to think of publishing by and by. With admirable detachment, he admitted that this was one of those "gravest plans that look so comical sometimes that we can scarce believe we ourselves are in earnest," and he was prepared to be not much annoyed if it were never realized. But it prospered along the lines he was seeking to follow, not just something that might be said but something not previously said that was yet true. In September, 1836, in an edition of five hundred copies, "Nature" was published and he was launched on a new career. His public life and his private life now both of widened dimension—the new book following closely on the new marriage—he could put down steadily deeper familial roots in the most congenial of situations.

Sorrow, however, continued to dog Emerson's footsteps after his removal to Concord. The felicity of his marriage was augmented by the birth within a decade of four children. They were all well formed, lively, and intelligent, and their parents took the keenest interest in their upbringing. Yet hearth happiness was periodically broken by misfortune. Emerson's younger brother Charles was stricken with advanced consumption and died in 1836. In 1842 an even crueller blow fell when young Waldo, the oldest child, richly gifted and dearer to his father than any other person could be, was destroyed by scarlet fever after an illness of only a few days.

Irrespective, however, of the vicissitudes which struck his family, Emerson continued to push ahead with his career. His lectures brought him a steadily wider reputation, and he published a number of important volumes of essays which spread his name abroad. His activities were broken by a second trip in 1847, after an absence of fifteen years, to England. Already able to profit from a slight reputation there, thanks in no small part to Carlyle, he was kept busy on this new visit in following an extensive lecture itinerary arranged by an admirer, an influential owner and publisher of newspapers encountered in Edinburgh a half generation before. He enjoyed the opportunity to try out new ideas on new audiences, and he was stimulated by his travel, which allowed him to see much more of the island than he had previously known and to meet personally many of its inhabitants illustrious in industry, science, and the arts. He went to exhibitions, attended lectures, talked tête-á-tête with writers, and participated in protracted breakfasts and banquets.

For years Emerson occupied a post as elder statesman of American thought and as dean of American letters. In 1871, appropriately lauded by a reviewer in *The Louisville Commercial* as the father of American radicalism, he was additionally—and rightly—said to be distinguished by a sobriety and sanity far beyond the reach of the most conservative of American conservatives. He was elected in 1864 a Fellow of the American Academy of Arts and Sciences and would have been one of the charter members of the National Academy of Literature and Art had Congress passed the bill allowing it to materialize. In 1867, when after a lapse of thirty years he was asked again to deliver the Phi Beta Kappa address, he was honored by Harvard College with the degree of Doctor of Letters. His virtues were eventually sung by eminent figures of various lands. During the term of his visit in England in 1848 he was elected an honorary member of the Athenaeum and of the Reform Club. In 1874 he was nominated by a student party for the rectorship of the University of Glasgow, an honorary post which would have exacted of him only an annual address but which finally went to Disraeli by a plurality of about two hundred votes.

In his sixties Emerson's powers quickly declined. Recognizing at once that the ebb had set in, he adapted himself to it with philosophic serenity. In 1872, late one July night, his house caught fire, and although no papers of value were destroyed, so much damage to the structure was done before the blaze was extinguished that he and his family had to be removed to the Old Manse, then occupied by a cousin. Friends generously came to his aid and raised a sum of money large enough not only to repair the house but to send him abroad for diversion during its restoration. His slight powers of concentration, along with his slowness of speech and weakened memory, made the trip not altogether a thing of pleasure, but, well taken care of by a daughter, even though his strength was taxed by an itinerary which took him as far as Egypt, whose colossal architectural remains he had long wanted to see, he found things to enjoy. He visited England for a third and final time and rejoiced in the renewal in flesh of old friendships, as well as in the making of new and illustrious acquaintances. On his return to the United

States he had the happiness of being greeted at the little Concord railway station by a large delegation of fellow citizens, who escorted him back to his rebuilt home in triumphal procession.

Emerson's last years were marked by exemplary simplicity and sweetness. To the end he loved his Concord house and garden, and the fields, the river, and the woods which lay beyond. He was tenderly devoted to his family and continued to enjoy his friends, handicapped though he was by his impaired powers. One of his last coherent statements was a poignant ejaculation over his son Waldo, dead forty years before, "Oh that beautiful boy!" Emerson died on April 27, 1882. For his funeral multitudes of tribute-payers streamed into Concord by train, by coach, in wagon, and on foot, making, Henry James said, the most striking popular manifestation he had ever seen over the death of a man of letters.

The outward events of Emerson's life were few; the inward were many and ultimately of consequence to mankind through his lectures and writings. Since it was during his decades in Concord that he attained the summit of his powers and created a way of life which in its grace and humanity became a legend, it is appropriate to pay closer attention to that chapter of his biography and to its relation to the broader features of his historical period.

Emerson's setting was an age of revolution—the beginning, in fact, of a long period of revolution of which the world has not yet seen the end—the great democratic revolution. No doubt every age is at once unique and like every other. Emerson himself smilingly recognized this when he observed that "no matter how many centuries of culture . . . the new man always finds himself standing on the brink of chaos, always in a crisis" (W, VII, 163-64)—as though there had ever been a time when the world had had enough of the right kind of men, of the right kind of women. It has "always had the same bankrupt look, to foregoing ages as to us, as of a failed world just re-collecting its old withered forces to begin again and try to do a little business." The year 1803, the year of his birth, was only twenty-seven years after 1776, and the American Revolution, which began in that year, had inaugurated a cataclysmic break with the past, whose effects strongly impressed his mind as Emerson grew up.

The Revolution had been a repudiation of an outworn political and social order—of a centralized monarchy dependent for its support and prestige on a moneyed and privileged aristocracy, exclusive claimants, by the accident of birth, to title, affluence, cultivation, and power. All that Thomas Jefferson had deplored as tinsel aristocracy, which he had made it his life's aim to destroy, was eventually destroyed: the tyrannical power of arrogant autocrats, the prerogatives and titles of the highborn, the discriminatory institutions of primogeniture and entail. For Emerson in 1837 an age of revolution was the only period one would desire to be born in—"when the old and the new stand side by side and admit of being compared; when the energies of all men are searched by fear and by hope; when the historic glories of the old can be compensated by the rich possibilities of the new era" (W, I, 110). He took Jeffersonian pleasure in the "movement which effected the elevation of what was called the lowest class in the state" and in the reflection that from now on the only aristocracy would be an aristocracy of worth, determined by moral considerations alone, and that the new conditions of society would allow all persons development and achievement limited only by their abilities. The air was aflame with promise and confidence, and Thomas Paine's words, "We have it in our power to begin the world over again," sum up succinctly the idealism of the new enterprise in America. It was more than a matter affecting cabinets, ministers, and votes; it was an unprecedented way of life.

Another aspect of the Revolution, more strictly intellectual, was the growth of science. Of increasing importance were the freshly collected data about man and his terrestrial and cosmic environment. Already by the time Emerson gave his Phi Beta Kappa address to the students of Harvard College (1837), indeed by the time of his first visit to Paris, geological researches were yielding startling evidences of the antiquity of the earth and of its occupation by living creatures. Ideas of an evolutionary cast had already sprouted, and in little more than two decades the publication of Darwin's *Origin of Species* (1859) would, like the sudden emergence of a prodigious mountain, alter forever the intellectual terrain of mankind. The Romans and Greeks had become of less and less relevancy, and the place they occupied in men's minds drastically diminished. To Thomas Jefferson, however, they had been indispensable, and education had been almost altogether acquired by a mastery of the philosophers, historians, political thinkers, and poets of ancient times. But his age was the last which held the lights of antiquity to be necessary to the illumination of contemporary life and which urged its young men to ignite their candles with the flame of Aristotle, Plato, Thucydides, Plutarch, Seneca, and Cicero. Although the education Emerson received at Harvard, only a generation after Jefferson's letter (1785) on education to Peter Carr, was still essentially that of the eighteenth century, classically oriented, the example of Benjamin Franklin had already shown the world what could be achieved in intellect, personality, and character by a man never formally introduced to the world of Latin and Greek culture.

The early decades of the nineteenth century are also commonly known as the age of Romanticism, in contradistinction to the age of Classicism, or the Rationalist Enlightenment, preceding it. Although Romanticism, which flowered in this country somewhat later than in Europe, was a reaction against certain habits of thought of the era which had gone before, it nevertheless owed its existence to other modes of thought which had simultaneously developed alongside them. Among these one ought to distinguish a predilection among certain people for feeling rather than for reason, for either of two kinds of nonrational force, above reason or below it. On the one hand were persons who loved exaltation and happy awe and believed man made by nature to experience it; on the other, individuals given to gloomy, eerie, or macabre excitement, who found the roots of their addiction to it also in human nature. The first group prized intuition; the second, subliminal impulse. The first proclaimed man destined for harmony and union with his fellows and the means to the highest cultivation of his faculties to be suprarational inspiration; the opposite school, convinced, sadly or cynically, of man's essential alienation and of his capacity for destruction, maintained that the chief thing to reckon with was subrational instinct. Yet they were both Romantic.

The Romantic believers in man were related to eighteenth-century deists and acquired their faith in suprarational experience from breathing currents of metaphysical idealism blowing from Germany. The heroic late eighteenth-century deist Thomas

Paine, for example, had represented the rationalism of his age in happy combination with feeling. He had believed in the study of nature. One examined the universe with his reason and discovered it to be a stupendously grand and complex machine, indescribable in its conception and in the harmony of its operation. Realizing, rationally, that it was the work of God—the only work of God knowable by man—one dismissed the Bible and all books on religious subjects as speculations about God, as no more than hearsay, and turned to nature as the only true theology, to learn God of it. Reason told him then that wisdom, power, munificence, and mercy, visibly reflected in the cosmos, were attributes of the Creator, which, being a rational creature, he aspired to cultivate in himself. As a result of the whole experience, he could not fail to be moved by feelings of thankfulness, humility, and jubilation. And Paine's own paragraphs, as he described how religion derived from science and morality from rationality, often vibrated with fervor.

The Romantics who were kin of Paine lifted up their eyes to the hills or the stars no less religiously, but the experience they sought was not the same. An ineffable power within, about, and behind all objects of vision was what had been impressed on their consciousness, and they desired communion with it, believing it to be divine. Attracted by the invisible rather than the visible, by what they could feel rather than see, by the potency residing in things which made them significant and mysteriously related to man, with Blake they looked through, not with, the eye.

The Romantics who believed man to be actuated by the forces weltering below reason rather than by those transcending it were descended from the votaries of mortuary and macabre emotion in the eighteenth century. Yet they had a coincidental point of contact with their differently hued contemporaries—nature—to which they were no less in the habit of turning, and with no less conviction. They saw nature, however, not as ordered benignity but as organized chaos and man as shaped for ruin, of himself as well as his fellows. Disbelieving in happiness as the crown of life and liberty, they revealed the sad mystery of existence: man's impenetrable isolation from his fellows and his need of violence. In their preoccupation with the dark and abysmal qualities of human nature, they can appropriately be called "Twilight Romantics." The others, whose imagination inhabited the day rather than the night, are "Sunlight Romantics." To the somber group in America belong Poe, Hawthorne, and Melville; to the sanguine, Emerson, poet of morning.

The Revolution was, of course, not confined to politics or modes of thought in philosophy and religion. It was also industrial, changing the face of the nation with its manufacturing cities, its canals and railroads, and willy-nilly, though perhaps in ways of which most people were unaware, impinging on individual behavior and social structure. Between Emerson's birth in 1803 and his death in 1882, three wars involving Americans were fought (in 1812 against England, in 1846 against Mexico, and in 1861 between the states). The Middle West was linked to the East by a network of traversable waterways and steel rails, which increased economic wealth immeasurably by intercourse between the developing hinterland and the urban centers of the seaboard, already whirring with the machines of their expanding factories. Gold was discovered in the Far West, an event which led to its colonization and national assimilation, cemented by the construction of a vast transcontinental railway, the locomotive eventually superseding the water barge as the means of commercial traffic. With the growth of the population over great areas of land hitherto unpenetrated and the inevitable differences of interest between those who tilled the land and those who manipulated its fruits in industry, disparities of wealth arose which seriously involved the monetary policies of the nation. And, in the cities themselves, feared by Jefferson before the end of the preceding century as breeding places for rabble, arose an exploited class of troglodytes, toiling by day in gloomy workshops and sleeping by night in dreary hovels, which, refusing to accept inhumanity as its permanent lot, precipitated one of the longest lasting and most distinguishing features of the century—the struggle between capital and labor.

The nineteenth century was, as Emerson said many times and in many ways, "The Philosophic" or "Reflective Era." Its subjectivity, more than anything else, had caused the decline of the old-fashioned religion of Calvinism for denying the direct relation of the person to his Creator indispensable to a modern mind. Its introversion, often touched by morbidity and prurience, had found its consummate literary expression in Goethe's *Faust*, whose hero was a Hamlet enlightened by science. Its individualism, the essence of the democratic spirit, was as sleepless as intrepid and called all things into question—all relations, all institutions, all dogmas. Because idiosyncrasy led inevitably to analysis, the mental climate was continually in ferment and in the Western world society was undergoing change, the outcome of which no one could foresee. Recurrently the spirit of revolution, after its great upsurges of 1776 and 1789, struggled to topple reactionary governments in the Old World, yet, for the most part, without success.

Even in the United States, a free and politically sophisticated nation, discontent was widespread, not only over political grievances such as the continued enslavement of the Negro, but also over social conditions, over educational methods and religious traditions, over domestic relations—over all kinds of habit or practice, in short, small or large, which determined the character of daily life and determined it wrong. Man was made for something better than what was: this was everywhere the central conviction; and the second, its corollary, was that the something better could not be attained by further adherence to old ways. The decades of the 1820's, 1830's, and 1840's were profoundly agitated by the search for new ways.

Some persons, convinced that large cities were the chief foe to humanity, advocated that like-minded men and women secede from them and in small numbers in wholesome surroundings resettle themselves, where, free to start their enterprise from scratch, they could strive for an ideal way of life with a better chance of realizing it, out from under the threat of mechanization, with the sexes equal and the races equal, and with children educated through an exercise of their minds on real things about them in the world. They thought more highly of human nature than preceding generations had done, and they expected more of it. Intentional communities, drawing on the ideas of utopian thinkers from Plato to Fourier, flourished in this country in the middle of the century as they never had before and never have since.

In various places Emerson described the fermentative character of the times as it revealed itself in New England. He was always —for the most part amusedly—alert to the tendency of idealism to become extremism, fertile parent of bizarrerie, crackpotism, and bigotry.

The key to the period appeared to be that the mind had become aware of itself. . . . The former generations acted under the belief that a shining social prosperity was the beatitude of man, and sacrificed uniformly the citizen to the State. The modern mind believed that the nation existed for the individual, for the guardianship and education of every man. . . . This perception is a sword such as was never drawn before. . . . The social sentiments are weak; the sentiment of patriotism is weak; veneration is low; the natural affections feebler than they were. People grow philosophical about native land and parents and relations. There is an universal resistance to ties and ligaments once supposed essential to civil society. The new race is stiff, heady, and rebellious; they are fanatics in freedom; they hate tolls, taxes, turnpikes, banks, hierarchies, governors, yea, almost laws. They have a neck of unspeakable tenderness; it winces at a hair. They rebel against theological as against political dogmas. . . . (W, X, 326-27)

What a fertility of projects for the salvation of the world! One apostle thought all men should go to farming, and another that no man should buy or sell, that the use of money was the cardinal evil; another that the mischief was in our diet, that we eat and drink damnation. These made unleavened bread, and were foes to the death to fermentation. . . . Others attacked the system of agriculture, the use of animal manures in farming, and the tyranny of man over brute nature. . . . Others assailed particular vocations, as that of the lawyer, that of the merchant, of the manufacturer, of the clergyman, of the scholar. Others attacked the institution of marriage as the fountain of social evils. Others devoted themselves to the worrying of churches and meetings for public worship. (W, III, 252-53)

Emerson could not himself join a community, although he followed closely the fortunes of two nearby, Brook Farm and Fruitlands, both founded by friends of his whose high motives and character he could not but admire. Brook Farm, of which the brilliant Margaret Fuller was a member and in which, incongruously, elegiac Nathaniel Hawthorne played a temporary role, lasted for about six years. Fruitlands, the product of the revolutionary ideas of Bronson Alcott, whose daughter Louisa May later piquantly described it in her *Transcendental Wild Oats,* collapsed, because of the impracticality of its citizens, after six months. Emerson, inveterately individualistic, stood apart from all such ventures, though he wished them well. It would have been madness, he said, to raise the siege of his little hencoop and march off instead to that of a pretended Babylon. Although

UNIVERSITY OF WINNIPEG
LIBRARY
DISCARDED
515 Portage Avenue
Winnipeg, Manitoba, R3B 2E9

his sympathies were with what he called the Party of Hope against that of Memory, with the Movement rather than the Establishment, he found the best of communities partial in its aims, dealing with virtue as though it were piecemeal. He preferred to remain in the self rather than the community, "the establishment better than the establishment," conducting it in the best way. No society could ever be so large as one man. In friendship a person multiplied himself to two; mortgaged to a group of twenty he dwarfed himself to less than one. Communitarians deluded themselves with the idea that although there was no concert in one, there could be concert in two. "I have failed and you have failed, but perhaps together, we shall not fail" (W, III, 261 ff.). No person could renovate society who was not himself renovated.

Louisa May Alcott's title, *Transcendental Wild Oats*, was one guaranteed to appeal to the public. Her father's excesses, although intellectual, had been as far from rational judgment as those of a young man given to sensual indulgence and sexual license—in the eyes of society they were absurdities of precisely the only kind of which Transcendentalists were capable. "Transcendentalism" was a popular term of derision for a brand of thought among a particular group of dissenters from the status quo whose loftiness seemed pretentious highflownness, whose frequently erudite and metaphysical expressions seemed unintelligible logorrhea and whose behavior, deriving from convictions about the oneness of all creatures and the importance of love in realizing it, appeared fatuous exhibitionism. "Transcendental," in a strict philosophical sense, had to do with the special brand of German metaphysics of Immanuel Kant and his followers. In a less technical sense the term had simply to do with those things in life which transcended the material—with spiritual things, in short. Plato's Truth, Goodness, and Beauty are transcendent things. So is the Christian's "beauty of holiness" or "peace that passeth understanding." And any person who sought to direct his life by such things, believing them to be the ultimate reality, who was devoted to the life of the mind, was in effect a Transcendentalist, simply one species of reformer or revolutionary, in an epoch of reform and revolution, more religious or philosophical than others. As Emerson described him, the perfect Transcendentalist, daily in the most intimate connection with nature and living frugally, would lean entirely on his own character and eat angels' food; for him life would be nothing but a succession of miracles. Needless to say, he did not exist.

Transcendentalism was often termed "the Newness" because its exponents seemed characteristically given to novelty in thought and innovation in behavior. In part, the appellation was right, because Emerson was forever hymning the advent of the new, sure that in proportion as one imitated the past and heeded the impulsion of the spirit, he would do now what the spirit had impelled men to do in the past—think in new terms and do in new forms. Insofar, however, as it implied something derogatory, which it generally did, it was altogether wrong for the principal literary spokesmen of the Transcendentalists. Emerson, Thoreau, and Margaret Fuller were not weavers of a lunatic fringe, not wild-eyed zealots, not boondoggling strainers at gnats. Even Bronson Alcott, whose inflated prose was unfortunately no less often fatuous than his verse was vacuous, was a thinker of elevation, to whom Emerson frequently acknowledged his indebtedness, and a citizen of courage and initiative. While it is easy to remember the ludicrousness of Alcott's Fruitlands fiasco, it is also easy to forget his noble pacifism, shown in his conscientious refusal to pay his poll tax several years before Thoreau's more famous refusal, and the extraordinary progressive Temple School he kept in Boston, in which he aimed at a genuinely democratic education, training minds to think through the Socratic method and refusing to discriminate against Negroes —a stand which ultimately forced him to close his doors because of lost patronage. The Transcendentalists took seriously the self-evident truth of the Declaration of Independence that all men were created equal and Jesus' new commandment to men that they love one another. They were unwilling to settle any longer for a society which tolerated luxury as well as squalor, made corruption the subject of its jokes, and did something about injustice only in treating it in fictional form. When the worst extravagances of Transcendentalist expression are finally counterbalanced by its best utterances and the fullness of its vision of life is finally glimpsed in relation to America's national ideal, Emerson's prediction may turn out to have been right—that the history of genius and religion in his times would be the history of the Transcendental tendency.

It was his Transcendentalism which brought Emerson into a journalistic relation with society through *The Dial*, a periodical which he helped found in 1840 and for two years edited, until its death in 1844. Although as a Transcendental organ *The Dial* never had more than three hundred subscribers, it allowed distinguished if eccentric minds in prose and verse to be heard for the first time and indicated what might be done another time by avant-garde intellectuals in a publication devoted to art and philosophy as well as to social and political matters. It was an effort to give voice and solidarity to hundreds of remote and obscure souls, chance readers, actuated by a revolutionary faith they themselves were unable to articulate—persons of "no external organization, no badge, no creed, no name," who did "not vote, or print, or even meet together," who did "not know each other's faces or names," who were "united only in a common love of truth."

Emerson's establishment of himself at Concord was his solution to the problem of society or solitude about which he had thought for years. Settled on the edge of a village, he could have companionship without crowds. Yet near the city of Boston, the "happy town beside the sea, whose roads lead everywhere to all," upon whose civilized intellectual associations and traditions he was as dependent as Samuel Johnson upon those of London, he could find the busy hum of men whenever he craved it. He could enjoy solitude in his degree of seclusion without the loneliness of isolation, simply by remaining in his library-study or by walking to the shade and quiet of his favorite property, Walden woods, only a couple of miles away.

The pine branches of Walden woods, however, seemed to him to wave in reproof every time he took the little train into Boston for library pleasure or business. He was not worried over the invasion of the Concord countryside by the railroad. He found, fancifully, that from a car behind a speeding locomotive men and trees and barns whizzing by caused "the very permanence of matter" to be compromised. Although no less a foe than Matthew Arnold of machinery, he nevertheless remained an interested follower of inventions. Ingeniousness of whatever kind fascinated him, and he loved to see man exercising his creative gifts vigorously, on a scale commensurate with that of nature. The making of the photographic camera and the spectroscope,

the opening of the first trans-Alpine tunnel, the digging of the
Suez and Panama canals, the laying of the trans-Atlantic cable
(which matched "God's equator with a zone of Art"), the completion of the American transcontinental railroad—all were heroic
achievements in his sight.

The art of living, about which he had preached so often in
his early days, Emerson found pleasure in practicing. Grace,
affection, and dignity distinguished the discipline of his household. Fearful always of the tyranny of things in a society increasingly industrialized and materialistic, he nevertheless loved
the things with which he surrounded himself, few and carefully
chosen. He was a respecter of what he termed prudence:

> Scorn not thou the love of parts,
> And the articles of arts.
> Grandeur of the perfect sphere
> Thanks the atoms that cohere. (W, IX, 280)

Among these things were copies of steel engravings of some
Raphael paintings and Michelangelo sculptures, in their time-
tarnished black and white now uninspiring if not unsightly but
for him potent reminders of the greatness of their originals,
which he had disturbedly seen. There was also a small Aeolian
harp which he was accustomed to hang in his window and which,
as he wrote at his desk, played a music more intelligible than that
of the concert hall.

Weekdays in the house went according to schedule, not complicated but regular. Mornings, Emerson, rising early, was accustomed to spend in his work, giving himself a respite, however, in the late forenoon with a short reading in Plato or one
of the oriental scriptures or with a brief walk out of doors.
Afternoons he spent walking or receiving visitors or in company
with house guests. Creative tasks he could undertake only in
the morning, when ideas were fresh and the mind resilient, when
the imagination and the spirit were quickened by the spectacle
and promise of a new day. In the evening, he maintained, after
his dinner every man was a conservative; the rise of the day
was for achievement, the decline for relaxation. "In the morning, mountains; in the evening, fountains." Although Sunday
school and the Sunday sermon were invariably deadening to

spirituality and he stayed away from both, the institution of the sweetly "odoriferous Sabbath," Emerson believed to have been of priceless effect on human character; he deplored its passing and would not relinquish it himself. He loved the ending of the week of bustle and work with a day of quiet and contemplative, grateful leisure. Its interposition fifty-two times a year made a rhythm altogether humane and elevating.

The refreshment of tranquil Sunday walks in the country or of family prayer or devotional reading was often heightened by the presence of close friends, whose social tone chimed with his own. Not many, for his reserve was a barrier to intimacy, they were dear to him, and he looked forward with undiminished eagerness to every visit they paid him—members of a little "circle of godlike men and women variously related to each other" but all sharing "a lofty intelligence" and believing that they were to dignify to one another the needs and offices of their daily life by affection, courage, and intelligence. These persons included Thoreau; Bronson Alcott, Platonic reformer of education; Margaret Fuller, passionate feminist-intellectualist; Elizabeth Peabody, bookstore proprietress and lover of art; William Ellery Channing, nature-loving, poetic nephew of the great Unitarian preacher of the same name; William Henry Channing, his brother; Frederic Hedge, penetrating, philosophical minister and student of German thought; Elizabeth Hoar, fiancée to Emerson's deceased brother Charles; and Theodore Parker, impetuous, erudite humanitarian minister. In spite of repeated disappointments to Emerson's high expectations (he admitted that perhaps the high style of friendship he demanded was impossible to flesh and blood), they brought atmosphere with them, a thing more important for a man than for the moon to have, and their minds, outpacing his own, occasionally opened up new vistas, lifted him, and caused his eyes to see with the penetration of divinity. Even he once in a while could become "alert and inventive and add rhyme and reason to what was (otherwise) drudgery." Other friends, not of the deeply intimate kind, he had in increasing number as he grew older and his fame spread—women and men, young and old, lettered and unlettered, famous and unknown. His excitement over meeting a new person of ability never left him, for the possibilities of life in what was unanticipated were enormous. "I never know,

in addressing myself to a new individual, what may befall me.
I carry the keys of my castle in my hand, ready to throw them
at the feet of my lord, whenever and in what disguise soever he
shall appear" (W, III, 53).

The freedom to enjoy his friends, however, or to pursue his
own work was much abridged by Emerson's overgenerous giving
of his days to "monotones," each of whom, in the words of Dr.
Channing, was an encyclopedist thoroughly versed in "L'Histoire
Universelle de Moi-Même." These were persons ostensibly desiring to propound their own solutions for the world's problems
but driven actually to belabor him with their particular malad-
justments. Unconnected though he personally was in thought
and act from the absurdities or impostures of extremism, Emerson was not free of the imputation of association with eccentric-
ity. The more widely he became known as the apostle of the
individual, the more he was taken by persons out of step, for
whatever reason, with government or society, or disaffected from
the church, to be their champion. Had not his utterances declared him to be of their kind? Had not his endowments ordained
him to be their voice? And so from everywhere they descended
on Concord to seek him out.

It was Emerson who had written shortly after relinquishing
his pulpit at the Second Church, "I like the sayers of No better
than the sayers of Yes" (J, III, 122). And not long after his
removal to Concord he had delivered an address to the ministerial students in the Harvard Divinity School which raised such
a storm of controversy that he was not invited back again for
thirty years. During the two decades preceding the Civil War
an exalted embodiment of individualism and sower of the seed
of self-reliance, he often—most strongly and memorably in his
famous essay of the same name—scathed society with his sarcasm:
"Society everywhere is in conspiracy against the manhood of
every one of its members. Society is a joint-stock company, in
which the members agree, for the better securing of his bread
to each shareholder, to surrender the liberty and culture of the
eater" (W, II, 49-50). Self-reliance meant nonconformity, a refusal to accept the materialistic values of most men and women,
the corrupt politics of their venal legislators, and the sterile
dogmas of their timid churchmen. "Whoso would be a man, must
be a nonconformist." "Nothing is at last sacred but the integrity

of your own mind." This principle, whatever else remained, lay in the consciousness of his readers like an inextinguishable coal, inciting them to manful assertions of their independence.

Yet Emerson's magnanimity disallowed him to close his door or his ear to tendentious importuners, tedious though they happened to be. A man's richness could be measured by his humanity, and humanity meant a friendly disposition to give hospitality to the queer, the outcast, even to the insane. He had set himself to harbor the madness he could not share. He tried, as he put it, to take every one by his best handle, to encounter him on the highest, most genial level possible, confident that an atmosphere of affirmation and accord would allow the mind to open most freely and the give-and-take to lead to some good. Opposition and denial sharpened tempers without clarifying thought.

Patience-trying as were the "monotones," they at least had the commendation of trying to live the particular reforms they preached, going bearded or barefoot or penniless, eating vegetarian or sleeping celibate. Although Emerson disbelieved in the talismanic value of particular reforms, he also knew that reform in general was meaningless, even when applied to an individual life.

Believing in the virtue for every man of some degree of manual labor in the soil, a restorative allowing him to preserve an organic tie with nature otherwise destroyed by an industrialized society, he set himself to do his own gardening. But he was unfit for it physically and temperamentally, and his work was bad. Realizing also that he was wasting time rightly spent on intellectual tasks, he gave it up and turned it over to persons professionally engaged. He continued to use a hoe or sickle but only as therapy, so that, as he wrote in his poem "Musketaquid," all his hurts, his garden spade could heal. He remained always a little on the defensive, however, knowing how easily the scholar-gardener, stooping to pull a weed and finding that behind it were ten others, which, in turn, were seen to hide still a bad," he would say facetiously, "but land is worse"; and, "Whoever sees my garden discovers that I must have some other garden" (W, VII, 384).

Concerned, along with his idealistic, intellectual wife, over the hundred more, could be "duped by a dandelion." "No land is problem of labor in modern society and the need everywhere of democratic relations, he sought to erase the barrier between his family and its few servants. Instead of eating their meals in the kitchen, the workers were invited to join the Emersons at the dining-room table. Embarrassed at the prospect, however, they declined, so that reform came to nothing. Shortly after Bronson Alcott came to Concord, Emerson in agreement with his wife invited him to bring his family to live in their house, half of which gratis would belong to the Alcotts and half to the Emersons, the oven and the potato pot for use jointly, but the cradle not. Community with a hundred families he could not brook, but community with one family of his own kind and choice under the same roof he would try. Mrs. Alcott decided against the offer.

Emerson cherished his feeling of membership in the community of Concord. Citizen as well as resident, he was always interested in what went on in the local school and library no less than what happened in the street. He continued to identify himself with the spiritual life of the town, participating in ceremonies which commemorated significant moments in its past and preserved them for the edification of the future, writing his famous "shot-heard-round-the-world" poem, sung as a hymn to the tune of "Old Hundred," for the dedication of the Battle Monument on July 4, 1837; speaking at the opening of the Sleepy Hollow Cemetery in 1855; delivering an address for the unveiling of the Soldiers Monument in 1869; and, with a short talk, blessing the opening of Concord's Free Public Library in 1873. Through his words he united himself to the little stream of history that would some day bind all local inhabitants together. He went regularly to the town meetings, where, although he almost never spoke, he watched and listened acutely, admiring the various kinds of character and force in those who debated, proud of the homely good sense and pithy speech which produced right decisions. He felt the kinship of those men—callus handed, straight thinking, independent—to the figures of ancient Athens and Rome.

During the 1850's Emerson's attention was drawn, with increasing feeling, to national affairs. Through the years he had been, like Socrates and Jesus in their time, mistrustful of the claims of society to rectitude and to right. Recollecting his own crisis in the ministry, Emerson knew how insidious in church, in government, and in school were the influences undermining integrity and courage in individuals, although church, government, and school could be said to include within their fold decent, respectable folk aplenty. Institutions and organizations, created as means to ends, had a way of cowing man with their pretensions to being ends. They sought to tyrannize over him, demanding his time and money when they could not command his mind. He who would remain independent had to resist them, whether they asked for his dollar on the street corner or knocked for it at his door, whether they came with a petition for him to sign or confronted him with a committee to join. Society was like a wave in the ocean; it seemed to move, but what really moved was an invisible impulsion beneath, all the particles of which it was composed remaining exactly the same and in the same position as before: "All men plume themselves on the improvement of society, and no man improves" (W, II, 84).

Emerson had pledged himself, in his capacity as faithful and illuminating recorder of affairs in his segment of the globe, to remain detached from social causes and political movements, but without becoming a recluse: "It is easy in the world to live after the world's opinion; it is easy in solitude to live after our own; but the great man is he who in the midst of the crowd keeps with perfect sweetness the independence of solitude" (W, II, 53-54).

Temperance fighters, feminist agitators, communitarians, vegetarians, Socialists, pacifists—no such people, although he gave them now more, now less intellectual sympathy and moral support, were to count on his enlistment in their ranks. They were partial in their aim, too embroiled in activity, like soldiers in the smoke of the battle, to see the eventual goal to be won. Even abolitionism was a cause from which he kept himself uncommitted. Let others strive to free black men; he needed to free thoughts. In spite of his abhorrence of slavery, "the greatest calamity in the universe," which had led him twice to invite abolitionist speakers to the Second Church during his ministry there and to offer hospitality to the English abolitionist Harriet Martineau when, on a visit to Boston in 1835 she ran the risk of being mobbed, he remained independent of the movement.

As the years passed, however, he saw with increasing alarm

the growth of the powers of slavery and the incapacity of even the strongest men in the federal government to oppose it. Although "stirrings in the philanthropic mud" gave him no peace and he had resolved to let the republic alone until the republic came to him, it was apparent with the passage of the Fugitive Slave Act in 1850 that it had come. He could any day be coerced into revealing the movements of runaway slaves, could be drafted into a gang to hunt them down. Battle was the only recourse. For the next ten years he was an intransigent platform foe of slavery, and for an additional ten years beyond that he remained critically, though compassionately, attentive to the big decisions of policy affecting the nation's destiny made in Washington. What went on in Washington he could not ignore; Abraham Lincoln, an uncultured unknown from the corn fields of the Middle West, at first seemed to him cause for despair, but through the grand patience, courage, and compassion of his nature, by the time of his assassination he had taken on the stature of a Plutarchan man, "a heroic figure in the center of a heroic epoch" and "the true representative of this continent" (W, XI, 335).

Concerned always over the quality of the life of the nation, Emerson never lost his faith in its future. He had ample opportunity to ask himself whether conditions as they were on the frontier justified his faith. By 1850, his lectures carrying him already as far into the West as St. Louis, Missouri, and Galena, Illinois, he could see the impoverished dusty clearings which passed as farms and the raw mud streets, littered with pigs and tobacco-chewing toughs, lined with saloons and unpainted frame shacks, which made the squalid settlements called towns. In Springfield, Illinois, in 1853, where it rained and thawed incessantly so that if one stepped off the narrow street he went up to his shoulders in muck, he was lodged in a house whose fellow boarders were legislators and two or three former governors—he was not quite sure; "But in the prairie we are all new men just come, and must not stand for trifles" (C, II, 567). Yet there was something being born in the crudity and occasional cruelty of the West which would eventually augur well for man; and, as he had realized when he was only nineteen, in spite of its grossness and immaturity, the United States, removed from the contamination of a tyrannical past which still infected the countries of Europe and the East, enjoyed a comparative purity. It was as true in 1853 as in 1823 that to America monarchs of the world looked with apprehension, and peoples, with hope. In a lecture entitled "The Fortune of the Republic" (his equivalent of Whitman's "Democratic Vistas"), first given in 1863 but repeated with modifications even as late as 1878 in one of his last platform appearances, after listing honestly the many defects of character and corruptions of performance still handicapping the land ("The spirit of our political economy is low and degrading." "The country is governed in bar-rooms, and in the mind of bar-rooms." "Our great men succumb . . . to the forms of the day . . ."), he affirmed the destiny of America to be to produce freedom and "exalted manhood" for the world: "I wish to see America not like the old powers of the earth, grasping, exclusive and narrow, but a benefactor such as no country ever was, hospitable to all nations, legislating for all nationalities" (W, XI, 531).

CHAPTER 2

The Development of Emerson's Thought in His Early Manhood

THE famous remark by the French eighteenth-century naturalist Comte Buffon is as true of a writer living as of a writer
writing: *"le style est l'homme même"* ("Style is the man himself"). In a sense, then, to study the quality, the style, of Emerson's life is to comprehend the nature of his thought. He was
as exemplary in his days in Concord as was, on the other side
of the ocean, "the saint of Rationalism," John Stuart Mill, in the
tranquillity of his home at Blackheath. Socrates, before the
Athenian Assembly, sought to vindicate himself by an appeal
to his visible person and to the qualities which emanated from
it, presumably because his embodiment of virtue was of more
consequence than his teachings about it. "The character of Lord
Morley's power"—so went a dictum about one of the famous
protégés of Mill— "is the power of Lord Morley's character." So
with Emerson. You did not go to hear Emerson lecture; you
went to hear Emerson. Indeed an individual once, arriving for
a lecture after it had already been given, consoled himself with
the reflection that it was better to miss Emerson than hear anybody else.

Yet the character of Emerson would not have been what it
was had he not thought as he did. While nobody's conduct is
the precise sum total of his ideas, what he does is necessarily
related to what inhabits his mind. What were the beliefs actuating Emerson in the decades of his Concord residency? What
was the view of life translating itself with such felicity into
word and deed? Before undertaking to ascertain this, however,
it is important to have a closer glimpse of the cast of his mind
during the crucial years of his early manhood by taking stock
of some of its leading ideas. What were the convictions that
impelled him in his twenty-ninth year to take the most mo-

mentous step of his life and leave the Christian ministry? What were the growing philosophical conceptions of deity and nature and of man's relation to them both which determined him on a path of independence at that time and later, in full flower, made him the renowned apostle of self-reliance?

The earliest seeds of the development of Emerson's mind are found in his two college dissertations, on Socrates and on the contemporary state of ethical philosophy. Socrates, part poet and part philosopher, admirable incarnator of fortitude, temperance, and prudence, was to Emerson distinguished by his great fund of "plain good sense" which had "enabled him to investigate his own character, to learn the natural tendency and bias of his own genius, and thus to perfectly control his mental energies." Whether, with his daemon and his claim to divine inspiration, he could have been a forerunner of Jesus, it was futile to ask, since such speculations did not lead to truth but served only to bewilder. What counted was that with the right kind of patriotism he had extended his wisdom to

the body of the people in the first city of the world, and communicated to his disciples not a hieroglyphical scripture to amuse the learned and awe the ignorant, but practical rules of life, adapted immediately to their condition and character, and little infected by the dogmas of the age. (TUE)

Without doubt he had "employed his reason to unveil the sublime purposes of Providence," and the lofty equanimity of his death, in which there was no trace of melancholy, left one no choice but to "bestow upon the pagan the praise of a perfect man."

In his discussion of ethical philosophy, significantly Emerson ascribed a strong value to the moral sense, innate and distinct from the conscious ratiocinative faculty. Where the will of God is concerned, for instance, we cannot *know* that it intends "the greatest possible happiness" for man. Although we reason from adaptation and analogy, "the object of these reasonings is [only] to confirm the decision of the moral faculty," which is the "original principle of our nature—an intuition by which we directly determine the merit or demerit of an action." Emerson refuted the doctrine that men are selfish and by nature tend "to savage-

ness and stupidity," maintaining that the faculties by which
they are impelled to the highest possible degree of activity are
precisely those which prompt them to "social intercourse, where
alone they have their widest range." And finally, in relating the
idea of democracy to the practice of virtue, he asserted that
God did not want an odious aristocracy based on "distinctions
of intellect and the pride of erudition," which were too often
profaned, but preferred a wide distribution of "humble energies . . . entirely devoted to the cause of virtue." "A series of
humble efforts was more meritorious than solitary miracles of
virtue." Under the excitement of great circumstance and with
the assurance of public applause, even a man without fixed
principles of virtue may rise to great sacrifice. It is more difficult,
removed from the stimulus of theatrical moment, to live through
the commonplace of today, tomorrow, and the day ever after
with courage, patience, generosity, and grace.

In the next decade and a half the main ideas of both utterances continued to expand and bear collateral fruit. The primacy
of the intuitive elements in psychological and spiritual experience
became steadily more revealed to him, along with the increased
extent of their domain and their influence in daily life. As for
the image of Socrates, incarnator of fully developed manhood
distinct from the almost solely spiritual embodiment of Jesus,
it remained priceless to Emerson, and the principle of wisdom
as a thing liberated from obscurantist metaphysics and receivable
by the body of people actuated him to the end of his life. However, in spite of his conviction that "the people know as much
and reason as well as we do," he did not intend to conform to
their mind. One's attitude toward them was necessarily double.
Talking with a workman or shopkeeper, one was impressed by
the rightness of his thinking on a particular political issue or
business practice; yet during the antics of an election campaign,
one could not escape the conclusion that public opinion would
bear any amount of nonsense. That one of the people showed
good sense in a particular conversation only showed that all
people had a faculty for right reason, hardly that they reasoned
right all the time. It was to this faculty that the man of thought
and books, the scholar, should address himself, for it needed
cultivation and enlargement.

Throughout the period of his teaching and his ministry Em-

erson's mind returned to certain major themes in such a way
that their dimensions were always slightly enlarged, their features a little more sharply defined through being shown from an
altered vantage point or in a new ray of light. His was an intelligence gracefully and with controlled impetus describing ever-
widening circles, or arcs indicating circles, not always fully
defined but seeming to grow out of one another on steadily
higher levels so that the thought, in the aspiration governing it,
spiraled perpetually upward. In a broad sense there are three
matters which in the ministerial years claimed his attention; the
proper attitude toward life in the face of the problem of evil
in the world and of the situation of the individual in it (hopelessly determined or free?); the proper end of religion and the
nature of Christianity; and the nature of God, or the idea of
divinity, and in relation to it the identity and position of Jesus.
These fields of thought, in spite of their overlapping, are best
considered in such a sequential relation as this.

From his late college days on Emerson praised life as good
and the proper attitude toward it as joy. What sane man, invited
to a banquet, would sit pouting in a corner, sucking his thumb?
Since the affair was kindly intended he would do better to par-
ticipate happily and "carry forward the brilliant game." Remembering always that the Greek word meant beauty, everyone
during his brief moment in the world before disappearing into
the abyss, should lift his hands and say, "Kosmos!" Already fond
of quoting Saint Augustine's "Let others dispute; I will wonder,"
the young celebrant of life maintained that we are born with
the instinct to revere and to adore, and that whoever slights it
makes his life barren. In admiration, which is close to love and
one of the "mainsprings of our progressive nature," life expands
because all our powers are open. In resentment or fear, which
are related to hate, life contracts for our faculties clench on
themselves and freeze. The mind by its very nature must go
out of itself and apply its affections to others. We know by
the way we feel whether we are living or dying. God has created
us to live, that is, to be happy, and has shaped the universe also
to that end, for the wider and more closely Emerson looked the
more he saw the system of things essentially to be one of
harmonies.

Often, however, fear and weakness swept over him at the

realization of evil in the world. About its origin, like other sensitive young men he thought very much. The book answer, that
it had come into the world with the sin of Adam, was less cred-
itable than the honest admission that our nature was incompetent
to explain its existence. A partially satisfactory explanation lay
in a kind of compensation, according to which nothing is known
until its opposite is experienced; we never know health until
we have endured sickness. Another justification, acceptable only
to the Christian, was in the nature of this life as probation for
the one to come. But the appalling enigma lay heavily on his
mind. What of the slave "born in chains [and] living in stripes
and toil," who had never heard of virtue and died cursing God
and man? What could justify the wretchedness of his life and
the horror to follow it? The diversity and magnitude of human
misery, Emerson knew to be frightful. Could a Benevolent Spirit
continue to introduce onto the stage of existence millions of new
beings, in incessant series to blunder, live in suffering, and go
on to damnation? Calvinism, with its doctrine of predestination,
although admittedly one hypothesis to solve the problem, was as
bad as the problem itself. Mankind seemed in such examples
abjectly helpless, its very lack of freedom stamping as evil all
the more vividly the system of things.

If on the other hand one regarded individuals illustrious in
achievement, one was inclined to view man as free and the
universe as good. But perhaps no single man was in every respect
solely responsible for his deeds, no matter how great. The issue
seemed to admit of minute gradations, to be not at all resolvable
in absolute terms. The Christian, Emerson maintained at the
beginning of his preaching career, could not but see man as
wholly obligated to God. "Nothing . . . can destroy, nothing
abridge, the claim of obedience which a Creator advances upon
his creatures." No man is his own but belongs to the Creator,
who has shaped him as a clod and then breathed His own divine
life into him. Having come from God, being a part of God, he
is absolutely God's. There is no such thing as "entire license to
go right or to go wrong" (J, I, 251-53). We are free only to do
right, which is what God wills us to do.

With those who would minimize even that degree of freedom
by the argument that it was inadequately small in the face of
the might of the temptation of sin, Emerson, only recently out

of college, disagreed. There was, true, "a huge and disproportionate abundance of evil on earth," but it had not been made more attractive than good. Even if evil were ten times more seductive than it was, it was impossible to understand how any man, once having rightly seen the loveliness of virtue and known the indescribable satisfaction that comes from its practice, could deliberately choose not to do it.

His own life, however, he came to observe as a schoolteacher, was slight and unpredictable. Of all his waking hours each day there were only a "few strong moments" when he knew himself to be living; and of his growth, although he could see that he had grown, he could say only that it was sporadic and unaccountable. To what an extent was he free when he had to confess that he grew by jumps in periods of intense thought and feeling, followed by stretches of barrenness, and that the leaps upward were dependent on circumstances often without his control? Picking up "unawares the Master Key, whose wards and springs open every door," he was a "surprised adventurer" who could only go on "astonished from cell to cell, from chamber to chamber gratified . . . overawed" (J, II, 94-95). He shaped his own fortunes, it seemed, not at all, but in everything obeyed a strong necessity. Suppose a period of suspended action should last forever and thought never return. Who could endure an apathetic blank as his immortality? "Eternity is only desirable when regarded as the career of an inquisitive mind" (J, II, 136). Alas, we are no more than scarecrows.

The pendulum of his thought, as of his feelings, in human fashion oscillated. He persisted in the conviction that if a mind could attain to sufficient perspective, seeing the operation of the entire universe, it would understand the mystery. In his brighter moments, of which there were many, he maintained that Heraclitus and his like, always seeing miscarriage and misfortune, were wrong: "True philosophy hath a clearer light, and remarks amid the vast disproportions of human condition a great equalization of happiness; an intimate intermingling of pleasure with every gradation, down to the very lowest of all" (J, I, 198). The very prodigality of the gift of life itself, through eons of time to billions of creatures in air and sea as well as on land, endowing them with shape and color and function and impelling them with resistless urge to activity and instinctual satisfaction, was proof of the benevolence of God. Which of those creatures was not pleased with the gift of life and loath to lose it? He himself, although he had known the abasement and pain of sickness, once emerged from it, had decided not to think on necessity or on the problem of evil in the world, not to pester his imagination with "what is done unseen, with the burden that is put in the contrary scale, with the sowing of the death-seed in the place of the nettle that was rooted up." He was "a more cheerful philosopher, . . . rather anxious to thank Oromasdes than to fear Ahriman" (J, II, 71).

Still he was troubled by the impediment imposed on some lives by accident, of stunted abilities, of sickness, of outward circumstance, which prevented them from attaining their desired ends and could not but be bowed to. In a low moment in his twenty-first year he concluded that, as nearly as he could see,

Time & Chance hold on their old way & we shape ourselves to them as well as we can. Young men & old soon find that these ancient principles, whether they shall call them fates or providences are the lords of life, to whose ordinations they must conform themselves. . . . The seed may be the best that ever was planted, but if it fall on stony ground it will not grow. (L, I, 148)

Perhaps the soundest conclusion to draw from the widest possible observation of things was that "the world . . . holds more dominion than it yields—both the natural and moral system." Both inescapable plan and freedom to act characterized the cosmos, for it was a "harmonious whole, combined and overruled by a sublime Necessity, which embraces in its mighty circle the freedom of the individuals, and without subtracting from any, directs all to their appropriate ends" (J, I, 199). And every man, therefore, longing to make something of himself and to rise in life, found himself in the situation of the ancient Macedonian conqueror—"as to the old knot of human liberty, our Alexanders must still *cut* its Gordian twines" (L, I, 138). Emerson, himself such an Alexander, urged his congregation never to despond, never to think of man as helpless or to view him as a pawn. "We hear a great deal of the empire of circumstances over the mind, but not enough of the empire of the mind over circumstances." Circumstances no more made the man than air made sound or than the wind brought the ship into harbor. And every person could exert influence as well as receive it.

That individuals had potentiality of development meant also that they must bear responsibility for not developing. It was idle to talk about the ills of society in an abstract, or collective sense, and equally idle to discuss plans for its renovation through systems of legislation, through institutions and organizations. What was done wrong at large was only a magnification of what was done at home. Instead of bewailing the profligacy of public morals, we ought to "lay our hands on our own breasts and say, *We are the men.*" "This is the way to reform states. You compel people to be better by being better yourself" (YES, 78-81).

Most men and women, blind to what lay about them, lived not only joylessly but like animals. "We would have them live like men." The whole object of the universe being the formation of character, it was the duty of the church to reveal how character should be formed. Life might be a banquet, but, unless he was educated to a knowledge of foods and how best to eat them, a man could not properly enjoy it. One must incessantly watch his habits, for the bubble of the present was every moment hardening into the flint of the past. Spontaneity needed to be wedded to regularity. The rules Emerson required, he must not be mastered by. In order to get "the most sweetness out of time," he must wear the easy dress of order not the straitjacket of method.

Rightly understood, "The great art which religion teaches, is the art of conducting life well . . . in the very best manner, [as] if there were no future state" (YES, 99). Religion was invaluable because for ordinary persons, who would never be in situations where greatness was called for, it could make the meanest offices of every day interesting by introducing the "sacred relation of God into the use of every faculty." Of Emerson's more than one hundred and seventy sermons, the one preached more often than any other was "On Showing Piety at Home," in which he sought to inspire his listeners with the desire to rise in their daily life to the dignity of angels. If we need an occasion and many onlookers to excite our virtue, it is only a sign "that we fear men more than God and respect men more than we respect ourselves" (YES, 16). The great test of character is to be fine at home—cheerful, affectionate, generous, and witty; the hardest of all human tasks is to live "a single hour of perfect purity."

Since the purification of life was the end of religion, "Philosopher or Christian, whatever faith you teach, live by it." And Emerson as a young man was convinced that Christianity was the best avenue to such an end, for on the grounds of its power to transform character, it could be seen historically to have been superior to any other faith. But Christianity, taught always as an academic subject involving emperors, bishops, popes, coronations, elections, synods, and creeds, put its emphasis on things— things already done and therefore dead—rather than on persons now alive and on God, perennially alive. In the language of a mystic, we did wrong in our historical emphasis by "putting Time between God and us"; we ought to "account every moment of the existence of the Universe as a new Creation, and *all* as a revelation proceeding each moment from the Divinity to the mind of the observer" (L, I, 174). We ought to judge Christianity not for what it was and meant to others but for what it is now and what it says to us, putting out of mind all its "pretensions on which the dust of 16 or 18 centuries has gathered." To go to church unfailingly, to read the Bible assiduously, to discuss theological problems learnedly was not to be religious; only to do good was. Deeds, not words, have always been the test of righteousness. Only Christianity could lead one to live "in the daily exercise of the purest and most expanded affections."

The best means to transformation of character Christianity might be, enabling men and women to live daily in the "purest and most expanded affections," but the particular brand of Christianity to which Emerson subscribed needs to be established. How in the perspective of the centuries of Christianity is the faith with which he entered the ministry to be placed? What changes during his years of maturation did it undergo? To say that the intellectual climate into which he was born was still colored in some respects by the perpetuation at a popular level of a theology already outgrown by the best New England minds —Calvinistic Puritanism—or that the church to which he attached himself in Boston was a Unitarian church, is not to say much if one does not know what Calvinism or Unitarianism was. Even to say that Emerson's early notion of the deity was of the Christian deity since he was a birthright member of a Christian society is not to speak very precisely, as a brief survey of some features of Christian thought reveals.

The Christian deity has not always been the same from one period of history to another or from one group of believers to another. Even in the New Testament the deity reveals, in the hands of His various apostle-commentators as well as in the reported remarks of Jesus about Him, qualities diverse enough to allow Him to appear to interpreters of different temperament in different guise. There is the deity who is the loving and forgiving father, and there is the deity who is the angry and unrelenting punisher. There is the deity whose will even a child can understand, and there is the deity whose precepts defy elucidation by the subtlest of sacred scholars. There is the deity whose worship is simple, but also the deity belief in whom can only be propagated through an institutionalized church buttressed by a complicated structure of legalisms. There is the deity whose principal will for His creatures is for their earthly good, and alongside Him the deity whose preoccupation toward them seems to be with their eventual beatitude in heaven; the deity, that is, who wants His creatures to live with one another in charity and in so doing to establish a society on earth like that in heaven ("Thy kingdom come on earth as it is in Heaven") and the deity intent on reminding his creatures of the supreme importance of the ultimate mysteries—the nature of the soul, the nature of death, and the indescribable events to be experienced by the soul after death. Jesus, in other words, taught a social gospel, according to which we must feed the hungry, clothe the naked, and heal the sick; and he also talked a "philosophy" of wonders, of things which altogether surpassed human understanding. From the beginning, then, Christianity has exhibited a double face. It has been at once a religion for this life and for another life, for the earth and for a place above the earth, of altruism (emphasizing benefit to others) and of autoism (emphasizing benefit to one's self), of humanitarianism and of eschatology.

For centuries, for various reasons Christianity—no longer the body of belief of the New Testament, but that body of belief amplified by theologians, who were the early Church Fathers— remained a religion whose chief emphasis was eschatological. During the period of the Renaissance, however, reformist think-

ers, reflecting the new importance of applying reason critically
to traditional beliefs as well as to matters of daily life and to
the features of the natural universe—an importance deriving
from the discovery of the intellectual achievements of the ancient Greeks—began to call into question not only the unex-
emplary lives lived by the representatives of the institution
which was the custodian of the holy faith but also the remoteness of that faith from actual life. The Church was declared
both corrupt in its practices and obscurantist in its teachings;
it perpetuated metaphysical doctrines not only unintelligible to
human reason but also repugnant to human nature. The doctrine
of the Trinity, for instance, involving the Homoousian idea,
according to which Jesus the Son and God the Father were of
the same substance and Jesus was simultaneously human and
not human, was declared by some speculative radicals, among
them Faustus Socinus, a sixteenth century Italian, to be meaningless. Additional dogmas inherited from early Christian centuries, such as original sin and total depravity (that is, ineradicable and overwhelming inclination to wickedness and total
ineffectuality of the human will in any effort to better the human
situation) were rejected as abhorrent.

In spite of growing currents of such rationalism, however,
John Calvin of Geneva, Switzerland, himself a sixteenth-century
reformer of the faith of a very special kind, created a new brand
of Christianity, substantially derived from Saint Augustine,
which not only perpetuated those very same dogmas but crowned
them with a new one of predestination—namely, that God, for
some reason which no human being would ever know, had, eons
ago, arbitrarily decided the ultimate destiny of the endless millions of mortal creatures he was about to create, by decreeing
that many of them would go after death automatically to hell
for eternal punishment and some would be sent instead to heaven
for blissful reward. For Calvin, it seemed, many were called
and few indeed chosen; yet, in spite of its outrage to human
dignity and the human sense of justice—since the doom of human
beings had no necessary relation to their merit, to whether they
had lived well or ill—his theology was widespread and of incalculable influence for more than a century.

In the United States, Jonathan Edwards in the first half of
the eighteenth century gave eloquently elegiac expression to

the stern tenets of Calvinism. Edwards as a Calvinist spokesman, however, was an anachronism, at least a half century behind his time. The Salem Witch Trials, for example, which were conducted by authoritarian Calvinist judges, had taken place in 1692, and by 1758, the year of Edwards' death, they could be remembered only with revulsion by enlightened minds. "Enlightened," because the middle of the eighteenth century was the apogee of the Enlightenment, a new age in which the tendencies manifested two hundred years earlier by Renaissance radical thinkers were achieving their consummation. The eighteenth century boasted a new religion, a new brand of Christianity known as deism, considered more consonant with the facts of human nature and of external nature, as more-than-human power was evidenced in it. Deism was the faith of a rationalist and included in the roster of its believers many illustrious names. In America, Benjamin Franklin was a deist, as were Thomas Paine and Thomas Jefferson. Like Jefferson, every deist could pride himself on being "a true Christian"—a follower, that is, of Jesus Christ of Nazareth—distinct from the pseudo-Christians or "Platonists," who still subscribed to metaphysical absurdities like that of the Trinity, according to which one was one and at the same time three. For the deist, what Jesus had said about restoring the sick and succoring the poor and naked was important; what he had said about the soul and death and a hereafter was unimportant. Deism valued the social gospel and not the eschatological doctrine. To the tribunal of reason the deist summoned every preconception, religious as well as philosophical and political, for examination and evaluation. Only that tribunal was infallible and could be called supreme. Revelation of the traditional theological kind led men into extremism of opinion and persecution of one another, which was manifest abomination. In contrast, reason taught moderation and tolerance.

By the time of Emerson's birth in 1803, anti-Trinitarian feelings, which were at least three hundred years old, inhabited the breasts of many men—so many, in fact, that they composed a special population among Christians, a new and special church, the Unitarian Church. Unitarianism, needless to say, emphasizing a unitary deity, or God as the one being who was divine, owed much to the deism which had preceded it. Emerson as a young man stigmatizing the idea of the Trinity as a sort of intellectual

scarecrow with which the Almighty would never mock the
intelligences of his worshipers was voicing his revulsion in terms
very much like those of Thomas Jefferson a generation earlier.
Unitarianism hymned the order and harmony of the natural
universe as evidences of the might and intelligence of God but
above all as signs of His mercy and benignity. God as provi-
dential God could not be overvalued; He had provided abun-
dantly for His creatures in creating the cosmos. Reverencing the
kindness of God, the Unitarian at the same time, along with the
deist, was grateful that He did not make revelations of Himself,
either internal or external, any longer. To do so would be only
to intervene needlessly in human affairs, which would be resolved in the long run harmoniously by man himself, who had
not only the immeasurably precious revelation of God made
centuries ago in the form of the Bible with which to be guided
but also the Godly gift of reason. The Unitarian, although he
denied his divinity, reverenced Jesus, as the deist had, for his
lofty morals and sublime philanthropy. He went beyond the
deist, however, in his attentive reading of the Scriptures, his
practice of prayer, and his considerable thought to the nature
of the soul and its immortality. He believed that God required
to be worshiped in corporate ritual in church edifices, whereas
for the deist the doing of good works outside any church was
the worship most acceptable to Him.

Emerson early made up his mind about the various religious
currents of his day. Always sensitive and concerned over human
values in a historical context, he was quite ready to give Puritanism its due. To the achievement of the new America, as the
latest instance of the growth of mankind, the Puritan character
had been indispensable. To these shores from England the
Puritans had brought both "their pride of intellectual power"
and that of "indomitable purpose." Leveling forests, wresting
rocks from the soil, building schools and colleges as well as
churches, believing in the destiny of the mind as something
more than a counter of pence and a rationalizer of sensuality,
they had shown that the "theory of the strong impulse" was
true. "The energy of an abused people, whose eyes the light of
books and progress of knowledge had just opened, has a better
title to immortality than that vulgar physical energy" of Gothic
or Scandinavian ancestors, always praised (J, I, 307). And this

energy had been consummately shown in the rational attainment
of Jonathan Edwards. Wrong as the Puritan notion of God had
been, it was nevertheless right in its ascription to Him of rationality and power. Emerson could not brook the notion of a God
"who was kind and good because he knew no better; who was
infinitely gentle as brutes are gentle" (J, I, 286). He revered—
and thought most men did—"the Providence of God as the benign
and natural *result* of his omniscience." Yet Calvinism, with its
emphasis on human depravity and, in Edwards' phrase, its "awful
doctrine of God's Sovereignty," according to which mankind was
immutably divided into a handful of the elect and hordes of the
damned, although it had served New England well, had rightly
seen its day. There had been something valuable in the way its
severities of belief and sternness of discipline had accommodated
themselves to the hardness of New England soil and the rigors
of its climate; and Emerson, though he abhorred the idea of
predestination—as his admirable little tribute to his grandfather
Dr. Ripley later showed—never lost his admiration of the sturdy
characters it had bred. But he was forever mindful of the deplorably anthropomorphic and parochial nature of the deity it
established even in the minds of its ministers.

As its minister from March, 1829, until December, 1832, Emerson was quite aware that the features of the Unitarian faith
of the Second Church of Boston, in comparison with the drama
of Calvinism, were thin and bleached, but his own construction
of the doctrine that could be preached under its name he hoped
would compensate for its attenuation. Unitarianism, reflecting
the growing scientific temper of the new century and its humanitarianism as well, appealed strongly to reformist minds.
Such a mind had been that of Emerson's father; such a mind
was his own. Although it respected the authority of the Scriptures as the sole divine Revelation, Unitarianism maintained that
they should be always open to the scrutiny of reason. Yet from
this claim it excepted the miracles of the New Testament, presumably on the ground that although Jesus was only man he
had been licensed by God to perform stupendous feats as necessary and incontrovertible signs of divine authority. As a consequence of their attitude toward miracles, Unitarians venerated
the Sacrament of the Lord's Supper. And this veneration was
the rock on which Emerson's Unitarian attachment split in pieces.

To understand why Emerson's hope of accommodating his increasingly liberal religious views to the demands of his Unitarian pulpit came to nothing, one must examine the growth of his idea of God and his conception of that part of the human psyche, called the soul, to which God appeals.

In his reflections on his spiritual life Emerson valued increasingly what he had declared in his Bowdoin dissertation of 1821 to be important in human religious experience—the moral faculty. It was not only the innate principle—the intuition—by which one knew what things were good and what bad. It was also that part of the self capable of illumination and expansion in moments of discovery, altogether transforming the quality of one's being and enabling him, in a happy suspension oblivious of time and space and self, to inhabit what could only be called eternity. The moral sense must be of divine origin since it seemed to be "more essential to our constitution than any other feeling whatever" and even "to be implied in consciousness." Even of the chaos of dreams it sat, wakeful, as judge. Its promptings it appeared to have from a participation in "the counsels of the eternal world," and one sensed Platonically from them that his soul "was but an emanation from the Abyss of Deity, and about to return whence it flowed" (J, I, 163-64).

Emerson was led to conclude that often the most important decisions of his life were made by something situated in an undiscernible recess of his being acting upon considerations of which he was often unaware and in ways he could not fathom. At the time of his entering the ministry, he realized with the wonder of a mystic the involuntary chain of "little coincidences in little things" responsible for his decision. In each man's history there must be such changes betokening the operation of a power within him not his own and higher than his own, causing the mind to stand

... forth in alarm with all her faculties, suspicious of a Presence which it behoves her deeply to respect—touched not more with awe than with curiosity, if perhaps some secret revelation is not about to be vouchsafed. . . . These are not the State Reasons by which we can enforce the burdensome doctrine of a Deity on the world, but make often, I apprehend, the body of evidence on which private conviction is built. (L, I, 170)

The doctrine of a deity, however, was in no way burdensome to Emerson. The mind touched with poetry must have a God, and the heart would reveal one if history did not. The evidence of feeling, of intuition, was incontrovertible.

My days are made up of the irregular succession of a very few different tones of feeling. These are my feasts and fasts. Each has his harbinger, some subtle sign by which I know when to prepare for its coming. Among these some are favourites, and some are to me as the Eumenides. But one of them is the sweet asylum where my greatest happiness is laid in. . . . (J, II, 219)

It was "like the life of angels to live in" the asylum when disaster struck, for it was nothing less than the presence of God. The humble celebrant could only marvel at the mystery, as sublime in wretchedness as in happiness, perhaps more nearly knowable in wretchedness than in happiness. During his illness, the seeming ruin of all his earthly chances, the depredation of suffering, and the "grievous dependence on other men which suffering brings with it" had alarmed him with their exposure of a system of necessity previously unapprehended. At the same time, "These suggest the possibility of relations more intimate and more awful than friendship and love. They bring to light a system of feelings whose existence was not suspected before; they place [one] in a connexion with God that furnishes a solution of the mystery of his being" (J, II, 180). The sublime relations, at once intimate and awful, were with immutable, imperishable ideas (features of the Eternal Divine), not unrelated to human friendship, truth, and love but far transcending them in perfection, and to live in them was to become invulnerable to the tragic havoc of pain and treachery and failure of life.

It gave Emerson pleasure to reflect on "the mighty image of God within the Soul." Intuitively we know that God exists; indeed, men have known it ever since the beginning of history, for such an intuition, not limited by time or geography or society, we can see to have affected thought in India and China before Greece and Palestine. Yet "we are not born to any image of perfect virtue." Ideas, like bodies, are subject to growth, and the moral sense is not exempt from education. We need the

examples of great ethical teachers of the past, whose ideas of
virtue and of divinity excite it. God "can be nothing less than
our own highest conception, and our conceptions continually
soar higher—both the man's and the age's. So that the best man
of our time is a nobler moral exhibition than the *God* of a much
ruder time" (J, II, 273-74).

By the time of his ministry, Emerson conceived of the relation
between man and God as one of loving dependency. As a child
by the umbilical cord is connected to its mother, so we by the
moral sense are tied to God. Yet in all this there is no anthropomorphism. God, in effect, because of His love can be called
our Father, our "most effectual friend"; but in a less personal
sense He is not so much the observer of our actions as "the
potent principle" binding them together, not so much the reader
of our thoughts as "the active creator" aiding them into being.
Strictly speaking, every human faculty is "but a mode of his
action"; our reason is God and our virtue is God, and only the
freedom to use them is our own. God, then, is "an object worthy
of endless study and love, whom to know aright is life eternal."

Of the ethical teachers of mankind the greatest had been
Jesus, God's "highly authorized and highly honored servant."
He had understood that prayer is not vulgar petition on the part
of a creature far removed from his creator but conversation between a lesser mind and a greater. He had prayed, "Thy kingdom come, Thy will be done, on earth as it is in Heaven," but
he had already taught that the kingdom of heaven was within
man. It is because God is "the most elevated conception of
character that can be formed . . . the individual's own soul
carried out to perfection," infinitely good, wise, just, and beautiful, that when the individual opens his mind to God in prayer,
the degrees of goodness, wisdom, justice, and beauty already
within him are enlarged and his affections are purified and
expanded.

Jesus had indeed shown the way and been the light. Thinking
of the possibility of the coming of the kingdom on earth, Emerson would wax as jubilant as Milton two centuries earlier,
who had hymned the transformation of society solely through
a following of the freedom proclaimed by the charming piper and
poet of Galilee. "If the principles of Jesus could take possession
of all breasts, life would not be vile. Society would be pure but

not puritanical." Men and women as they were, at best "half-faced friends of God," were awkward in religion and holy without beauty. But as for Christianity, "In its source it is the all fair. A community of Christians would be a field of splendid occasions, exciting recollections, purposes; grand characters and epical situations that would leave the loftiest fiction, of prose and verse, far beneath it. . . . (J, II, 373).

Every person, Emerson had concluded before entering the ministry, had possibilities of uniqueness. It should be the duty of Christian ministers to exhibit this priceless individualization of human personality, but they were signal only as failures. If they avoided "that general language and general manner" in which they strove "to hide all that is peculiar" and said "only what was uppermost in their own minds after their own individual manner," they would be interesting. But they always seemed to be ashamed of themselves and so were dull.

Individualism not only made thought interesting; it made it authoritative. Jesus was both arresting and influential because he spoke with authority—an authority derived from consulting only his own breast and his own mind, not the recorded sentiments and thoughts of others. And yet, paradoxically, the firmest particularity in thought was at once the surest universality. How often, when we had heard a new melody or seen a new landscape, was it revealed to us flashingly that we had heard or seen it before. Similarly, the words of a wise and eloquent man, which excited us and made us tremble with delight, sounded as old as ourselves. We had listened to them all sometime, somewhere before. "It is God in you that responds to God without," concluded Emerson confidently. Deploring what he called pepper-corn aims and rejoicing over the number of persons of quality in life and history to draw his admiration and love, he was determined to "go buoyed up as high as sentiments of Heaven" would allow and not to "huckster with sense and custom, but treat with princes only—a sovereign with a sovereign" (J, II, 393). The princes—the sovereigns—were discovered all to have been—and to be—individuals, persons distinguished by cultivation of the self. And yet, paradoxically, each, although par excellence a self, was unselfish. The example of Jesus was of help in elucidating this further paradox. What did it mean to think? It was "to receive truth immediately from God without any medium." It was living faith. Dead faith, on the other hand, was taking facts on trust. To rely on one's self, then, was the height of humility and piety, not pride; it was "an unwillingness to learn of any but God himself."

Not only was each person "born with a peculiar character or . . . a peculiar determination to some one pursuit or one sort of usefulness," but all the powers he had were "extremely susceptible of cultivation"; his soul was "an infinite spiritual estate": "If God has made us with such intention as revelation discloses, then it must be that there are in each of us all the elements of moral and intellectual excellence . . ." (YES, 106). And each could, if he really acted out his self, attain "a perfect character." The more finished a character was, "the more striking its individuality"; and the more individualized all men's characters, then the better the state of the world, for it would approximate the infinite diversity of nature, in which not only was an oak different from a pine and a violet from a daisy but no oak or pine, or violet or daisy, was the duplicate of any other. It was evident that to be self-reliant in the quest for individuality meant to distinguish between the two selves, the "low and partial self" and the "whole self"—the self that Jesus had in mind when he asked what it profited a man to gain the world if he lost his soul. There was nothing in self-reliance incompatible with religion. It not only did not contravene a "spirit of dependence and piety toward God," it *was* dependence in piety on God.

Day after day during his pastorate the incredible truth of the paradoxes of self-reliance unveiled itself to Emerson, and he embraced it with ever more ardor. Let every "man scorn to imitate any being, let him fully trust his own share of God's goodness," and he would be led on to perfection. The revelation even seemed to close the awful gap between the splendid heroes of humanity and the wretched specimens whose only distinction was that they were counted by the million, for it meant that the meanest living soul had potentialities higher than the realizations of character hitherto achieved by the greatest men.

Every effort should be made to awaken early in children the sense of ideal behavior through arousing the affections and the instinct for admiration. And with his fine historical sense, citing Socrates, Jesus, the Stoics, the martyrs of the early Christian Church, Alfred, Luther, Newton, and Laplace and other astronomers, Emerson exhorted every parent and every teacher to show the child "the world as God's work; as the house in which wise and great and brave men have dwelled, that with all the evil, almost every spot of it is made venerable by their history ... (YES, 52).

But of this truth education took no heed, repeating as it did musty maxims and cultivating puppet piety through its mistaken attachment to trivial forms of behavior. One needed to be on guard against the tendency of society to magnify trifles, to remember that the human mind was capable of a grand view, and accordingly to aim always at a "great simplicity of living, and dress, and simplicity of character." One was not to ask, "What will people think?" but to recall that Jesus had rebuked the officiousness and conventional solicitude of Martha and, therefore, like him, to despise trifles. One was not to punish a child for dirtying his coat—"Do not teach him to be dainty in his food or nice of his dress"—or let him wonder about the disapproval of neighbors, for this was to develop in him an apprehension over material and superficial things: "I know it is difficult to walk in the world with these lofty views, for life is cast among little things. And society is full of superstitions and makes an outcry when its forms or idols are contemned" (YES, 53). But if one kept in mind the strength that was more than his own, he could so walk.

Little things, however, from another point of view, even when ugly and mean, are of value. Pascal had taken pleasure in exposing the juxtaposition of the sublime and the vile in human life, but Pascal's was not the final word; "there is not a thing so poor and refuse in the world but that has some aspects and connexions which are grand" (J, II, 173). In the reflection of life in literature little things are priceless. An anecdote or an aphorism can "give better insight into the depths of past centuries than grave and voluminous chronicles." To know which way the wind is blowing, one does not throw up a stone, he throws a straw. And in the course of a day the fortuitous consequences flowing from the homeliest, seemingly most trivial things are inexpressible —a movement, an expression, a tone of voice on the part of someone nearby. The diurnal contributes to the eternal. In moments of fear or weakness we look on the faces of our friends and, seeing good nature and courage there, take heart.

As for the life hereafter, truth, goodness, justice, love, beauty—
it was only such principles that were divine, were eternal, and
in proportion as we lived by them we lived in them and hence
in eternity. The spiritual part of us, our reason in its largest
sense, which comprehended those indestructible spiritual qualities, must also be therefore indestructible. Hence, immortality
was living in the spirit here and now, on this earth. With his
emphasis increasingly on the possibilities of eternity in this life,
"the real heaven" after which we should seek, Emerson sought
to rid men's minds of conventional notions about "the other life"
in a place called heaven. But, if the kingdom of heaven was
within us, so also was the kingdom of hell. To the ineluctable
law of compensation at work in life creating heaven or hell, it
was imperative to open men's and women's eyes: "Go where
you will, you shall work out with great fidelity your own effect
. . . everything takes the line of our thought." A peevish man is
always being crossed; a benevolent is forever blessed; a sensual
is incessantly sensualized. "So is this the law of all action. All
things are double, one against another. Love and you shall be
loved. Hate and you shall be hated" (YES, 101-2).

The natural world became steadily more important in Emerson's frame of things. "Providence supports, but does not spoil
its children" (J, II, 11). He took increasing pleasure as he looked
about him in what seemed, no matter how slight, evidence of
nature's "progressive adaptation to human wants." In Switzerland, for example, men covered their houses with larch shingles,
which, as the sun warmed them, leaked pitch, with the result
that cracks between them were filled and the whole roof was
rendered waterproof (J, II, 82). In his ministerial maturity he
revealed the growth of a habit of thinking analogically. As a
tree must bear its fruit and an animal produce its young, so
correspondingly must the human soul do good deeds or it will
wither and die. Man is born for virtue and only by the daily
practice of good, in the smallest of things, keeps his soul alive,
for a soul unexercised is as doomed as the muscles of a horse
fed but never worked. A popinjay blows with the wind, but the
thundercloud sails against it; so the individual, heeding the
prompting of "great sentiments," should act "right against the
voice, it may be, of the whole world." The circulation of the
blood is an elemental fact, and so is gravitation; yet we take

them for granted. Man's capacity to be addressed on moral grounds is no less elemental and no less casually accepted. Great things only by our indifference are rendered unimportant.

Nature was revealed in a different light through Emerson's budding interest in science, the effects of which, he was coming to see about the time of his resignation from the church, impinged on man's art and his religion as well as on his economics and politics. He was amazed at the audacity of astronomers, who had projected their reason into the farthest stretches of the universe to weigh the remotest masses and plot their motions. "Not a white spot but is a lump of suns—the roe, the milt of light and life." And as one contemplated the possibility of life on other earths, revolving endlessly around other suns, one was exalted by the immensity of the plan and wincingly aware of the pitiable narrowness of the orthodox Christian view of the world, focused on a single sphere. "Who can be a Calvinist, or who an atheist? God has opened this knowledge to us to correct our theology and educate the mind" (J, II, 487). Copernican astronomy should have blasted anthropomorphism away forever in exposing the incredibility of the great scheme for the salvation of man. To creatures of another globe what meaning would inhere in the story of a God who so loved this world that He gave His only begotten son to be born on this particular ball of earth in a manger in Bethlehem, tempted by Satan in a desert beside the Sea of Galilee, and finally resurrected after crucifixion on a hill outside Jerusalem? "The Sermon on the Mount must be true throughout all the space which the eye sees and the brain imagines, but St. Paul's epistles, the Jewish Christianity would be unintelligible" (J, II, 491). The whole idea of inspiration was universalized by the enlarged vision of astronomy. One saw that there was "one light through a thousand stars" and only "one spirit through myriad mouths." Every word of truth, every true thought, every realization of beauty, every right act by any man in any time or any place was from God. Enlightened comparatively though Unitarians were, their Christianity was just as much ecclesianity as that of other denominations, only a set of churchified rites in mistaken idolatry of the spiritual teacher of Nazareth, and within a few years Emerson could no longer stomach it. In his very first year at the Second Church, reminding his flock of "the blessed law of heaven . . . that our nature should

be progressive," which meant that like certain animals who cast
their shell or skin we also needed periodically to change the
government, laws, or customs we were born into, he had invited
a reconsideration of the purpose of Jesus in holding the Last
Supper. Jesus had seemed to intend it to be a permanent memorial but when or how often was not at all clear. And although
he had requested his disciples to eat bread and drink wine in
memory of him, he had said nothing of his divinity in relation
to those substances nor hinted that when eaten and drunk they
would be transubstantiated.

Emerson could not but think that Jesus would "be better loved
by not being adored," by being lowered from the unnatural
place in human opinion which for ages he had occupied. "Now
that the Scriptures are read with purged eyes, it is seen that he
is only to be loved for so much goodness and wisdom as dwelt
in him, which are the only properties for which a sound human
mind can love any person" (YES, 195). Jesus, however, even if
not divine had been of incalculable worth to mankind. Although
"there had been many other moral teachers before him yet had
no one devoted himself with this entireness to the higher interest
of the human race or expressed the rule of life in anything like
so just and comprehensive and significant a manner" (YES,
96-97). In calling himself the truth and the light, however, he
was asking us to believe not in him as a divine person but in
the way to the truth and the light which he had exemplified. He
had derived his power from the frequency and the extent to
which in humble prayer he had opened his mind to the mind of
the Creator. The same authority he had had, then, any of us
could also have in proportion as we possessed ourselves in communion with the divine "of the truth which was in him." Jesus
had not monopolized it.

As for the miracles, which were the basis for the exaltation
by Unitarians of the Holy Communion, Emerson concluded
coolly that "a miracle is a lower species of evidence. It speaks
to unbelief. It speaks to ignorance." The best kinds of evidence,
in the experience of wise and pious Christians, were not external
but internal—those of the mind and heart. To speculate on the
marvelous in scriptural narrative was foolishly to turn one's
mind away from life. "All our life is a miracle. Ourselves are the
greatest miracle of all." That a person lives is more astounding

than that another has been resurrected (YES, 122). And where Jesus in particular was concerned, the truth of his example as a man God-ennobled through prayer was his miracle.

Such was the nature of Emerson's view of life; such were the leading ideas that constituted it at the time he seceded from the church and embarked on lecturing for his career. He himself, on shipboard returning from Europe, had summed them up succinctly in a single paragraph as the faith which he was prepared to preach to other men as distinctively his own:

It is the old revelation, that perfect beauty is perfect goodness, it is the development of the wonderful congruities of the moral law of human nature. . . . A man contains all that is needful to his government within himself. He is made a law unto himself. He only can do himself any good or any harm. Nothing can be given to him or taken from him but always there is a compensation. There is a correspondence between the human soul and everything that exists in the world; more properly, everything that is known to man. Instead of studying things without the principles of them, all may be penetrated unto within him. Every act puts the agent in a new condition. The purpose of life seems to be to acquaint a man with himself. He is not to live to the future as described to him, but to live to the real future by living to the real present. The highest revelation is that God is in every man. (J, III, 200-201)

One of Emerson's early biographers, James Elliot Cabot, who knew him well, was of the opinion that to try to track down the origins of his ideas was futile:

Here and there we find a trace of influence from some book, particularly those he read in early youth, Berkeley, Hume, Coleridge, Sampson Reed's "Growth of the Mind;" but, in general, to look for the source of any way of thinking of his in the Neoplatonists, or in any of the books he read, seems to me like tracing the origin of Jacob Behmen's illumination to the glitter of the pewter tankard, which, he says, awakened in him the consciousness of divine things. (C, I, 291)

There is some truth in this. Emerson was more than most an intellectual vagrant and never managed fully to control his "omnivorous curiosity and facility of new undertaking." Like Samuel Johnson, who never read books through but prided himself on tearing their heart out, he penetrated with a sort of intuition to whatever he was spiritually in need of at the moment he picked up a book. He maintained that there was much of American history in Aristophanes, rightly read, and confessed that his way of dealing with a book did an injustice to its author, for he attacked it for its lusters—its flashes of insight into human experience, which in quotable form helped him crystallize his own random, undefined thoughts. Systematic treatises, he could not read. Every thoughtful man, to be sure, had looked into a metaphysical book, but what thoughtful man had ever looked twice? With Hawthorne he could say that works of theology were, for the most part, volumes of stupendous impertinence.

Emerson was a great eclectic and in his wide-ranging and vivacious touching of books owed stimulation to the expression of innumerable other minds. He was like the often-cited bee, visiting an infinitude of flowers and during only momentary contact with them extracting the nectar which was their essence. It would be impossible, even in a lifetime, to reveal explicitly the sources of the vast composite of thoughts that inhabited his mind. One of his admirers, exclaiming over the manysidedness of his mind, said that, except for the sordid and morbid, in whatever domain of human experience you penetrated, you found that, like Shakespeare, he had already been there before you. Impressible, suggestible as he was, creature so largely of intuition, his intelligence could take fire from a sight fleetingly glimpsed or a sound for an instant heard. No wonder his response to the grand exposition of plants and animals in Paris in 1833 was so electrifying and of such consequence. After it he did not, in a sense, need to read any treatise explaining how the subtleties of morphological or structural similarity in organisms revealed their kinship and their tendency to grow into one another, out of simplicity toward increasing complexity. He was like the preacher who, when asked whether he believed in baptism through immersion, answered that the question was irrelevant: he had seen it done. Evolution inhered in what lay before his eyes in the world about him as well as on the printed page.

The idea of the moral sense, for example, one of Emerson's leading convictions from the time he entered college: how did he come by it? Was it from reading the Earl of Shaftesbury, considered by many scholars to be its first enunciator in the eighteenth century? Or was it through a passage by Thomas

Jefferson, a later propagator of it: "I sincerely then believe . . . in the general existence of a moral instinct. I think it the brightest gem with which the human character is studded, and the want of it as more degrading than the most hideous of the bodily deformities?" (To T. Law, 1814). Or in a sentence by a humble Quaker, John Woolman: "I was early convinced . . . that as the mind was moved by an inward principle to love God as an invisible, incomprehensible Being, so, by the same principle it was moved to love him in all his manifestations in the visible world" *(Journal)*.

The belief in such a faculty, in short, widespread during the late eighteenth century, must have been subscribed to and often talked about by persons of conscience in the little sphere in which Emerson moved in the early nineteenth century. That the moral sense came to mean for him not only a touchstone for separating virtue from vice but the mystical activity of the soul, as in the Quaker conception, inviting him into the presence of God or opening the door to quiet rapture when he was suffused with beauty, only illustrates the germinative hospitality of his mind. What collateral ideas from what other readings in his early years contributed to such an expansion of the concept one can only speculate about. Saint Augustine and the seventeenth-century poet George Herbert in his college days, it seems likely, fostered its growth.

Searching for sources was to Emerson like peeling off the successive layers of the skin of an onion. One thought that in a Renaissance humanist he had the source of an idea relating, say, animal natures to human physiognomy, only to discover thereafter the same idea in a sermon by a medieval preacher—and beyond that in a satirical Roman poet of the first century. Could not one presume, then, that it had been previously entertained also by a Greek nature philosopher—and before him by an Egyptian astrologer? Was any stopping point to be found? At bottom, although interested in their antiquity, Emerson was not interested in the origin of ideas. Too much value attached to originators. Men should cultivate a high-minded and dispassionate interest in what was said, not in who said it. Once I understand an idea of Plato's, it is as important to me as it was to Plato, and then all question of person becomes irrelevant. No matter who first sang poetic words, Shakespeare or Jonson or Donne, "it is we at last who sing."

Yet, in spite of the degree of authoritativeness in the biographer Cabot's judgment (1887) about the lack of explicit connection between Emerson and his reading, scholarship on Emerson in the last quarter of a century has devoted itself increasingly, and with steady illumination, to the relation between his thought and that of published works of interest to him in his development.

In addition to the Bible and whatever writers on Christian theology he was indebted to, the Emerson of 1832 had been principally influenced, it appears, by some of the Greek pre-Socratic philosophers and by Plato, by Plutarch and the Neo-platonists, by Berkeley, Locke, and Hume, by modern German thought, by Coleridge and Swedenborg, by George Fox and Quakers generally, and by a Boston contemporary, Sampson Reed.

Emerson's introduction to the Greeks had occurred in college through a late seventeenth-century volume by the Englishman Ralph Cudworth, *The True Intellectual System of the Universe*, which was distinguished by a commentary that he thought deadly at the time but also by a storehouse of quotations that he found irresistible. In the fall of 1830 his interest in the Greeks was additionally stimulated by his reading in the comprehensive *Histoire Comparée des Systèmes de Philosophie* by Joseph-Marie de Gérando, through which his mind, confronting initially the teachings of Confucius and Zoroaster, was also strongly attracted to the thought of the East, of increasing importance to him in later years. Of the ideas of the pre-Socratics it was Pythagoras' conviction of the sublime beauty of the world ("Kosmos!") and Heraclitus' idea of reality as flux that were principally adopted by him. As for Plutarch, both his *Lives* and *Morals* were works about whose ethical worth to humanity he could hardly say too much. They enabled him to develop the martial virtues of patience and silent courage in the face of the vicissitudes of life, necessary to complement his childlike innocence and readiness to sing among its delights. Emerson never knew a good translation of Plato, but in spite of the impediment of bad ones he glimpsed enough of the beauty and intellectual excitement of the dialogues to be permanently stamped by their view of life; and although his Platonism was largely colored by the thought of the Alexandrian Neoplatonists, to whose ideas as reported by Plutarch he was led directly by de Gérando, he was fond of saying that it was a memorable day in a young man's life when he read "The Symposium" for the first time. From the body of Neoplatonic thought, to which he became devoted, his mind was most susceptible to Plotinus' teaching of the efflux of spirit in nature.

Through Plato Emerson had come to see what was divine not as person but as idea, not as a being but as being. Such qualities as Truth, Beauty, and Goodness were divine—were timeless and omnipresent. They thus invaded every sensitive mind century after century with irresistible attraction and revealed themselves as supremely lovely and faultless things. Truth, Beauty, and Goodness were aspects of an ultimate, disembodied, depersonalized force or intelligence, and all the shapes of things by which human beings were surrounded on earth during their lifetimes were transitory, faulty copies of originals, ideas residing in utter flawlessness in that intelligence. Plato had taught that the ideas which haunted men's minds—justice, love, honesty, piety, patriotism, and the rest, of which in all earthly history there had been only incomplete examples—were in their perfect form inaccessibly removed from them, centered as they were in the one universal, creative intelligence. Men must be forever content with their botched approximations to such essences, compensated for their ineffective performance as judges, lovers, artists, worshipers, and patriots only by the knowledge that in some place the things they aspired to existed absolutely.

Plotinus, however, had shown men a way to escape from their shriveled insularity. He had accepted Plato's idea that the creative intelligence was one and universal—but he had taught that it flowed ceaselessly outward through all of nature, its own creation although far below intellect and soul in value, and then rhythmically flowed back into itself at the center of all being. Man, one of its creatures, could identify himself with it during its efflux and in that identification mystically see the pristine forms of justice and truth, love, beauty, piety, and patriotism. Plato had said that the work of the best human artist was but a pale shadow of a shadow of its original, a copy of a copy, a replica at two removes. The tree on the painter's canvas was a representation, badly done even when well done, of the tree in

nature, which itself was a representation, imperfect, of the idea
of tree in the divine mind. According to the theory of Plotinus,
however, with the reality of the idea entering his mind when
he was one with the divine mind, the artist himself became a
creator on a near-divine level.

Berkeley, Locke, and Hume Emerson had also encountered in
his student days at Harvard. Locke and Hume were of value
mostly in stimulating him to refutations of their beliefs. Hume,
whose work, he said, had been written to destroy all relation
between cause and effect, to efface "memory, judgment, and
finally our own consciousness" and to reduce the laws of morals
to "idle dreams and fantasies," had with his "pernicious ingenuity" committed "an outrage upon the feelings of human nature."
Even if his philosophy were true, Emerson maintained as an
undergraduate, mankind with its moral system would be content
to remain deceived, for its deception was sublime. Yet he would
not speak slightingly of Hume; he was a great man. Berkeley,
whom, along with Hume, he was constrained as an undergraduate
to consider a fabricator of "visionary schemes," had nevertheless
stirred Emerson profoundly, exposing to him, apparently for the
first time, the subtle relations between thought and external
thing and revealing with electrifying brilliance the sovereign
power of the mind.

By 1832 contemporary German thought was more than a little
on Emerson's mind, the great Goethe along with certain less
encyclopedic figures. Germany was the center of erudition and
scholarship for the Western world, to which young American
men of promise, aspiring to reputation in fields of learning,
needed to go for thorough preparation. Emerson himself had
once thought of going, to study theology, but had been prevented by poverty. In October, 1830, he set down in his *Journal*
a list of quotations from Goethe which reflected ideas close to
his own on such things as self-reliance, the universe speaking
directly through the heart, eclecticism, and the whole in the
part. He followed learned journals, domestic as well as imported,
which carried pieces on aspects of the sphere of German intellect. In 1827 in *The Edinburgh Review* he encountered an
epochal survey by the extraordinary Thomas Carlyle of the
phenomenon of contemporary Germanism. And in 1832, when
in *Fraser's Magazine* a new and altogether unprecedented work

by Carlyle, *Sartor Resartus*, was serialized, he read it with the same prodigious excitement, cutting out the instalments to lend to friends and to preserve, not only for what they disclosed, in a turbulently unique style, of the inner world of their author, but also for their continued revelation of the growth of the psyche of modern Germany.

Ideas akin to those of Plato and Plotinus were in vigorous circulation in Germany in the years of Emerson's maturity, in the dissemination of the thought of certain philosophers, notably Johann Gottlieb Fichte, Friedrich Schleiermacher, and Friedrich Wilhelm Schelling. Although their speculation, cast in the form of system, made volumes to which by nature he was antipathetic, and although the language in which they were written was not one in which he was at home, he easily made their acquaintance secondhand. The German philosophers were preoccupied with such issues as the self and the not-self, the individual ego and the absolute ego, subject and object, matter and spirit, reality and ideality, art and morality, the relation of man to nature and the relation of both to the underlying, interpenetrating force of the universe. (Carlyle himself in Goethean terms had described nature as a garment of God woven on the loom of Time.) They showed, in short, that one of the essential features of the Romantic mind everywhere was its impulsion to link the sense of individual identity to a sense of cosmic identity.

Coleridge, to whom he had at least been exposed as early as 1819, was a thinker, himself much influenced by the new German thought, whom Emerson had come to revere by the time of his rupture with the Second Church. The lofty pitch of his intelligence, with its Platonic coloration little inclined to the transitory world but devoted to the imperishable ideas of Truth, Beauty, and Goodness, and its wonderful capacity for subtle distinction and apt definition, were qualities continuously inspiring. Coleridge's revelatory differentiation between the Reason and the Understanding had become one of the standard instruments of Emerson's own mode of thought:

Reason is the highest faculty of the soul—what we mean often by the soul itself; it never *reasons*, never proves, it simply perceives; it is vision. The Understanding toils all the time, compares, contrives, adds, argues, near sighted but strong-sighted, dwelling in the present the expedient the customary. Beasts have some understanding but no Reason. Reason is potentially perfect in every man—Understanding in very different degrees of strength. (L, I, 412-13)

Coleridge, in sum, was a modern incarnation of the highest of all attainments, spiritualized mind. In pages to which Emerson was profoundly indebted for his adult understanding of Shakespeare, he had defined what he called the esemplastic power of the imagination as sovereign among human faculties, for in fusing disparate features of the natural world in metaphorical images it produced things altogether new in the universe and illuminated man to himself. It showed man taking nature into himself and shaping it in different combinations; it was divine creativity operative at the finite level.

In Swedenborg, encountered after his college days, Emerson seemed to value most, along with his emblematic reading of the book of nature, the new and germinal spiritual interpretation of the Scriptures. Some years later, however, after he had published a bold and arresting essay on Swedenborg and been taken to task for its erroneous judgments by a Swedenborg scholar, he is said to have admitted that he did not really know Swedenborg's writings; after trying them several times, he still found them, alas, unreadable.

As for the Quakers, at the time of his seclusion in the mountains over the crisis of the Lord's Supper, Emerson was reading intensively a life of George Fox, the seventeenth-century founder of Quakerism. In Fox was the revelation of greatness in the humblest of circumstances, of nobility in lowliness.

We wish to hold these fellow minds as mirrors before ourselves to learn the deepest secret of our capacity. We wish not only to mark the extraordinary but to find the common and natural motions of the soul, what the cook, the peasant, and the soldier say. . . . Portraits of common men who have accomplished much do human nature a kindness in showing it how much it can do of itself. (EL, I, 165)

Emerson profited richly from a personal association with the Society of Friends that dated back to 1827. The Quaker ideas of the worth of the single person; of the seed of God's spirit as planted in every man and woman, capable of enlargement in silent communion with the divine; of the world as essentially good and of love as a force able to transform evil; of religion, in John Woolman's phrase, as a way of life "where practice doth harmonize with principle"; of simplicity as the element in speech, dress, and manner which rightly led to truth and revealed the tendency of forms to ossify belief and practice, setting men apart from one another—these were all ideas potently congenial to his mind. He came to think of himself as more a Quaker than anything else. Quakers prized the present above the past and believed truth to be still infinitely revealable to spiritual seekers. Their conviction that daily life was something sacramental could not but recommend itself to a young man whose central wish for his parishioners was that they should dignify and beautify the humblest of their activities.

Sampson Reed's "Observations on Growth of the Mind," published in 1826, was for Emerson "a noble pamphlet" after his own heart, "the best thing since Plato of Plato's kind." For some years to come, defining his age as that of "the first person singular," destined to achieve the reform of Reformation, he would include Reed for America, along with Mme. de Staël for France, Wordsworth for England, and Swedenborg for Germany, as one of the principal exponents of "Transcendentalism," or the new tendency of "Metaphysics and Ethics to look inwards." Reed, a graduate of Harvard and fledgling Swedenborgian minister three years older than Emerson, believed in a subtle relation between mind and nature, the cultivation of which was indispensable to right education. Convinced that mankind was on the threshold of a new and lofty development which would bring each person, in "the timid subdued, awed condition of the brute," to gaze "on the erect and godlike form of man," he was, although often oracular, in certain convictions very much like Emerson:

It is not for time or space to set limits to the effects of the life of a single man.

The doctrine of the immortality of the soul is simply "I in my Father, and ye in me and I in you." It is the union of the Divine, with the human . . . through the connecting medium of Divine Truth. (Cn, 12, 25)

After 1832, and particularly during the 1840's, Emerson's

readings in science were of great importance in rounding out his
view of life, and in constituting the extraordinary amalgam that
was his thought. Although he always had difficulty in reading the
works of scientists themselves, even in 1871 complaining that
physicists in general repelled him—only their anecdotes when
they were men of ideas awakened his curiosity and delight—he
loved to keep abreast of developments in geology, biology, and
astronomical physics, which he could do easily through the
volumes of interpreter-popularizers. The geological discoveries
of Charles Lyell meant much to him, as did also Lamarckian
evolutionary ideas; and the *Vestiges of Creation* by Robert Chambers in 1845 was later of inestimable value in providing him
with the concept of arrested development and in reflecting a
view of the fairness of the universe vis-à-vis man which paralleled
his own.

It is apparent that in certain of its currents the intellectual
climate of his times was propitious for the birth of Emerson's
mature religious thought. Various metaphysicians, poets, and
critics, indebted in one way or another to Plato, the most germinal of all Western thinkers, were altogether absorbed by the
conviction that in man was something not physical and not
perishable which could be put in relation with a corresponding
something inhering in all the physical things that made the
natural universe—a relation of such a kind that by it both man's
understanding of life and his capacity to live life more fruitfully
would be immeasurably enlarged. It was a widening of perspective that was sought, with the subtlest human minds giving
themselves to acute scrutiny of the connection between the
many and the one, the partial and the whole, the finite and the
infinite, the temporal and the eternal. They were impatient with
the imperfection of man through the centuries—an imperfection
of being resulting from an imperfection of knowledge. Too little
was known about man because, in a sense, there had been too
little desire to know anything about him—anything of consequence, that is. For ages there had been too low an idea of man.
The new conviction was that a loftier idea could be not only
spread among men but enacted by them. Even scientists acted on
a desire to enlarge man by enlarging the bounds of what was to
be known about him—in relation not only to his predecessors on
the earth, animal as well as human, but also to the elemental

forces which had shaped his sphere and to the astral bodies, numberless, which peopled what once had been called the void. It was a cosmos-embracing tendency, physical as well as metaphysical, in the face of which Unitarian dogmas were lamentably sterile and petty; it would reflect itself in Emerson's mature conception of divinity, to be fully described for the first time in his "Nature."

CHAPTER 3

Emerson's Mature Thought

THE three series of lectures, on science, biography, and literature, which began Emerson's lyceum career and occupied him from 1833 to 1836 naturally reflected the interests and convictions which were the substance of his mind on his return from England and as well the new ideas attracting him. But he wisely refrained from publishing them. No man ought to bring his children into company naked, he had written, or bring more children into the world than he could clothe; neither should a writer publish his thoughts "until they embody themselves in fit outward illustrations" (J, III, 468). The lectures, hurriedly put together, were not fit outward illustrations, yet as additional trial suits of clothing for his ideas they were of use in helping him decide afterward on their final attire. "It is a law of Wit that whoso can make a good sentence can make a good book," he wrote; and to offer the reader a fine quotation was like offering a fine apple to indicate the quality of the tree that bore it. But a good sentence was made up of the right words, with which at bottom a writer must be preoccupied. And with sentences and words, "infinitely repellent particles," he struggled, apprehensive of premature expression, as ineffectual as the untimely springing of a trap. Even in talk his concern over *le mot juste* was revealed; he was not a good conversationalist, said Oliver Wendell Holmes, for he was too deliberate, like a man crossing a stream on boulders, always searching where to place his foot next.

With the appearance of "Nature" in 1836, however, Emerson embarked on a new phase of his career, in the role of prophet saying only things that were of moment to himself. From now on periodically the best things he uttered from a platform, refined, would appear in print. Several collegiate addresses, delivered between 1837 and 1841, further revealed that he had attained the height of his powers—that the stream was pristine and its movement at once true and musically rhythmical. In these beautiful and epochal pieces is unfolded Emerson's fully developed religious thought, his radically new idea of the divine in relation to the life of the individual and of the nation. The door to an ascertainment of the magnitude and quality of Emerson's complete mature thought opens through an examination of "Nature," "The American Scholar," "The Divinity School Address," and "The Method of Nature."

Intellectually the tendency of Emerson's era seemed dismayingly toward atomization, pulverization. Driven by a need to analyze and evaluate every concept inherited from previous generations, men had dismantled almost all the traditional structures of thought. Not long after leaving Harvard he had been struck by the contradictory fact that although on the one hand history revealed progress, in that "cannibal Saracens" had given way to critical scholars, and talismans and the charlatanry of superstition to the safety lamp, the compass, and the press—on the other what appeared was retrogression. In philosophy exegetes seemed only to have torn and rent Plato's gorgeous fabric, leaving us no wiser; and in religion, laudably impelled to do away with imperfection, reformers had knocked down idol after idol until faith was "very bare and very cold." "From Eden to America the apples of the tree of knowledge are but bitter fruit in the end" (J, I, 359). With the once lofty edifice of Christianity leveled to the ground, by what ideals were men from now on to be expected to live? What was to keep them from utter nihilism? From his long years of probation Emerson believed himself to have emerged in possession of the new faith that must take the place of the old. Yet with characteristic genial, gentle self-depreciation he described the aim of his first published essay as no more than "bringing a pebble or two to the edification of the new temple whilst so many wise hands are demolishing the old" (L, I, 447).

"Nature" opened with a noble paragraph, whose initial sentences, though not scored sonorously for full orchestra fortissimo, were no less arresting than if they had been written by Thomas Paine: "Our age is retrospective. It builds the sepulchres of the fathers. It writes biographies, histories, and criticism. The foregoing generations beheld God and nature face to face; we, through their eyes. Why should not we also enjoy an original relation to the universe?" (W, I, 3). This is as much a call to arms as the famous beginning of "Common Sense"; and the sudden, startling demand, "Why should not we also enjoy an original relation to the universe?," is as electrifying as "These are the times that try men's souls." It rings in the mind. As Paine had berated "sunshine patriots," so Emerson sought to inspirit "parlor soldiers," afraid to encounter the possibilities of life.

The whole of "Nature" exists to define "an original relation to the universe," for the unfolding of that definition is at the same time the revelation of the new temple of faith erected over the rubble of the old. Yet before he could disclose what he meant by an original relation to the universe, Emerson had to answer a more immediate question—the philosophical question of the nature of nature—since the universe is nature, and no one can have any relation to a thing he does not understand.

Was nature substantial and fixed or insubstantial and illusory? Was the materialist right in believing all visible and touchable things to be what he saw them to be and in paying them delighted homage? Or was the philosophical idealist right in maintaining that although there were things around man constituting what he called nature, it was impossible to know them, their qualities of shape, color, and behavior all arbitrarily created and ascribed to them by the mind? Did nature exist apart from man or only in man's mind? The question had been important to Emerson ever since his encounter in his Harvard days with Bishop Berkeley; and his reading in the pre-Socratic and Neoplatonic philosophers, among whom Plotinus was to remain a beloved figure, had strengthened his preoccupation with it.

His position embraced both materialism and philosophical idealism; nature was both fact and idea, both thing and mind. The roses, the pine trees, the redbirds, the rivers, the mountains, the clouds—all in sight from his window and all offering themselves for fuller delectation if he would but emerge from his study and come out in person among them—were what they appeared to be, and to mingle his existence with theirs was one of the most precious pursuits of his life. "I have no hostility to nature, but a child's love to it. I expand in the warm day like corn and melons. Let us speak her fair. I do not wish to fling stones at my beautiful mother, nor soil my gentle nest" (W, I, 59).

The elements of nature were symbols. In their physicality they offered beauty to man and were of use in many ways; in what underlay their physicality they reflected something of the divine intelligence, the Universal Mind, which had created all things, which *was* all things. They had, then, a double reality—one evidenced by man's senses and another, higher by far, affirmable only by his mind.

For Emerson everything that the eye beholds was an objectification of thought. Everywhere in society everyday evidence of this smote him with force. The commonest objects, things which the rest of us take for granted, at most acknowledging their usefulness and admiring now and then their grace or beauty, their might or efficiency, moved him reverentially, for he saw them as signs of the mystical translation of the invisible into the visible, of the word become flesh. A chair, for example, was originally an idea in some man's mind; now it is a fact, the idea materialized. Yet it is the idea materialized on the smallest scale; it has thousands of counterparts, replicas of itself, and indeed the great factory which manufactures them and the thousands of stores and salesmen through which they are distributed and sold are all features of the physical realization of the same idea—CHAIR. The idea of slavery, of one man owning another and having his entire life and services to command, first eventuated perniciously in a single person's summarily so disposing of the being of one other person; yet by Emerson's time it had achieved embodiment on a grand scale, for it was an institution with millions of human lives involved in its ground plan and a gigantic corps of policemen, lawyers, judges, and statesmen, utilizing a complicated superstructure of legal statutes in its operation. Such things, commonplace for us, were for Emerson causes of wonder.

What was true in the human realm must then be true also in the sphere of nature. Everything about him must be miracle—must be investiture of the thought of a mind, but of a mind superior to that of man. Indeed man himself must be a materialization of an idea once conceived by it. Hence Emerson's distinction that man was a projection of the universal mind in the conscious, whereas nature was its projection in the unconscious,

and his declaration that this was "the true position of nature
in regard to man, wherein to establish man all right education
tends."

What Emerson said in full and poetic detail in "Nature" was a
consummation of what he had first said in his lectures on science
several years earlier, that, beyond its various kinds of utilitarian
profit, the supreme value of natural history was in giving us aid
in supernatural history. He devoted an entire section of his new
work to "Language," making explicit what had been for some
time one of his principal convictions—that language shows a
"radical correspondence between visible things and human
thoughts" and "all spiritual facts are represented by natural symbols." Language is emblematic, and, in proportion as a man lives
close to nature, the way he talks will reveal an immediate dependence on it. "Every word which is used to express a moral
or intellectual fact, if traced to its root, is found to be borrowed
from some material appearance. *Right* means *straight! wrong*
means *twisted.* Spirit primarily means *wind*" (W, I, 25). The
best thought is not abstract but metaphorical, expressing itself
in images and figures of speech:

An enraged man is a lion, a cunning man is a fox, a firm man is a rock,
a learned man is a torch. . . . Who looks upon a river in a meditative
hour and is not reminded of the flux of all things? Throw a stone into
the stream, and the circles that propagate themselves are the beautiful
type of all influence. (W, I, 26-27)

Nature was a vast "metaphor of the human mind," the laws of
its spiritual operation answering "to those of matter as face to
face in a glass" (W, I, 32-33). Proverbial sayings like "a rolling
stone gathers no moss" and "a bird in the hand is worth two in
the bush" illustrated this, as did also axioms straight out of
physics:

Thus, "the whole is greater than its part"; "reaction is equal to action";
"the smallest weight may be made to lift the greatest, the difference
of weight being compensated by time"; and many the like propositions,
which have an ethical as well as physical sense. (W, I, 33)

What was new in "Nature" and showed Emerson's position to
be far advanced beyond the thought of the earlier lectures was,

in addition to the careful unfolding of the illustration linking idealism and materialism, what he now said in a mystical vein. Of what good was it to man, it might have been asked, to know that he differed from nature in being a projection of the divine in the conscious and that when he thought metaphorically he was using a fact of the natural world to describe a truth of his own moral world? Would he not always remain detached from nature, unable to trust his perceptions about her? Not at all. A product with her of the one supreme intelligence, by giving himself over to the intuitive features of the portion of that intelligence which he embodied, man could unite with the inarticulate spirit pulsating within the attractive phenomena of nature all about him. The divine in such moments of ecstasy would flow directly into him. His mind, spiritualized by this extraordinary identification, would see the underlying significance of nature's lovely and useful constituents and attain a larger knowledge of itself and of the universe. Nature was "the organ through which the universal spirit speaks to the individual, and strives to lead the individual back to it." Like the vast sky this Universal Spirit, or soul, was forever arching in benignancy over him; and like the air, of which the sky was made, it was ready to flow into him in as deep drafts as he could take. Emerson described briefly his own transformation in such moments: "Standing on the bare ground—my head bathed by the blithe air and uplifted into infinite space—all mean egotism vanishes. I become a transparent eye-ball; I am nothing; I see all; the currents of the Universal Being circulate through me . . ." (W, I, 10).

It was this experience, then, which was in Emerson's mind at the very outset of the little work when he propounded the memorable question, "Why should not we also enjoy an original relation to the universe?" The value of such a relation was immeasurable. It was original, first, in putting man in direct connection with the origin of all life, the primal source of being. It was original also in that its effect was on the original part of man: he was mind before he was body, spirit before he was flesh. It was original additionally in involving man in adoration, a state of mind which, in the history of the race, preceded skepticism. It was original finally because its consequence was to make each man an original creature, a unique person, an individual.

This all may seem indifferent to many readers to whom it is intelligible. What is so remarkable, it may be asked, about Emerson's insistence on a relation between man and the divine, between a human being and whatever it is that is suprahuman, responsible for the universe, its operation as well as creation? Have not all Christian churches for generations been equally insistent on the same thing? Has not the Bible for centuries reminded man unremittingly of the same thing—"I will lift up mine eyes to the hills from whence cometh my help" and "Love the Lord thy God with all thy heart, with all thy mind, and with all thy soul." The answer is that what Christian churches have been preaching is not what Emerson was advocating; the difference lies in the meaning of "relation."

Traditionally, Christianity has propagated a faith based on dualism—that is, on the fact of man and God as two separate beings, inhabiting disparate worlds, one low and one high, capable of approximation to each other but never of union. Man has always been in a relation to God, being the creature of a creator, but in prayer or worship although he could make the relation a near one, narrowing the gap between him and the Almighty, he could never become one with Him. In profound and humble meditation, man, "down here," could solicit and win the ear of God, "up there," and sometimes believe that his petition was being heeded. This was the sum of his relation. For Emerson man and God were not thus separate. God was not a person; nor was he a being. God was being in its highest and most intelligential form, therefore divine. But the divine was not "up there" in contradistinction to the mortal "down here." The divine was everywhere, already in small part within man himself and every moment all about him. Blessed was the day when one learned that "above" and "within" were synonyms. In right worship man opened himself to the currents of divinity surrounding him so that the small portion of it already his became larger. The relation, then, which Emerson urged his readers to seek was not simply relation; it was identification. Worship was communion, man becoming one with God.

The only counterpart to this in traditional Christianity has been in the sacrament of the Eucharist, the rite of Holy Communion, patterned after the Last Supper of Jesus with his disciples. In it, the individual worshiper becomes, as it were, one with God by taking into himself a bit of God's substance, with the result that he is enlarged and strengthened, a better because more spiritual person than he was before. But God's substance enters him through his ingestion of a wafer of bread and a sip of wine, which represent the body and blood of Jesus, the Son of God. The communion, then, the becoming one with God, is, strictly speaking, accomplished at one remove, is secondhand. Although he had various reasons for rejecting it Emerson objected to this sacrament not only because of its barbarousness, considering the eating of Jesus a sort of cannibalism, but also because it was based on the assumption that only Jesus was the Son of God. In his sight every man was the son of God, and every act of worship, irrespective of where it befell—in a field or woods, in one's own living room or on one's porch—was communion, and he never tired of saying that communion was exaltation because in it man saw with the eyes of God. No wonder he defined prayer as he did, seeing it always as rejoicing rather than prudential supplication or selfish petition:

Prayer that craves a particular commodity, anything less than all good, is vicious. Prayer is the contemplation of the facts of life from the highest point of view. It is the soliloquy of a beholding and jubilant soul. It is the spirit of God pronouncing his works good. But prayer as a means of effecting a private end is meanness and theft. It supposes dualism and not unity in nature and consciousness. (W, II, 77)

Since mankind began men and women, no doubt, have periodically been overcome by a sense of the inadequacy of their own unaided powers, by despondency at a realization of the deplorable smallness of what they could see in comparison with what they needed to see in order to make their lot better than it was. They have sought to invoke the assistance of power greater than their own, not only to invoke it, but also to bring it into themselves and possess it. Certainly such a desire, to be stronger in order to do more and do better, has been as considerable a motive underlying the perpetuation of supernatural religions as fear and self-abasement, leading men to the invention of rites, often monstrous, such as human sacrifice with which to propitiate inimical nonhuman forces. The eating by a band of tribesmen of the testicles of a bull and their performance afterward of a dance while enclosed within his hide, so that the more-than-human muscular strength and sexual potency of the beast may enter them, his worshipers, is perhaps more gross a rite than the Christian Holy Communion, but one whose purpose is essentially the same. Christianity has improved upon the savage function by refining it; it has substituted, as gains sought, spiritual for physical things, and it has, correspondingly, replaced the physical body of the agent of the transformation with a symbol.

Emerson, who delighted always in revealing the superiority of things of the spirit and things of the mind to things of the flesh, was intent on disclosing in this instance the falling short even of the Christian practice, the intermediate stage in the evolution of thought which it could be said to occupy. Communion needed to be seen as altogether a spiritual event; if things physical had no place in it, no more did symbols of things physical. Since it was altogether a spiritual event, no mediator had any place in it; it was not necessary that a Christian go through Jesus in order to get to God. With the universe rightly understood, any worshiper could go directly to God and become God by taking God into himself.

"Nature," then, was distinguished by its mystical development of an idea important in the last of the sermons five years before. The prayer which in them was described as enlarging conversation of the human mind with the mind of God had here become magnifying union with the Universal Being. The divine was still the divine, but it was more often than not referred to by a name not so likely as "God" to evoke associations of personality and it was not so localized. In fact, according to Emerson's developed thought, largely pantheistic, the divine was everywhere in nature, which meant that although it was approached through nature as an intermediary, its apprehension was much wider in scope, the individual in his transcending experience becoming one not only with a Being but with all Being. In all of this is seen the influence of Plotinus, from whom, in fact, the first edition of the little essay had borne as its epigraph a quotation: "Nature is but an image or imitation of wisdom, the last thing of the soul: Nature being a thing which doth only do, but not know."

But the conception of the divine in this whole exposition reveals an extraordinary fusion of ideas from Plato and Christianity (and from Quakerism as well) with those of Plotinus. In the

· emphasis on ideas in the mind relating to virtue or right conduct, Emerson is Platonic. (How, never having seen an instance of perfect justice, can man recognize that some things he does are more just than others? Because in his intellect are recollections, although imperfect, of the absolute justice his soul has known before birth in the state of the eternal.) In his belief in man's ability to know such qualities as justice in their fullness through meditative absorption in nature, Emerson is Plotinal. In his stress on the importance of employing the illumination one has gained not only for his own ethical betterment but for the improvement of mankind—in affirming the need of turning right knowledge into right conduct—he is both Platonic and Christian. And in his conviction that from the illuminative experience will come the strength to make deed out of illumination he seems to be Christian.

With the attainment of his adult belief, Emerson had at last found the way of enabling the kingdom to come on earth as it was in heaven. Christians by the million, he knew, every day repeated the phrase from the Lord's Prayer without ever thinking of its meaning. It meant to bring to pass among men the degrees of honesty, intelligence, justice, beauty, affection, generosity, and fidelity that characterized the order of things in the region of God. If such a state were reached, the same harmony would characterize human society as distinguished heaven. But it would be reached only in proportion as individual men and women were honest, intelligent, just, and the rest. How could each know what things were honest, intelligent, and just? And how could he get the strength to do them after he knew? Platonists also had believed in the existence of another order of things, the equivalent of the Christian heaven, where such qualities existed in sublime perfection, but they had not taught a means whereby they could be brought down to earth and made to prevail there. Plotinus had shown Emerson the means, overlooked by Platonists and only faultily glimpsed by Christians.

The whole idea of communion with the divine through nature, while he may in various respects have given distinctive utterance to it, was not in modern times original with Emerson. First singer of it on this continent he may have been, but other poets on the other side of the ocean, even in the parent country England, had already expressed it. It was an idea of special attraction

to Romantic minds, and Romanticism had flowered earlier in the
Old World than in the New. Wordsworth preeminently among
older English contemporaries had voiced it in eloquent terms
again and again, but the sharpest statement of its value to him is
to be found in a quatrain not at all eloquent, in which the two
kinds of enlightenment, rational and suprarational, are explicitly
juxtaposed:

> One impulse from a vernal wood
> May teach you more of man,
> Of moral evil and of good,
> Than all the sages can.
> (From "The Tables Turned")

One contemplates a great tree, losing all sense of his own human
identity, feeling himself into the life within the mighty trunk
until time is suspended and in his quiet rapture the impulses
that animate it become his own. From such an experience he
emerges finally, more nearly whole and fulfilled than he was
before, elevated by a revelation which he could never have experienced in reading all the volumes of Plato, Aristotle, Saint
Thomas Aquinas, and Immanuel Kant combined. From the invisible spirit of the tree, integrity, quiet strength, patience, single-
ness of purpose, and harmony with the cosmos have all flowed
into him.

The relation of this mystical identification to certain kinds of
oriental communion is apparent. For Wordsworth the tree, oak
or elm or willow, took the place of the navel, through whose
contemplation, in gradual suspension of consciousness, a Buddhist worshiper could feel his way back into his mother's womb
and, beyond it, into the womb of all Being, from an immersion
in which he gained renewal and depth of vision and tranquillity
and oneness of soul.

Yet, although Wordsworth had preceded Emerson in poetically
preaching the gospel of communion with nature, he had not
depicted it in comparable detail or with such Platonic overtones
or such effects of individualization. Nor had he revealed its value
in any association like that which was peculiar to Emerson.
Emerson, it is true, was addressing himself in "Nature" to the
individual, intent on showing him how to give his life meaning.

But his context was more than private. He was also addressing his entire generation, exhorting all of his contemporaries, Americans, alive like him in the most exciting, most propitious of times, to cut the umbilical cord to the past, to become emancipated from tradition, to live prospectively rather than retrospectively—on insight and revelation, not rote and convention. His goal was, by implication, national regeneration.

"The American Scholar"

In 1837 the United States, only two generations removed from the establishment of its nationhood, was still a raw and crude country. When, having won its political independence, would it achieve intellectual and cultural independence? This question vexed, and was destined to continue for generations to vex, sensitive, patriotic minds. Would America ever have her own literature? Was there indeed any such thing as a national literature? Although Poe could sneer at the idea and Longfellow diplomatically plead for a universal literature which would encompass ipso facto qualities of national character, Emerson unequivocally believed in national literatures and declared that America would eventually have one, "great absentee" though it was, realizable through travail only in some indefinable future. Other men of letters, Washington Irving and Nathaniel Hawthorne, for example, repelled by the immature state of their native land—still in the building stage, the qualities it asked for among its citizenry were practical and workaday, not imaginative—could be inspired only by the Old World. Where shovelmen and carpenters, engineers and inventors, teachers and lawmakers were hourly in demand, what place was there for an artist who would shape fiction or conceive poems? For him who would create, no inspiration could come, in Irving's words, from "the commonplace realities of the present" but only from "the shadowy grandeurs of the past," rich with historical and legendary association. It was Emerson's nature to deny all this and his mission to state eloquently and inspiringly that in the very commonplaceness by which the artist was surrounded lay the thing he sought, unique and wondrous. In his address on "The American Scholar" to the Phi Beta Kappa Society of Harvard College he made his first public statement of the theme.

Emerson's scholar is a peculiar genus; he is not the scholar

generally conceived—not the book-learned man, not a restorer
of texts, not an emendator, not a cataloguer or commentator.
Men who spend their lives with books he depreciates as biblio-
maniacs. The American Scholar he is talking about is in a broad
sense the American Man—Everyman in the United States, capable
of thought and able to read. Such an identification he had made
several years before, at the outset of his career as lecturer: "I
say then that every man as far as he is a man is capable of being
addressed as an intellectual being is to some extent a scholar.
The sailor has his song & his Robinson Crusoe & bible and every
house in this city a closet or a shelf of books . . ." (EL, I, 466).

In short, he is—or could be—Man Thinking. Every man should
remember that he is man before he is anything else and that the
essential dignity of his nature lies in thought. Therefore Man
Thinking should be everywhere. One should find Man Thinking
with books, but, alas, too often one finds the bookworm. Instead
of Man Thinking on the farm one finds the farmer, and in place
of Man Thinking in the manufacture of wheels, only the wheel-
wright.

In a more restrictive sense the American Scholar is the American Man of the high degree of intellectual life and leisure necessary to do what Emerson maintains he ought to do to be worthy
of his title—to catalogue the "obscure and nebulous stars of the
human mind, which as yet no man has thought of as such." His
work is "the study and the communication of principles, the
making those instincts prevalent, the conversion of his world"
(W, I, 100-15). He is an acute and compassionate student of
life, not of the printed word. He observes and sounds the present
instead of burying himself in the past, and he aims to guide
men into the future. Whatever book he writes will be of value,
but once read it will have served its day; out of it other books
should not be made. No book should ever grow out of anything
but its writer's own intense reading of life. Some persons in
history, great and heroic, have, it is true, known almost nothing
but books, but they are prodigious exceptions; for the great
generality of men, a printed page means something only when
the mind with which they read it has already been "braced by
labor and invention," by thoughtful contact with life.

Adhering to a clearly defined plan, Emerson discusses the
threefold education of the scholar—by nature, by the past or

books, and by action—and in a final section considers his duties.

The value of nature is in its occult tie to man, in the correspondence between its inner life and that of man, so that "nature is the opposite of the soul, answering to it part for part. One is seal and one is print." Man Thinking soon realizes that "the ancient precept, 'Know thyself,' and the modern precept, 'Study nature,' become at last one maxim." As for books, although originally translations of the world into thought by persons who had known joy and suffering, they are now only bloodless and thin comments on those translations. They seem to be contrivances for perpetuating the past and impeding the movement of life. Since rightly books are "for nothing but to inspire," it is necessary for every generation to write its own. The Scholar must be a "grand affirmer of the present tense": "Meek young men grow up in libraries, believing it their duty to accept the views which Cicero, which Locke, which Bacon, have given; forgetful that Cicero, Locke, and Bacon were only young men in libraries when they wrote those books" (W, I, 89). About the relation of action to thought Emerson had long before made up his mind, when he removed himself from the ministry. Books being valuable only as they inspire, it follows that their ideas are worth precisely what they incite their readers to do. A good book is life translated into thought, but it exists to turn thought back into life. Only when it is lived does one's thought become truth. It is not necessary for the Scholar to be a man of overt, body-moving action—an industrialist, a merchant, a politician— but it is indispensable to him to live: "A great soul will be strong to think. Does he lack organ or medium to impart his truths? He can still fall back on this elemental force of living them. This is a total act. Thinking is a partial act" (W, I, 99).

The American Scholar, rightly a student of nature, rightly a reader of books and rightly a liver of truth, was to cherish his office as a benefactor of mankind. Tranquilly removed from the bustle of life but never passively divorced from it, his end was not solipsistic satisfaction but enlightenment for others; he was "to cheer, to raise, and to guide men by showing them facts amidst appearances" (W, I, 100). His scope must be broad and his procedure serene. Trying always to see things under the aspect of eternity, he must never be swayed by popular commotion. "Let him not quit his belief that a popgun is a popgun, though the ancient and honorable of the earth affirm it to be the crack of doom" (W, I, 102). His elevation was not isolation; he did not inhabit an ivory tower. Nor was his disinterestedness cowardice. In order to see the popgun when raised and identify its report when fired, he could not have his head buried, ostrich-like, in the sand. He must keep his judicial eye on society and as critic take a stand on vexatious issues of politics or religion. His divergent opinion meant, of course, occasional danger and frequent misunderstanding; he would be thought by society, in his hostility to its low ideals, to be in a state of hostility to *it*. He would, however, endure with sweetness that misconstruction of his attitude, and quietly, manfully suffer retaliation, if vented upon him. He was a gentlemanly radical, ready to die for his principles but not to brawl in the street for them. Jesus and Socrates had undergone martyrdom.

Self-trust was the essential characteristic of Man Thinking. He stood on his own feet and considered right the path on which they carried him. He was independent and self-reliant, making his decisions with the assurance that the sounding of his own private mind and heart was at the same time the penetration of the Universal Mind. One read Plato or Shakespeare or Goethe, Voltaire or Plotinus, and again and again encountered ideas which he had himself thought though never fully enunciated; the discovery revealed to him that there was one mind of which all minds were particles, one man of which all men were incarnations. To repair repeatedly to the recesses of one's being was to be increasingly in contact with the source-spring of truth—to repair to it, that is, in solitude and in identification with nature:

The books which once we valued more than the apple of the eye, we have quite exhausted. What is that but saying that we have come up with the point of view which the universal mind took through the eyes of one scribe; we have been that man and passed on. . . . The human mind cannot be enshrined in a person who shall set a barrier on any one side to this unbounded unboundable empire. It is one central fire, which, flaming now out of the lips of Etna, lightens the capes of Sicily, and now out of the throat of Vesuvius, illuminates the towers and vineyards of Naples. It is one light which beams out of a thousand stars. It is one soul which animates all men. (W, I, 108)

Turning his eyes in sharper focus on the native scene, Emerson deplored the widespread waste of America's young men. Instead of knowing himself joyfully to be Man Thinking, every youth, college graduate or not, on coming of age, felt himself to be despairingly nothing, an anonymity, one of millions constituting "the mass," "the herd." In addition to the pressure of population and the dehumanization of industry, he was weighed down by materialism of motive. The very possession of conscience, he discovered, was in the workaday world a disqualification for success:

Young men of the fairest promise, who begin life upon our shores, inflated by the mountain winds, shined upon by all the stars of God, find the earth below not in unison with these, but are hindered from action by the disgust which the principles on which business is managed inspire, and turn drudges, or die of disgust, some of them suicides. (W, I, 114)

The younger generation, however, was not to be suffered longer to destroy itself in alienation from society; the mind of the country must be arrested in its appalling occupation of eating upon itself. Emerson called attention to countervailing tendencies of the reflective or philosophical age: its discovery of sublimity and beauty in things near, low, and common; and its emphasis on the individual person, its growing, and accurate, supposition that out of insulation would come unity, that in proportion as men were independent of one another, freely pursuing their work and their domestic interest, society would be whole and strong. Such a society, it might be argued, would, like a gigantic jigsaw puzzle, be interesting and enduring from the complicated interlocking of its many parts, every one with particular identity, different from every other, its very unity dependent upon their diversity. "The union is only perfect when all the uniters are isolated" (W, III, 267).

Such tendencies, it was important to reveal to the young, along with the truth that in every man was the fount of all knowledge and power, as well as the means for tapping it. The means to national redemption and fulfillment were, in short, in the cultivation by individuals of the original relation to the universe described in "Nature"—the transparent-eyeball experience which would reveal to every man his infinitude. This was, in effect, Emerson's implicit meaning at various points earlier in his address—as in saying, for example, "Books are for the scholar's idle times. When he can read God directly, the hour is too precious to be wasted in other men's transcripts of their readings" (W, I, 91). The spreading of this revelation would give heart to young men and invigorate American society. America would indeed become a country of Men Thinking.

We will walk on our own feet; we will work with our own hands; we will speak our own minds. The study of letters shall be no longer a name for pity, for doubt, and for sensual indulgence. The dread of man and the love of man shall be a wall of defence and a wreath of joy around all. *A nation of men will for the first time exist,* because each believes himself inspired by the Divine Soul which also inspires all men. (W, I, 115; italics mine)

What relation between a resuscitated individual life and a new and creative national life, with distinctive arts, philosophy, and politics, was to be found in a transparent-eyeball experience? In proportion as a man knew the mystical dilation, he became wiser and all his powers more powerful. All possible truths about morality and religion, about art and science, about collective life and personal life inhered in the Universal Mind, and in those moments of quiet but rapturous absorption they communicated themselves to the reverential seeker, absorbed. "We must trust the perfection of the creation so far as to believe that whatever curiosity the order of things has awakened in our minds, the order of things can satisfy" (W, I, 3-4). The truths not previously inscribed by man in preceding generations—ideas and forms that were new—could be come by only in such a way. By himself, insulated—let him think as hard and long as he chose with his conscious rational mind—no man could ever be original. But insofar as he knew that original relation with nature, he was in a position, benefiting from its enlightenment, to set down something new in art or philosophy or politics or religion and so contribute to the growth of a culture, an American culture, which, not copying that of the French of the seventeenth century or of the Italians of the fifteenth or of the Romans of the time of Augustus or of the Greeks of the time of Pericles, would demonstrate no less than theirs an original relation with the universe. In fact, it would demonstrate more than theirs that desired relation. "Mr. President and Gentlemen, this confidence in the unsearched might of man belongs, by all motives, by all prophecy, by all preparation, to the American Scholar. We have listened too long to the courtly muses of Europe" (W, I, 114).

A country could be original only if its citizens were original; and its citizens would be original only if they were religious. What treatises were written, what poems composed, what paintings painted, what houses built, and what laws promulgated all depended on what, spiritually, every man and every woman became. This, then, was the evangel from the lips of the singer of the fields and woods of Concord. That every man and woman could know union with the Divine Spirit, he had no doubt. Made of it, by entering its current, they could imbibe it in large measures. "Who can set bounds to the possibilities of man? Once inhale the upper air, being admitted to behold the absolute natures of justice and truth, and we learn that man has access to the entire mind of the Creator, is himself the creator in the finite" (W, I, 64).

The life of the Creator could only be said to be one of perfection, in which all virtues, in whatever relations, made nothing but harmony. In entering that life, a man or woman for the time being was seeing through the eye of the Creator; and afterward, recalling the sublimity of its harmony, was impelled to re-create it in daily human life, in all personal affairs and all matters of business. The citizen, once so enlightened, wanted continuously to be enlightened; having once seen directly, sought always so to see. And in proportion as his sight was righted, asperities, pettinesses, discords of envy and hostility dropped away from him. The consequences of such a renewal on a national scale would be prodigious. To reform society, to restore the world, it was necessary only to redeem the soul. As Emerson had said in "Nature," once the axis of vision was coincident with the axis of things, one saw that the world was not lying broken and in heaps, but had unity. If all persons lived by the right idea of life, to which they had equal access, and with the right vision, which they could alike share, they would shape a pure society:

Build therefore your own world. As fast as you conform your life to the pure idea in your mind, that will unfold its great proportions. A correspondent revolution in things will attend the influx of the spirit. So fast will disagreeable appearances, swine, spiders, snakes, pests, mad-houses, prisons, enemies, vanish; they are temporary and shall be no more seen. (W, I, 76)

This was not an exhortation to his contemporaries to be wishful thinkers, to close their eyes to things offensive in society, although it is often read as though it were. There is nothing of Christian Science in it. Emerson never said that brute facts could be willed away or that wish should take the place of thought. It is a plea for right thinking and for right acting according to it. That men if they thought rightly would live rightly he was as confident as were Socrates and Plato, with whom he believed that no man was willingly deprived of the truth.

No less than Thomas Paine, Emerson held the conviction that Americans had it within their power to make the world over again. The founders of the nation less than two generations earlier had conceived the idea of an independent nation dedicated to freedom and the representative principle in politics, and acting courageously on it, had made it a reality. Emerson was fond of pointing out that the Declaration of Independence (made not of glittering generalities but of blazing ubiquities which would burn forever) was less an eloquent repudiation of the past than a hope for the future, in the face of all the evidence from the past which militated against it. He was as ready as any cynic to admit that life was base and that it had been base throughout history—but he was forever countering with the question, "But how did we find out that it was so?" The faculty in man which informed him of the base was that which knew the ideal; and whatever knew the ideal was capable of moving toward it. The achievement of the Founding Fathers was much; but it could never be crowned until all men and women, knowing the ideal more fully, translated it into their lives. The United States of America could thus become the first nation in history perfect in its original relation to the universe, where not only the arts flourished but also justice prevailed—where not only new poetry, philosophy, and religion *were* but also insane asylums, jails, exploitation, and wars were *not*—a land altogether of "beautiful faces, warm hearts, wise discourse, and heroic acts."

It is important to realize that the Puritans had earlier held the idea of this land as a thing of a special destiny, in which national feeling and religious devotion were in close relation. William Stoughton, one of their spokesmen, three hundred years ago declared:

This we must know, that the Lord's promises and expectations of great things have singled out New England, and all sorts and ranks of men amongst us, above any nation or people in the world; . . . If any people in the world have been lifted up to heaven as to advantages and privileges, we are the people. Name what you will under this head, and we have had it. (PM, 114-15)

When the religious leaders of the migrating Puritans first viewed these shores it was with awe and exultation that a new land had been preserved for them by God, where His Word, transplanted, might take root in a soil still uncontaminated by error and grow into a plant of perfection. The consummation of the Christian Good News, so long awaited by the war-weary and sin-burdened peoples of the Old World would occur in this hemisphere. The Kingdom would come on earth here, not there. Had God not wanted it to be so, He would not have delayed for so many centuries the disclosure of these virgin territories to His children. This was the Promised Land for the fleeing Puritans, as Israel had been more than two thousand years earlier to the Jewish refugees from Egypt.

The idea of a unique and consummating significance attaching to the new lands of the Western world is a very old one, ante-dating even the coming of the Puritans in the early seventeenth century. In fact, it can be traced all the way back to the legend of the disappearance of the fabled Atlantis among the ancient Greeks. Somewhere in the ocean far to the west, beyond the shores of Europe, the Greeks imagined, there had once been a land of plenty, justice, and bliss, which inexplicably no longer existed. Could it ever again be found? This question, generation after generation, occupied a fixed place in human speculation. That even before moralistic Anglo-Saxon Puritans thought of making homes for themselves across the Atlantic, Spanish conquerors, actuated by the thought of plunder not domicile, could be excited by the certainty of finding here the Fountain of Youth, illustrates the widespread, long-lived idea of another place exempt from the ravages of time and causes of human corruption which through the ages were all that mankind had known.

The kind of fulfillment of humanity's dreams or aspirations which would occur here varied from time to time and from people to people, depending on their nature. For the imperialistic conquistador it was a magical immortality allowing the ever youthful human being to live forever in sensual pleasure in voluptuous surroundings. For the religious seeker it was a way of life in which all the traditional Christian virtues would flower at last. For political idealists it was a way of life in which tyranny would cease at last. Thomas Paine in the late eighteenth century, exhorting colonists to revive their flagging spirits and fight the revolution through to a triumphant finish, reminded them jubilantly—anticlerical and disbeliever in revelation though he was— of the special nature of this continent in human history. That its discovery by Columbus in 1492 had preceded the Protestant Reformation in Germany in 1517 rather than followed it, say, in 1542 was according to the design of Almighty Providence, which had with perfect timeliness revealed it as a vast shelter to harbor fugitives from persecution in Europe.

Emerson, then, in 1837 exultantly chanting his original relation to the universe and proclaiming that if only the American citizenry lived by his Good News a healthy and just nation would for the first time come to be, was a marcher in a very long procession, whose front ranks had risen out of the mists of antiquity. And yet what he was saying about America's destiny was different, in its combining of religious and national elements, from what had ever been said before. The Puritans, almost two centuries before his time, did not have this land as a particular nation in mind when they rejoiced in the prospect of the coming of the Kingdom in the Atlantic colonies and in the importance to it of their pietistic lives. This land figured only as the place, the setting, where a mighty completion would take place; this land as a collectivity of human beings with an original way of life figured not at all. The completion to take place would be a consummation of something old, not the establishment of something new. It would be Christian, not American.

And in the distinction between these terms lies the difference between Emerson and his Puritan predecessors. Although the furthest thing from indifferent to various virtues traditionally cherished by the Christian church, he was, like Paine before him, intent on breaking with that church in emancipating himself from the past. And, in aspiring like him to make the world over again, he wanted to establish a way of life different in principle as well as practice from any previously tried—a way of life which involved a representative government on the widest possible scale (in this respect different from that of the Puritan theocracies) and which at the same time depended for its vitality on spiritual communion by every individual with the divine (in this respect, different from that of Paine). In each of its features, growth of the new venture would be invigorated by a sense of its special identity as a geographically and politically unique community, which on the highest level must be called national.

"Divinity School Address"

In "The American Scholar" Emerson cited what was wrong with the academic community in the United States; in his "Divinity School Address" he dealt with the religious community. In each instance the shortcoming he exposed was the same; both clergymen and teachers were cut off from life, and what they dispensed was not faith or learning, but information, at best second-hand and useful only in a mechanical sense to the intellect.

Like the schools, the churches of America were shackled by the past and by an addiction to books. Jesus, who had lived in the past, was kept there by theology, enshrined and embalmed as a divine person, instead of being viewed as a man surcharged with the Divine Spirit, to which his purity of mind and simplicity of life had given him large access, a man still, in every moment, brotherly related to us:

One man was true to what is in you and me. He saw that God incarnates himself in man, and evermore goes forth anew to take possession of his World. He said, in this jubilee of sublime emotion, "I am divine. Through me, God acts; through me, speaks. Would you see God, see me; or see thee, when thou also thinkest as I now think." (W, I, 128-29)

And God, having revealed himself and acted in what was called
His Only Begotten Son, was considered by clergymen to have
put a period after his once-and-for-all fiat and never again to
have entered human history. He too was a force fixed in the past.
The study of Christianity, in theological treatises as well as in
the Bible, was a continual looking backward; religion was something frozen, not still quick and flowing. "It is the office of a
true teacher to show us that God is, not was; that He speaketh,
not spake." From the pulpits on Sunday came words, impoverished and irrelevant, which gave no indication that their speakers
had ever lived—had ever loved or hated, waked or slept, eaten
or drunk. The way of Jesus was The Living Word; Christianity
was the Dead Word. Preachers wrestled vexatiously and vainly
with the miracles reputedly wrought by the superhuman Person
of Nazareth. Jesus, to be sure,

spoke of miracles; for he felt that man's life was a miracle, and all that
man doth, and he knew that this daily miracle shines as the character
ascends. But the word Miracle, as pronounced by Christian churches,
gives a false impression; it is Monster. It is not one with the blowing
clover and the falling rain. (W, I, 129)

It is "by his holy thoughts," and by them alone, that Jesus teaches
us. "To aim to convert a man by miracles is a profanation of
the soul" (W, I, 132).

What solution to the problem of petrifaction and formalism
could be found? Emerson saw no prospect of success in the
establishment of another cult with new rites and forms. Such an
undertaking, artificial and arbitrary, would collapse in deformities
and aberrations like those which had accompanied the failure
of the new goddess of reason in France during the Revolution
there. It would be better to breathe new life into the existing
forms of religion through a renewed dignity of the Sabbath and
through humanized preaching, which would be the utterance
of joy and love. But a transformation of the institution could
only follow a transformation of persons. Each minister must himself become "a newborn bard of the Holy Ghost," casting off all
conformity and acquainting "men at first hand with Deity" (W,
I, 146). He must become self-reliant and independent, discovering the infinitude of man through the ever opening life of

intuition so that he could introduce his parishioners to the marvelous fact—to the temple whose doors stood open, night and day, before every man. For to come to oneself was always to come to God in oneself. Then in the expansion of the mystical experience, every man would realize himself to be an illimitable soul and would be exalted by "the earth and heavens . . . passing into his mind; . . . drinking forever the soul of God." The restoration of religion, in short, like that of education or of any aspect of the good life, depended upon the establishment of an original relation to the universe.

"The Method of Nature"

"The Method of Nature," reflecting the growing importance of scientific thought for Emerson's mind, was an unprecedented piece, a hymned disquisition on nature, different from the quiet canticle sung under that title five years earlier. The first celebration of nature was Apollonian; the second is Dionysian. The first rejoiced in the calm of nature—its smooth and idyllic serenity and its cool, affectionate readiness to embrace man, to have him merge his mind in its beautiful order. The second proclaims the prodigious, unfathomable, ineffable energy of nature forever streaming, coursing, whirling through all that is—its ceaseless might, blinding to contemplate, in perpetual creation of new forms and species of forms, resistless and unstoppable. Characteristic passages from the two works, juxtaposed, make this clear:

> As a plant upon the earth, so a man rests upon the bosom of God; he is nourished by unfailing fountains, and draws at his need inexhaustible power. (W, I, 64)
> So must we admire in man the form of the formless, the concentration of the vast, the house of reason, the cave of memory. See the play of thoughts! What nimble gigantic creatures are these! What Saurians, what palaiotheria shall be named with these agile movers? (W, I, 205)

There had been awareness in the first essay of the marvelous plenitude that is the creation and of its activity, too, since the creation is perpetually self-repeating, but the plenitude had not been embraced orgiastically, its impetus not reflected in the very prose that reported it. It had emerged essentially fixed and static, something pictorial, for it was the total visible order of things, not the unspeakable, tumultuous fertility invisible within, that had engaged Emerson. He had beheld "the whole circle of persons and things, of actions and events, of country and religion, not as painfully accumulated, atom after atom, act after act, in an aged creeping Past, but as one vast picture which God paints on the instant eternity for the contemplation of the soul" (W, I, 60).

For the writing of the second work, Emerson had gone to a small hotel on the seashore and there, aware, as the ancient Greeks had been, of the cosmic rhythm of the sea's undulation and of the inexhaustible procreative power contained within its waters, had grown drunk on the kinesis of the spectacle. His address was a dithyramb. How could one analyze the method of nature when nature was a rushing stream never stopping to be observed?

We can never surprise nature in a corner; never find the end of a thread; never tell where to set the first stone. The bird hastens to lay her egg; the egg hastens to be a bird. The wholeness we admire in the order of the world is the result of infinite distribution. Its smoothness is the smoothness of the pitch of the cataract. Its permanence is a perpetual inchoation. Every natural fact is an emanation, and that from which it emanates is an emanation also, and from every emanation is a new emanation. If anything could stand still, it would be crushed and dissipated by the torrent it resisted, and if it were a mind, would be crazed. (W, I, 199)

Natura creatrix is an ecstasy, the universe of dynamism and progressive begetting. Vibrant with vitality, her one aim seems to be to achieve perfection, in doing ever better what she has been doing all along. She has not yet produced the perfect pine tree, nor has man ever seen one which wholly satisfied his eye; and if the species of pine tree, for some reason, does not admit of perfection, with no hesitation she will blot it out and create a new tree in its stead. The method of nature can only be defined as infinite creation for a universal, not a single, end.

Can ecstasy be adapted to man, transferred to the literary life? Man stands midway between visible nature and the intelligence which is its origin. He sees, however, that he is not the end

for which nature strives. In comparison with the splendid pro-
ductivity of nature, her unwearied ascent, in spirals of finer
forms upward toward a consummation beyond sight, how paltry,
how contemptible are the pursuits of even the most famous
members of his race—of a Louis XIV, *Le Roi Soleil,* for example,
a "solemn fop in wig and stars," wearing high heels to look tall,
talking high words to sound tall, but giving his mind to the
execution of secret fornications and vindictive political appoint-
ments or removals—or of his courtiers, dukes and marshals, *abbés*
and *mesdames,* in the most glorious court of the world, seated at
the gaming table, laying traps through lies to outwit and ruin
one another. Does such a planet rival nature's astronomy?

Yet man, "a necessary actor" on the scene, although he did
not will to play a part, is unable, having obligations to both the
pageant of beauty and the creator of it, only to stand and look
on. He senses he is not all he should be—that the things of which
he is made were once much better than they are in his person—
that nature can be used "as a convenient standard, and the metre
of our rise and fall." (Plato, to whom Emerson belonged, rather
than to Calvin, had also believed in the Fall of Man.) To dispel
his disquiet, to satisfy his need to be better than he is, he must
imitate nature, which means he must give himself to her. Her
method, in short, not only can but must become his. Suspending
his own will, silencing his own understanding, he must go to
her and enter her—or allow her to enter him (sometimes in the
same Emerson essay man goes out to nature, sometimes nature
comes into man, but in either case his mind is suffused with
her irradiating power). His repossession by her is his real birth.
And with this truth enunciated Emerson relates his message to
what he had initially promulgated in "Nature," but with dynamic
implications not contained there. "The doctrine of this Supreme
Presence is a cry of joy and exultation"; it is the "great reality,
which seems to drown all things in the deluge of its light" (W,
I, 222-23). Ecstasy, which is the law and cause of nature, must
become man's law too. His meddling self-consciousness will diminish; and whatever it is he was shaped by the Universal Will to
do, he will do with joy and love—joy in the simple fact of the
doing and love of the perfection toward which he feels it to
lead. Losing his desire to be a conspicuous or a separate person,
he will know the rapture of anonymous identification with the

creative force hurling itself through the vastnesses of space and the eons of time. Man's "health and greatness consist in his being the channel through which heaven flows to earth, in short, in the fulness in which an ecstatical state takes place in him" (W, I, 210).

Ecstasy for those of superior qualities results in art; poetry should be a rhapsody, and every poet in such a mystical experience, realizing his original relation to the universe, sees himself rightly as born "to deliver the thought of his heart from the universe to the universe" (W, I, 208). And it is not only art which gains from the transfiguration; making bread does also, and suckling a child, hoeing a field, or sweeping a room—even reforming society: "There is no office or function of man but is rightly discharged by this divine method . . ." (W, I, 211). The fault in social reformers is the lowness of their aim and the partiality of their reform, whereas if they allowed themselves to be filled with the ecstatic power of nature they would like her think in general, not in particular, terms and "aim at an infinite, not a special benefit" (W, I, 214): "the soul can be appeased not by a deed but by a tendency. It is in a hope that she feels her wings. You shall love rectitude, and not the disuse of money or the avoidance of trade, an unimpeded mind and not a monkish diet . . ." (W, I, 215). Emerson has been perhaps the only reformer in history with the sublime temerity to prescribe for the regeneration of society a program of ecstasy.

In "Nature" Emerson had been largely content to view the cataract, fixed and smooth, holding himself "off from a too trivial and microscopic study of the universal tablet" (W, I, 60). In "The Method of Nature" he penetrates the veil of white-foam water, sheeny with the sun, for a microscopic study and discovers a dizzying race of atoms. But what is extraordinary is that although nature knows no rest, and, like a rushing stream, sweeps forward to flood the ever widening abyss of the future, her speeding waters so teeming with life that there is not space for the insertion of one atom more, she still has place and time to receive man. What is also extraordinary is that, in the breathless acceleration of the Immense Impersonal, man discovers paradoxically "the lesson of an intimate divinity" (W, I, 221). "The Vast and the Divine," which uses any person glad to be used, whose love is abandonment and a depersonalized zeal for perfection, is at the same time, although not in an orthodox sense, "God in distribution, God rushing into multiform benefit" (W, I, 210), harboring in his bosom many more men than one, "biding their time and the needs and the beauty of all" (W, I, 208), and speaking rich and great wisdom in a voice that is "ravishing music." It is the "mighty and transcendent Soul" (W, I, 221). Whatever it has in mind as the great end of its ecstatic operation must be good; of that Emerson is intuitively sure. He trusts it wholly—its overspilling might is the only sanity of man, who needs it "against the heedlessness and against the contradiction of society" (W, I, 221).

Emerson is determined to annul the centuries-long divorce between the intellect and holiness. It is with his intellect (larger reason) that he has discovered the immanent force. His intellect is automatically true, and, since for a Platonist what is true is at the same time holy, and since the immanent force is one with the thing that has discovered it, then the immanent force is holy too, and what it has in store for man, he must rest unperturbedly on, in faith. Emerson was in the habit of pointing out that the difference between his necessity and the vulgarly considered fate was that his necessity was beneficent. But it is interesting to see that—far as he has come from his one-time theological position and remote though a scientific view of reality as a maelstrom of atoms seems to be from a religious picture of the world as a thing shaped by the hands of a loving Creator—he is still very close to where he started. Even in his ardor to surrender his individual will and find his happiness in the fullness with which as a faceless instrument he can be used, he is near to Christian mystics, to a Jonathan Edwards, for example, who knew ecstasy in being swallowed up in God and ravished by Him, for whom to lie out of God (to live in imperfection) was sin, and whose fulfillment was in the self-obliterating execution of God's will.

To the nature of the divine earlier described in "Nature," "The American Scholar," and "The Divinity School Address" Emerson has added a quality of power and dynamism, which will characterize it through the rest of his life. The divine not only is; it ceaselessly does. And it not only ceaselessly does; it does to some end, indefinable but good, working toward it in acts which are innumerable, progressive stages of change, many of them visible

in nature and measurable by man, thanks to the development
of techniques in modern science. Emerson has added, or, more
accurately, restored and developed, an attribute of the divine
in terms in which, in an astonishing fashion, before he became
aware of the revelations of science, he had very early at the age
of eighteen conceived of it:

The idea of *power* seems to have been everywhere at the bottom of
the Theology. . . . Cause and Effect is another name for the direction
of this sentiment. . . . It is a great flood which encircles the universe
and is poured out in unnumbered channels to feed the fountains of life
and the wants of Creation, but everywhere runs back again and is
swallowed up in its eternal source. That source is God. (J, I, 103-4)

At the time of his lectures on his return from England he had
stated, about the connection of the human being with suprahuman being, that even Alaric (Attila?), the scourge of God,
had opened "thus unto himself supernal influence" and added,
"Nothing seems less than an insulated man an ant an acorn is
each united to the World by a stream of relation which flows
through them" (EL, I, 424-5). It was a conception easily and
happily harmonized with the steady development of the evolutionary idea through the rest of the century. He would continue
to take delight in looking at the world in a way altogether different from that of his ancestors, contemplating as a fact at once
scientific and religious the innumerable species of living things
on the globe, the interaction between them and their environment, and the subtle and protracted evolvement through eons of
simple organisms into complex creatures. Supremely cause for
joy was man, the most complex creature, whose earthly tenancy
had not been allowed to occur until the earth was ready for him.
    The idea of a graduated scale in living forms, from simplest
vegetable organisms through sentient animals to complex intellective creatures, was not new in Emerson's time. According to
the concept of the Great Chain of Being, so important to the
view of life of educated, thoughtful men in the seventeenth and
eighteenth centuries, all things that made up the natural universe, ranked in beautifully articulated coherence from inert
stones to angels, exhibited the climactic organization of life in infinitesimal gradations from utter materiality to pure spirituality.

There was ascending order in such a plan but no ascent, for it was fixed and static. Every species making a link in the great chain was specially created and bore no necessary relation to any other. No species, even given the appropriate conditions, could evolve into another higher on the Chain. Nor were new species being created, for the whole hierarchy had been established for all time at the time of the single creation.

Just as Emerson's evolutionism differed from such a pattern in being dynamic, so also did his faith from the best old brand of Christianity. Most practicing Christians still believed that the essential elements of spiritual life were fixed by revelation centuries ago—in the Ten Commandments and in the teachings of Jesus. The Book of Revelation had closed, and the aim of life now was, looking backward, to live up to the demands of those ancient dicta. That new truth could be revealed still, almost nobody believed. But for Emerson it could be and to the commonest person. God was ready at any instant to disclose Himself anew, and any day bore possibilities of human transformation.

At the beginning of his short career as minister Emerson had summed up his function in the following passage:

What is the office of a Christian minister? 'Tis his to show the beauty of the moral laws of the universe; to explain the theory of a perfect life; to watch the Divinity in his world; to detect his footstep; to discern him in the history of the race of his children, by catching the tune from a patient listening to miscellaneous sounds; by threading out the unapparent plan in events crowding on events. (J, II, 262)

It is obvious from the epochal pieces just considered that Emerson the lecturer and writer was one with Emerson the preacher. He had exchanged the church pulpit for the platform lectern, but his aims remained the same. Wherever he spoke it was with the same intention of renewing life for those who listened by disclosing their relation to a world of beauty where law prevailed. He had resigned his churchly office because of his scruple against administering the sacrament of the Holy Communion; yet, in effect, in every one of his utterances, written or spoken, he continued to unveil the Host—not the symbols of the flesh and blood of Jesus of Nazareth but those of the person and spirit of every man and woman in his audience. He revealed them in their mystery to themselves. Ordinary men all had powers of which they were unaware. They seemed unawake, as though in a trance or makebelieve. They were like neuters in a hive of bees, every one of which was capable of transformation into the queen bee as soon as the sovereign was removed. He set himself to be the agent of their transformation and, through them, of a national metamorphosis. His exhortation in "The American Scholar" to young men to capitalize their native American potential was made with the conviction that to do so was, in the broadest, most human sense, their religious duty. To the end of his career he sought to rouse "the sluggard intellect of this continent" to "look from under its iron lids and fill the postponed expectation of the world with something better than the exertions of mechanical skill" (W, I, 81) by making his hearers believe in themselves through disclosing the infinitude of the private man.

Although in his *Journals,* letters, and lectures he was prolific, in the number of printed works under his name during his lifetime Emerson was hardly remarkable. In 1841 and 1844 appeared the extraordinary *Essays,* Series 1 and 2, and in 1847 *Poems.* In 1849 he brought out a revised edition of the lyrical "Nature" (1836) in company with a number of select addresses and lectures from the decade which had followed it. In 1850 he issued *Representative Men,* in which, in illustration, more or less, of an idea he had assimilated a quarter of a century earlier, that geniuses, not thinking their own thoughts or speaking their own words, were the organs or mouthpieces of their age, he aimed to show how in six supremely receptive intelligences—Plato, Swedenborg, Montaigne, Shakespeare, Napoleon, and Goethe—the World Soul had incarnated itself as the Philosopher, the Mystic, the Skeptic, the Poet, the Man of the World, and the Writer, respectively. *English Traits* in 1856 was the product of years of thought about England, as well as of considerable firsthand observation, and it depicted brilliantly the nature of contemporary Englishmen in relation to qualities of their ancestors and features of their history. It also revealed something of his ideas of history and of race. In 1860 and 1867 with *The Conduct of Life* and *May Day and Other Pieces,* respectively, he completed his career as publishing thinker. Unlike such prodigious artists as Michelangelo, J. S. Bach, and Verdi, he was not fertile and productive to the end of his life. In his last ten years he was incapable of intellectual activity in the strict sense of the term, and his creative period, in fact, was past by the time he was sixty. He had long since said what he had to say.

The titles of the essays that make up the two volumes of 1841 and 1844 and the third of 1860 are revealing:

1841	*1844*	*1860*
History	The Poet	Fate
Self-Reliance	Experience	Power
Compensation	Character	Wealth
Spiritual Laws	Manners	Culture
Love	Gifts	Behavior
Friendship	Nature	Worship
Prudence	Politics	Considerations
Heroism	Nominalist and	by the Way
The Over-Soul	Realist	Beauty
Circles	New England	Illusions
Intellect	Reformers	
Art		

Some essays obviously aim to deal with the big issues of life, to unfold thought on a vast scale in treating metaphysical matters—History, Compensation, Spiritual Laws, The Over-Soul, Circles, Intellect, Experience, Nature, Fate, and Illusions. Others suggest a discussion of man in relation to his fellows and to society—Love, Friendship, Prudence, Manners, Gifts, Politics, Wealth, Culture, Behavior, and Worship. Still others indicate an examination of man, so to speak, vis-à-vis himself—Self-Reliance, Heroism, Character, and Power. And a few, a leftover miscellany, seem to have to do with art or are topical—Art, Beauty, Nominalist and Realist, and New England Reformers. The distribution of the several kinds over the three volumes is more or less equal. Throughout his career Emerson dealt with the same kinds of subject in about the same proportion to one another and in the same fashion.

In a survey of his work one is struck by Emerson's fidelity to his early aim to see life through thought, to live in the world of thought, and by the consistency of his attitude, always one of joy and confidence untinged by authoritarianism. As a lover of truth he tried to keep himself unmoored and freely afloat, to abstain from dogmatism and to "recognize all the opposite negations between which, as walls, his being" was swung (W, II, 342). He lived each day in a perspective allowing him to attach the smallest thing to the largest, yet he could not describe his vision of life as definitive or ultimate. In a charming six-line fragment, rather like Robert Frost, he showed human beings their cosmic predicament and the inability of any one of them, himself included, to explain what it meant:

> Nature centres into balls,
> And her proud ephemerals,
> Fast to surface and outside,
> Scan the profile of the sphere;
> Knew they what that signified,
> A new genesis were here. (W, IX, 282)

In a sense, his own days although numerous and luminous, had not counted for any more than those of the most complacent loafer:

> I am not wiser for my age,
> Nor skilful by my grief;
> Life loiters at the book's first page,—
> Ah! could we turn the leaf. (W, IX, 295)

Plato had come close to explaining what it all meant and so, in his own way, had Shakespeare. Emerson longed for the penetration of mind and the might of speech that would allow him to reveal the final what-was-what to mankind:

> And as the light divides the dark
>   Through with living swords,
> So shall thou pierce the distant age
>   With adamantine words. (W, IX, 330)

His powers, however, were inadequate to the task, and so, he feared, were those of every man.

But never yet the man was found
Who could the mystery expound
Though Adam, born when oaks were young,
Endured, the Bible says, as long;
But when at last the patriarch died
The Gordian noose was still untied.
He left, though goodly centuries old,
Meek Nature's Secret still untold. (W, IX, 339)

The picture of the universe, and man's place in it, implicit in "The Method of Nature" remained true for Emerson for the rest of his days. The findings of science through his remaining four decades only confirmed its features. The universe was limitless, and, in incessant activity continuously begetting new forms, was moving, in a mode which man's comprehension could only represent as spiraling ascent, from rude to finer organization toward an ultimate fulfillment, a total perfection. Everything in existence at any given moment was involved in flux, in change—in the grand evolution toward the climactic *ne plus ultra*. The universe comprised an infinite number of solar systems, all formed by suns having hurled off from themselves their outer rings of diffuse ether, which had then condensed into tributary planets, earths, and moons. In the wake of this incredible physical parturition the central governing mind had detached from itself lesser minds for the rational creatures it had shaped, each with the same power of detaching from itself thoughts or intellections. The elements of the universe were thus linked by a marvelously complicated sphericity. Nature, originally a vast idea in the Universal Mind, was incarnated by it in the visible, palpable shapes we know in order to become a vast idea in our human minds also, in proportion as we understand it. "Nature is the incarnation of a thought, and turns to a thought again, as ice becomes water and gas" (W, III, 196). Her operation was distinguished with paradoxical simultaneity by two principal laws, motion or change, and rest or identity. Although she was always in flux, she was always the same; the many, fleeing, were really the one, perpetually remaining. (Related to that of illusion, this idea of the pre-Socratic Greek philosopher Heraclitus had lent itself to happy assimilation by modern scientific discovery.) In a second essay, "Nature" (1844), Emerson, reconciling to one another the Dionysian and Apollonian, or active and passive, aspects of things which he had earlier treated separately in "Nature" (1836) and "The Method of Nature" (1841), named them *natura naturans* and *natura naturata* (loosely, nature in realization and nature realized).

Not put off by the face of motion but remembering that she also wore a face of rest, man could understand nature through the mystical identification earlier described in the collegiate addresses. In moments of such Communion, the Universal Mind or Over-Soul, since it corresponded mirrorlike in every detail with the human soul in faculties of appetite, sentiment, rational cognition, and will, and was therefore reachable through the forms of nature, which it wore like a delicate garment, enclosed man, embraced him to the end that his own faculties, in intimate contact with their parental prototypes, were expanded and realized as they never otherwise would be. As we have already seen, it was this experience through which a person established an original relation to the universe. It enabled him to become self-reliant and develop those particular powers he was born into the world to develop—whether powers for farming, for raising children, for teaching, for doctoring, for creating in the arts, or for governing the state. In proportion as such individualism took place, nations became distinctive, strong, and great; and nature herself—for nature, having made the mason who builds the house, included cities as well as fields, forests, and mountains —moved a step further toward her consummation. In proportion as it did not, nature was dissatisfied and, because of the recalcitrance and blindness of her creatures, destroyed them to make room for others more intelligent and more cooperative. "Nature works in immense time, and spends individuals and races prodigally to prepare new individuals and races. The lower kinds are one after one extinguished; the higher forms come in" (W, XI, 525-26).

The universe, however, it must never be forgotten, was named by the Greeks *Kosmos,* or Beauty, and Emerson never outgrew the feeling that what was amazing was not that nature lay under the command of exhibiting beauty in particular places at particular moments but that she was beautiful everywhere always. Man did right to love her beautiful forms, yet he was not to give himself wholly to them in sensuous delight but rather to be on guard against them as a cup of enchantments and strive to "look at nature with a supernatural eye" (W, I, 213). Else, he was doomed to frustration. The forms themselves were as elusive as Proteus and in their loveliness always gave the "sense of still-ness that follows a pageant which has just gone by" (W, III, 192-93). Beauty could never be grasped.

The human soul, in realizing its attributes, would take on something of the beauty of nature and, in reabsorption into na-ture at death, know its immortality. The feelings of love, kind-ness, and fidelity which it experienced, the ideas it entertained of justice, cooperation, and beauty, were all in themselves in-destructible and eternal things and so also must be the faculties of the soul on which they acted. The constituents of the soul, as well as the qualities which engaged them, were immortal:

Jesus, living in these moral sentiments, heedless of sensual fortunes, heeding only the manifestations of these, never made the separation of the idea of duration from the essence of these attributes, nor uttered a syllable concerning the duration of the soul. It was left to his disciples to sever duration from the moral elements, and to teach the immortality of the soul as a doctrine, and maintain it by evidences. The moment the doctrine of the immortality is separately taught, man is already fallen. (W, II, 283-84)

Presumably those persons who in their lifetime had not exercised the attributes of their souls and had not, then, participated in the infinitude of the flowing of love and adoration, would never know anything of Emerson's immortality and would cease to be living even long before death, their faculties having atrophied through disuse.

As gravity in the physical universe held things together, so did truth sustain the moral realm. Without the cohesive power of truth chaos would reign in the mind and civilization would be impossible. For Emerson, the supreme truth about the system of things was that it was moral and went according to plan or law. Evidence of this was, as has already been seen, in the number of analogies demonstrating that on every hand physical laws were counterparts of moral laws and translatable into them. As scientists had shown that every gas was a vacuum for every other, so Emerson took pleasure in observing that, in human beings, states of mind, or interests, served as restorative vacuums for one another; Newton, for example, tiring of calculus turned to astronomy, tiring of astronomy turned to optics, and finally found refreshment from optics in chronology. Had scientists demonstrated that a drop of water in a tube under certain conditions could counterbalance the pressure of the entire ocean? So in a moral sense could a single individual withstand the effect of a whole people, as Socrates had done in Greece, Jesus in Palestine, Martin Luther in Germany.

To say that the universe was moral and existed for good was not to say, however, that it was soft or had been made to reward namby-pambies. It existed because it was power, and even the good it promoted was power. Nothing could be, let alone be done, without power. To put together required power; to part asunder required power. On the whole, putting together was good because it was formation, construction, and harmony; parting asunder was bad because it was separation and disharmony. Wicked men, insofar as they exhibited power in performing their deeds, were working along the lines of the universe, but inasmuch as they destroyed and sowed dissension, they were going against its principle. The universe sought always to realize its creative self more purely, more fully. Its line was positive, not negative; its direction up, not down. Since creation could only be the fruit of what we term the virtues—honesty, harmony, and love—men and women who lived increasingly by them, by qualities of the mind, were congenial to nature and at one with it. They were substituting intellective power, power of the spirit, for physical power and, even though infinitesimally, assisting in the evolution of the existing order into something better. "Liberation of the will from the sheaths and clogs of organization which . . . [man] has outgrown, is the end and aim of this world." (W, VI, 36). Yet all virtues must be practiced vigorously, and the virtuous man, in everything he did, must be confident and happily affirmative. What was called religion by the churches was effeminatizing and demoralizing; on the rightly minded man who lived serenely and surely, not tentative or apologetic and the furthest thing from pusillanimous, nature, never hesitant or uncertain, would look with favor, infusing into him ever more of her own sure and straight vitality.

Evil in the world was not absolute or a thing in itself but was privative, the absence of good, as cold was the absence of heat and darkness the absence of light. Yet although it might appear otherwise, doers of evil did not continue in life unscathed by their deeds. The mighty principle of undulation in the universe insured that every thing thought or done by man brought its own requital. Just as nothing in the world of affairs was ever bought for nothing, so in the moral world no act of mind or body was done without effect. Society might think that liars and swindlers moved from day to day in their covert deceit with impunity because no public exposure of their crookedness was ever made, but an enlightened man, seeing not with the understanding but with the intellect or reason, knew that retribution was forever overtaking them, not necessarily in outward circumstance, but in their real nature. A vicious man might persevere until death in his vice and malice, never stunningly confuted in "his nonsense before men and angels," but this did not mean that he had outwitted the law. Every departure from truth, every transgression of affection left its mark on the soul of the transgressor; he was perpetually deceasing from nature, whose motion was always toward integrity and unity. His malignity, his lies bred distrust in those about him and fear in himself; his neighbors, though perhaps with no word revealing it, never encountered him without suspicion and distaste; and his reaction, increasingly one of resentment over the rupture he had made, necessarily sought to palliate it by a stronger curtain of treachery. Every tyrant mistakenly depended for his safety on a strong bodyguard. Ultimately, in the eternal account, the only good or harm that befalls us, we do ourselves. Socrates and Jesus, though physically put to death, died unharmed because their souls were unstained by rancor or vindictiveness.

As for evil in the physical universe, it was true that great forces seemed inimical to man, striking cataclysmally at him in hurricane, tidal wave, or eruption, or enfeebling him insidiously through pestilence or disease; but on the whole, if the age-long perspective were taken into account, they were seen not to be destroyers of man. Emerson knew that nature in act vis-à-vis man was not the metaphysical entity so easily manipulated in an essay about her, and he often set himself to look her fully in the face, at once grim as well as ingratiating. "Let us not deny it up and down. Providence has a wild, rough, incalculable road to its end, and it is of no use to try to whitewash its huge, mixed instrumentalities, or to dress up that terrific benefactor in a clean shirt and white neckcloth of a student in divinity" (W, VI, 8). Yet man was endowed with powers of physical resistance and endurance that kept him firm on the earth; the pressure of the atmosphere, for example, was countervailed by pressure of air within his own body, and the chemistry of his blood availed to create immunities against toxic germs. "If the Universe have these savage accidents, our atoms are as savage in resistance" (W, VI, 24). Where the powers of his body did not suffice to enable him to withstand the seeming hostility of forces outside him, his intellect preserved him from them. He built ships and learned to swim to master the threat of the ocean. He drained swamps and saved himself from typhus; supplemented drainage with vaccination to ward off smallpox; thwarted scurvy by the simple expedient of lemon juice and right diet. Steam and electricity, giant forces, he was likewise learning, thanks to his brain, to transform into friendly servants.

Seeming adversity in the form of weak native constitution or temperament the individual could also circumvent or sublimate through elevation of mind. Physical handicaps confining persons to their homes could be made the means to an intellectual cultivation which otherwise they would never have been led to undertake; a cripple, for example, by virtue of his inactivity could develop an interest in immobile structures and become an architect. An oversensitive, shy man, unable to master the quick give-and-take of social conversation, could—as Emerson himself had done—utilize his solitude in perfecting his thoughts and giving them in writing a finish of expression they would never have known in ephemeral talk. Adversity, in short, could be turned to advantage. The law of polarity, of undulation, of compensation made it so. Evil was not only the absence of good; it was the means of good, could be turned into good. Physical suffering, by heightening mental activity, often led the sufferer to important discoveries about himself. And bereavement was just as often a carrier of benefit to the bereaved; "it commonly operates revolutions in our way of life, terminates an epoch of infancy or of youth which was waiting to be closed, breaks up a wonted occupation, or a household, or style of living, and allows the formation of new ones more friendly to the growth of character" (W, II, 126). That evil could be turned to good was as true on a national, or racial, as on an individual scale. The Crusades, for example, although causing an immeasurable destruction of property and loss of life, had put western Europe into contact with the Near East and brought about a fertilization of intellectual activity of incalculable worth to mankind. Where ancient history was concerned, Providence could be seen benignly to have used the scourge of war, "of earthquakes and changed water courses, to save underground through barbarous ages the relics of ancient art, and thus allows us to witness the upturning of the alphabets of old races, and the deciphering of forgotten languages, so to complete the annals of the forefathers of Asia, Africa, and Europe" (W, X, 303).

Where no gain to a generally reputed evil was yet seen to exist, Emerson was of the opinion that a higher state of knowledge and intellectual development could reveal one, sure in his faith that nature did nothing but for the beneficent end she had in mind and that therefore all occurrences, no matter how disastrous, being contained in a high order, were ministering to a good, remote yet certain. This faith led him to statements on occasion that seem to us extravagant—as that "most of the great results of history are brought about by discreditable means" and that "the benefit done by a good King Alfred or by a Howard, or Pestalozzi, or Elizabeth Fry, or Florence Nightingale, or any lover, lesser or larger," is as nothing "compared with the involuntary blessing wrought on nations by the selfish capitalists who built the Illinois, Michigan and the network of the Mississippi Valley [rail] roads; which have evoked not only all the wealth of the soil, but the energy of millions of men" (W, VI, 256). Sometimes in the late essays such asseverations leave the reader with the feeling that if good is automatically to prevail and all evil is miraculously disguised good, he need make no effort of his own to help the cause along. Once in a while Emerson, realizing this import, worked himself into a near-contradiction by trying to obviate it: "and though we should fold our arms,—which we cannot do, for our duty requires us to be the very hands of this guiding sentiment, and work in the present moment,—the evils we suffer will at last end themselves through the incessant opposition of Nature to everything hurtful" (W, X, 189).

To all that limited man in the universe Emerson gave the name of fate. External nature and internal nature, race and sex, environment and heredity he was continually aware of, intent on assessing accurately their relation to man. Yet although in the several essays, "Compensation," "Experience," and "Fate," in which he treated the adversely restrictive in life as honestly as possible, he seemed on occasion to admit that fate is omnipotent, he could not be absolute in his admission and at the last minute invariably affirmed the value of freedom in man. In "Experience," for example, he stated: "On its own level, or in view of nature, temperament is final. I see not, if one be once caught in this trap of so-called sciences, any escape for the man from the links of the chain of physical necessity. Given such an embryo, such a history must follow" (W, III, 54). But immediately he extricated himself from the links of the chain:

But it is impossible that the creative power should exclude itself. Into every intelligence there is a door which is never closed, through which the creator passes. The intellect, seeker of absolute truth, or the heart, lover of absolute good, intervenes for our succor, and at one whisper of these high powers we awake from ineffectual struggles with this nightmare.

Sometimes Emerson conceded that "in its last and loftiest ascensions, insight itself and the freedom of the will" was one of the obedient members of fate (W, VI, 21). Yet paradoxically he explained this to mean that, since it was forever causing man to choose and act, intellect annulled fate. "So far as a man thinks, he is free" (W, VI, 23). And he was honest enough to explain that he did not pursue such strictly speculative matters very far, believing them both insoluble and dispiriting. He trusted intuition and feeling; with Samuel Johnson, one suspects, he could say about free will that although all theory was against it all experience was for it. He was always conscious simultaneously of both freedom and fate, of individual will and necessity, and believed that man's sanity resided in the skill with which he could keep himself balanced on both, like the circus riders who rode agilely erect on two steeds at once or who nimbly leaped from one horse to another. His geometry spanned extreme points and reconciled them. Hence he could always say, as he said at the beginning of "Fate": "But if there be irresistible dictation, this dictation understands itself. If we must accept Fate, we are not less compelled to affirm liberty, the significance of the individual, the grandeur of duty, the power of character. This is true and that other is true" (W, VI, 4). During his life, however, depending on circumstances and their effect on him, his emphasis varied. Sometimes he had more to say for freedom, sometimes for necessity.

Where evil is concerned, however, many readers will feel Emerson's treatment of it to be evasive. He will seem to them to have done exactly what it used to weary him to see done by clergymen in the pulpit—to have announced an impartial examination of a vexatious question candidly raised and then to have given a prepared answer to it with the result that his performance, rehearsed, is nugatory and irrelevant. In *Representative Men,* for example, apropos of the degree of limitation on human achievement imposed by fate, he creates an adversary to oppose his idea that the great man is an inspiration to us to make ourselves infinite also:

The thoughtful youth laments the superfoetation of nature. "Generous and handsome," he says, "is your hero; but look at yonder poor Paddy, whose country is his wheelbarrow; look at his whole nation of Paddies." Why are the masses, from the dawn of history down, food for knives and powder? The idea dignifies a few leaders, who have sentiment, opinion, love, self-devotion; and they make war and death sacred;—but what for the wretches whom they hire and kill? The cheapness of man is every day's tragedy. (W, IV, 30-31)

What indeed for the wretches who are hired and killed every day? And one waits for Emerson, who here as in "Experience" and other serious inquiries into the matter, has set his heart on honesty, to throw some light on the significance of their brief lives and reveal how self-reliance relates to them. But what he proceeds to say is that "Society is a Pestalozzian school: all are teachers and pupils in turn." If in a gathering we observe that only a few persons shine, while dozens of others are present simply in supporting roles to fill in the scene, this is because we do not observe long enough. Tomorrow, and the day after, circumstances having changed, the extras have their turn as principals. There is an inevitable rotation of parts. "As to what we call the masses, and common men,—there are no common men. All men are at last of a size; and . . . every talent has its apotheosis somewhere." This is the answer he had returned his brother Charles years before when he was worried about the meagerness of his talent and the seeming impossibility of ever using it. Nothing, nothing was ever lost. But the question of the meaning of the existence of the "Paddies" remains unanswered.

In her intent to create ever better kinds of life, nature, indifferent to individuals and species alike, was melioristic. Meliorism meant progress, and of progress Emerson was never in doubt. The record of mankind, if viewed in the perspective of centuries or millennia, showed growth upward—not unbroken or continuous but, in a loose spiral sense, continual. Even in his days as minister this was a conviction he had propounded:

In the place of the unsupported virtues of solitary individuals that sparkle in the darkness of antiquity, of the little stingy rapacious intercourse of that day—a few Corinthians, a few Romans creeping round the shores of the Mediterranean for piracy and conquest, the nations of the globe are brought together [A.D. 1830] by pacific and equitable commerce; liberal humane Christian associations are correcting the manners and relieving the sufferings of vast masses of men. (YES, 197-98)

And he could point in his own nation to societies for the correction of prison discipline, for the humane treatment of seamen, for temperance and the enfranchisement of women, and for the abolition of slavery as incontrovertible signs of advancement. Such reforms, when not too much in the way of "melioration" was ascribed to them individually by their advocates, he continued to believe good and in accord with nature's aim, but their numerousness or their collective support did not at all mean that their adherents represented the finest strain of humanity of which homo sapiens was capable.

No nations in the nineteenth century were made of the stock which would be nature's ultimate product. "We still carry sticking to us some remains of the inferior quadruped organization. We call these millions men; but they are not yet men. Half engaged in the soil, pawing to get free, man needs all the music that can be brought to disengage him" (W, VI, 165). What the perfected stock would look like or where it would originate no one could say, but it would be distinguished by its capacity for living in the intellect and by its freedom from weaknesses physical or mental. "The age of the quadruped is to go out, the age of the brain and of the heart is to come in" (W, VI, 166). Still widespread over the globe were diseases and aberrations which showed bodies and minds far from perfect. Emerson liked the long view of human experience contained in the literature and philosophy of the Far East—its universality of vision and its valuation of thought as distinct from action, of being rather than doing—yet the great doctrines of fate and of the transmigration of souls, while strongly attractive, he was forced to modify. As we have seen, he could not subscribe to a fate or necessity which was pitilessly, impersonally omnipotent. Correspondingly, although he held to the idea of retribution (a form of compensation) in the world, he could not accept the oriental notion that persons presently alive but suffering from handicaps of whatever kind were being punished for sins they had individually committed in previous incarnations. They were instead the victims, more credibly, of the collective operation of cause and effect in nature.

The violations of the laws of nature by our predecessors and our contemporaries are punished in us also. The disease and deformity around us certify the infraction of natural, intellectual and moral laws, and often violation on violation to breed such compound misery. A lock-jaw that bends a man's head back to his heels; hydrophobia that makes him bark at his wife and babes; insanity that makes him eat grass; war, plague, cholera, famine, indicate a certain ferocity in nature, which, as it had its inlet by human crime, must have its outlet by human suffering. Unhappily no man exists who has not in his own person become to some amount a stockholder in the sin, and so made himself liable to a share in the expiation. (W, II, 249)

This picture in its grim details brings to mind perhaps the severity of the operation of the Old Testament Jehovah, jealous, retributive, and implacable, who punished the sins of offenders against Him even unto the third and fourth generation—or recalls the severity of the God of Calvinism, who worked toward a final culmination in His universe, undeterred by voices of human plaint. Indeed, the readiness of nature in accomplishing her end to scrap her creatures by the million is not dissimilar to the disposition of Calvin's deity to abandon in hell by the myriad those defective children not eligible to promote or share in His glorious millennium. Emerson called himself an optimist, and his name has come to be synonymous with optimism; yet it is plain that in connection with him the term has to be carefully qualified. The system of things in the universe was for the best, but at no time historically were conditions on earth the best—man never was, but always to be, blest.

Emerson saw the unfolding of history in a cyclical fashion. Even those peoples or nations not grossly imperfect and cut off quickly by nature, being below the standard of perfection, were numbered in their days. They waxed and waned and disappeared; they emerged from nothing, and after the wheel had come full circle, they returned into nothing. Their course was like that of the human individual: in their adolescence they were marked by animal spirits; in their maturity their physical vitality was matched with intellectual strength; and in their old age, settled and comfortable, they sought to have wealth and material possession do duty for creation of the mind. But in their heyday—while the happy wedding of body and intellect lasted—their peculiar genius could lead them to splendid achievements of the spirit in philosophy and the arts. England, for example, Emerson declared in his fascinating, racy *English Traits* (1856), had already contributed to the world and to the evolution of mankind what by nature the Anglo-Saxon race was capable of contributing. She was in her decline, which had set in about 1700, still prosperous and vigorous, to be sure—Emerson in his second visit in 1847 was impressed by the boisterousness of her sport, the alertness of her law, and her initiative in business and industry—but no longer creative in things of the mind. Her military strength high and her reputation for freedom and justice at its height still, with English political and juridical institutions being copied everywhere, she nevertheless had no new Bacon, no new Shakespeare to offer to the world. Those two supreme intelligences had been possible only in the Elizabethan period, when the World Soul had brought the national spirit to its fruition. The next climactic accomplishment of the Anglo-Saxon race, retempered by its amalgamation with other stocks, would occur in the New World in the United States, which, raw and undisciplined, was still in her ascent. Yet eventually, the law of melioration being what it was, the inscribing of a series of circles, each progressively capable of containing all the others, one could only conclude that even the United States would suffer eclipse and disappear into oblivion.

Races of mankind, then, like races of lesser animals, were limited by nature in their power to accomplish; each was subject to a particular arrested development. Every individual, however, owed it to his nation and to the human race to make as much of himself as he could, developing to the full his particular talent as well as his general faculties of thought and affection. The imagination of Jonathan Edwards was set on fire by the prospect of contributing to the future advancement of Christ's kingdom upon earth; that of Emerson by the need to further the progressive improvement of nature in the universe. Everywhere, however, too many human creatures lived, crawling between heaven and earth. Enormous and impoverished populations were "disgusting, like moving cheese, like hills of ants or of fleas—the more the worse" (W, IV, 4). The tendency toward national fulfillment and nature's perfection would be aided universally if there were more individuals, more aristocrats or men of character, of penetrating mind and active will. Emerson wanted not to concede anything to the pernicious masses, but to "tame, drill, divide and break them up," to draw single persons out of them. He wished that governments could limit their populations, preventing the drones from multiplying, to insure that every new person born could "be hailed as essential" (W, VI, 249).

Throughout history certain individuals, her "darlings," had been brought into being by nature, with extraordinary endowments at birth and a prodigious faculty for enlarging their powers by replenishment from the bottomless reservoir of the Universal Soul. These were vessels through whom the divine force, the creative might of nature, flowed superabundantly—representative men. Emerson had always been attracted by such heroes, by what they demonstrated of the possibilities of humanity superhumanized, but he seems never to have tried to find one for the climacteric of every nation in civilization; and even in *Representative Men* (1850), in spite of its beautifully written interpretations, there is little to show his five subjects as representative because they embodied par excellence ideas at a given time distinguishing their sectors of civilization. Montaigne, for example, he treats as a representative skeptic without any consideration of whether France, or western Europe, in the sixteenth century was predominantly skeptical in temper; and even to the word "skeptic" he gives an idiosyncratic definition.

Governments in the course of history could be shown to have improved. For thousands of years they had been determined by

the autocratic, or tyrannical, principle in man, and the telling of
their record would be nothing but one long account of fore-
bemoaned moan, of billions in abjection subservient to the
violence of a few in mastery. "This is the history of governments,
—one man does something which is to bind another" (W, III, 215).
In modern times, however, owing to the degree of enlightenment
of the human intellect about forces, human as well as extra-
human, a new principle, after periodically bursting its confines,
had come to prevail:

The Fultons and Watts of politics, believing in unity, saw that it was
a power, and by satisfying it (as justice satisfies everybody), through
a different disposition of society,—grouping it on a level instead of
piling it into a mountain—they have contrived to make of this terror
the most harmless and energetic form of a State. (W, VI, 34)

The state, however, even at its best in modern times, was in
Emerson's view an inferior contrivance for adjusting the claims
of property to those of the person. He saw signs of discontent
with it and of aspiration toward something better:

There is an instinctive sense, however obscure and yet inarticulate, that
the whole constitution of property, on its present tenures, is injurious,
and its influence on persons deteriorating and degrading; that truly
the only interest for the consideration of the State is persons; that
property will always follow persons; that the highest end of government is the culture of men; and that if men can be educated, the
institutions will share their improvement and the moral sentiment will
write the law of the land. (W, III, 204)

Although many people thought civilization to be nearing its
meridian, it was actually still "only at the cock-crowing and the
morning star." Emerson looked, like Marx, for the day when
the state would wither away and individuals would be all in all
to each other. Just as he said that he was more a poet than anything else and in religion more a Quaker than anything else,
so one could say that in politics he was more an anarchist than
anything else:

To educate the wise man the State exists, and with the appearance of
the wise man the State expires. The appearance of character makes the
State unnecessary. The wise man is the State. He needs no army, fort,

or navy,—he loves men too well; . . . He needs no library for he has not done thinking; no church, for he is a prophet; no statute-book, for he has the lawgiver; no money, for he is value; no road, for he is at home where he is; no experience, for the life of the creator shoots through him, and looks from his eyes. (W, III, 216)

To move slowly toward the end of the expiration of the state, it was necessary in the meanwhile to work on "the most religious and instructed men of the most religious and civil nations" to awaken in them "a reliance on the moral sentiment and a sufficient belief in the unity of things, to persuade them that society can be maintained without artificial restraints, as well as the solar system; or that the private citizen might be reasonable and a good neighbor, without the hint of a jail or a confiscation" (W, III, 220-21). The state would be renovated only on the principle of right and love. In the meantime, everywhere, "Good men must not obey the laws too well" (W, III, 208).

Emerson's own relation to the state during the decade which led to the Civil War is so important for what it reveals of his thought translated into his life that it deserves a few pages of special observation. His "good men must not obey the laws too well" was an injunction which influenced various young men, most notably Thoreau, to adopt open civil disobedience rather than comply with the demands of a government they believed to be iniquitous. He was himself in deed never civilly disobedient, but in word, which is a species of act, he often was. To incite others not to cooperate with the government is in effect not to cooperate with it oneself. Urging others to break the law is itself a breaking of the law. Emerson in many of the things he said would today be judged as culpable as certain dissident idealists who advise young men not to accept the law on compulsory military service.

Party spirit he reprobated for its juvenile enthusiasms and narrowness of aim. Parties themselves were formed according to circumstances rather than principle, their ends too often crass advantage for some economic interest and always susceptible to distortion and exploitation by an overweening personality. Conservatives in the United States by and large offered the best men as candidates but in their platforms, centered in property, the least desirable ideas; democrats, on the other hand, tended to vitiate the rightness of their ideas, always more consonant with the needs of the social situation and oriented toward reform, by the questionable character of their candidates.

The support of The Fugitive Slave Law in 1851 by Daniel Webster, long revered by him as a noble political leader and the one American who was a "finished work of Nature," left Emerson in indescribable dismay and wrath. If morality could be betrayed by the foremost minds of the nation, what decision was to be expected of the least? Although Webster had been a guest in his house and his brother William had years before begun his practice in the great man's law office, he spoke bitterly against him as a traitor to the land. "The fairest American fame ends in this filthy law. . . . All the drops of his blood have eyes that look downward" (W, XI, 201, 204).

And with equal sarcasm he described his disillusionment at the political reality of the day:

I thought it was this fair mystery, whose foundations are hidden in eternity, which made the basis of human society, and of law; and that to pretend anything else, as that the acquisition of property was the end of living, was to confound all distinctions, to make the world a greasy hotel, and instead of noble motives and inspirations, and a heaven of companions and angels around and before us, to leave us in a grimacing menagerie of monkeys and idiots. (W, XI, 189)

His revulsion four years earlier over the predatory war waged against Mexico by a coalition of politicians, "rabble" believing themselves above the moral law in their "Satanic effrontery," was matched now by the ferocity of his condemnation of the new law providing for the forcible extradition of runaway slaves back to their masters as a "filthy enactment" and his terse decision, "I will not obey it, by God." From public platforms he exhorted his listeners likewise not to obey it. "An immoral law makes it a man's duty to break it, at every hazard" (W, XI, 186). He never ceased to wince under the widespread use of "Manifest Destiny" in the expansion of the country (although he also saw the appropriation of the entire West by energetic Anglo-Saxons as inevitable), and in his old age he reprobated what he feared to be our imperialistic desire to take over the Sandwich Islands. American foreign policy, he maintained, ought always be humane, in emulation of that of William Penn.

An admirer of what Great Britain had done some years earlier to end slavery in the empire, Emerson advocated that the United States follow her example and emancipate all Negroes by indemnifying their owners. The cost, reckoned at various times as one thousand million dollars and two thousand million dollars, although astronomical, was not too great. Rightly appealed to, the moral citizenry of the United States would gladly assume any kind of sacrifice to defray the cost, so long as the shadow of the monster was wiped from their minds and the "accursed mountain of sorrow" was once and forever dug away out of the world. There could be no mistake about it; the ending of slavery was a great revolution—the second revolution of the United States, harder than that of the eighteenth century, which had bought its glory cheap, fighting an enemy three thousand miles away with a people which, although few, was united. The new struggle was infinitely complicated by party coils, powerful families, vast property interests, and sectional passions.

As the showdown of the war came nearer, Emerson was fearful that southerners, born into wealth and power and accustomed to command, had a native impetus which might defeat the north. Above the Mason-Dixon line, although with a juster cause and deeper moral nature, men were too prone to reflect before acting; yet if they could survive its initial handicaps, he had no doubt that their deliberativeness would carry them ultimately to victory. His aversion to the southern way of life and the mentality from which it grew he expressed on occasion with fierce invective, as when he said that southerners were deadly in treachery like cobras and had to be treated as such by having their fangs drawn. The two parts of the nation were alien to each other, one civilized, the other barbarous; they were separate nations, severed not by slavery but by climate and temperament. The South had never liked the North, and the North had liked the South only for selfish commercial advantage.

By his declaration in the middle 1830's that race in the case of the Negro was appallingly important, Emerson meant that the Negro's contemporary nature, inferior to that of some other races, was so by virtue of mistakes made, or faults committed, in the deep past by his ancestors. He was therefore expiating them by his inability to achieve what other peoples in the modern world were achieving, although his lesser quality was no justification at all of the enslavement inflicted on him by the white man. In 1844, however, in his admirable address celebrating the anniversary of the emancipation of the Negroes in the British West Indies, Emerson praised the action of the British government for having added a man to the human family and for having annihilated "the old indecent nonsense about the nature of the negro." The Negro race was revealed as, "more than any other, susceptible of rapid civilization"; exemplary in moderation, it mastered skills swiftly and had demonstrated its parity with the white race. It carried in its bosom a "moral genius" which was "an indispensable element of a new and coming civilization" (W, XI, 140 ff). And at the end of the brief celebration of the Emancipation Proclamation in 1862, referring to Negroes as an "ill-fated, much-injured race," benevolent, docile, and industrious, he prophesied that their "great talent for usefulness" would, "in a more moral age . . . give them a rank among nations" (W, XI, 326).

It was inevitable, given the discontent with current political practices, the zeal to abolish slavery, and the widespread desire for religious reform, which was leading many seekers back to the way of life of primitive Christians, that the issue of the non-violent resistance of evil, or pacifism, would become cardinal in the minds of some idealistic reformers. It was a widespread subject of prayer and discussion and had become "so distinct as to be a social thought," on which communities could be formed. Examples of nonviolent resistance Emerson had close at hand in Bronson Alcott and Henry Thoreau, who had gone to jail in 1846 rather than pay his state tax for support of the immoral Mexican War. Much attracted to the principle, although never a pacifist himself, he gave it considerable attention and, when he went to England in 1848, carried it along as a sort of conversational trump card, or wholesome moral thorn with which to prick the minds of progressive thinkers there.

War had the virtue of calling into question qualities of solidarity and stamina in a people and of drawing out in individuals those of courage, tenacity, and selflessness. Perhaps its chief benefit to a man lay in putting him on his own in the face of terrible immensities and making him self-responsible, self-reliant. Yet nonviolence accomplished the same ends, with the additional virtue that the pacifist, risking his life no less than the soldier, would, unlike him, desist from taking that of another. Before long, civilization would reach the point where it would decide matters of right and wrong with moral force alone; war would be outmoded and irrelevant. In the meantime it was necessary that the idea of nonviolence "pass out of thoughts into things," not by manifestos, organizations, or politics, but by private opinion, by "increased insight," which was "the spontaneous teaching, of the cultivated soul, in its secret experiences and meditation." All association of cowardice with nonviolent resistance needed to be removed from the popular mind, and the manly qualities of the fighter to be seen as attaching to the resister. (W, XI, 173ff.)

Emerson cogently rebutted the arguments customarily put forward to discredit the cause of the pacifist. It was simply untrue that in society men refrained from theft and murder only because they knew the musket, the halter, and the jail were standing ready to punish. If we put our trust in ideas we would see that the musket, the halter, and the jail, along with flags, fleets, and forts, were only in a sense "brute facts." More accurately, they were appearances—the reflections of a state of mind which was wrong; and since wrong ideas had brought them in, right ideas could drive them out. The arsenal only showed where man was *now*.

Addressing himself to American young people, Emerson flung a challenge to the rising generation: if the cry for a reform of abuses, heard everywhere, was real; if seekers truly were looking for a faith and hope, intellectual and religious, such as they had not yet found; if they continued to rely more, in study and in action, on the unexplored riches of the human constitution, on men and not books, on the present and not the past; if they could be brought to "think it unworthy to nestle into every abomination of the past" and could feel "the generous darings of austerity and virtue," then war had a short day and blood would cease to flow. The future of nonviolence lay here, in America, the only place on the globe in 1838 in which that particular "seed of benevolence" could be "laid in the furrow with tears of hope." Elsewhere no onward step could be taken without rebellion. (W, XI, 175)

It was to be another land altogether where in the twentieth-century the efficacy of nonviolent resistance on a national scale was first demonstrated; yet Emerson's prediction relating it to the United States was ultimately borne out in the success of the famous Birmingham bus boycott of 1955; and so the figure of Martin Luther King, alongside that of Mahatma Gandhi, has become historically not inconsiderable. It is interesting that the new tactic of civil disobedience should have been employed in the United States by the Negro, whose extraordinary moral qualities Emerson had come to recognize, and not by the white man, whose forebears he was directly addressing.

The problem of the relation to society of the intuition-directed individual will never be resolved. Society lives by rules; such a person by impulses. And such a person was Joan of Arc, was Anne Hutchinson, was, in fact, Jesus or Socrates. Can those who see visions, who hear voices, who feel leadings which the rest of us never know be suffered to live by their secret experiences? Samuel Johnson said no.

If a man . . . pretends to a principle of action of which I can know nothing, nay, not so much as that he has it, but only that he pretends to it, how can I tell what that person may be prompted to do? When a person professes to be governed by a written ascertained law, I can then know where to find him.

And Johnson's voice has been the voice of humanity's collective judgment. Society will go to pieces if spirit-directed idealists, particularly those who oppose war, are free to act as they are prompted. Even today in the United States although the law provides for exemption from military service of conscientious objectors, young men, to win such exemption, must show convincing evidence of their religious training and belief in a supreme being, such evidence being generally information which relates them satisfactorily to a conventionally recognized church or creed. It is hard to see how the Emerson of 1846 (or the Wordsworth of 1800) could be exempted, if they were among us.

Emerson's descent into the fray in some respects meant that he was guilty of the *trahison des clercs* deplored in our own century by the Frenchman Julien Benda and earlier decried by himself as behavior from which the true scholar should abstain, because it would lead to a confusion of ultimate benefits with immediate gains and a smirching of truth by expediency. It is not that he was wrong in declaring slavery wrong and himself a foe of it. No scholar is prerogatived to neutrality in the big moral issues that make a time of crisis. But he was wrong in broadcasting certain invidious subsidiary convictions to which his passionate hatred of slavery led him. In speaking hyperbolically in praise of John Brown after his rebellion he was, in effect, endorsing vigilantism, violent and inflammatory lawlessness as against dignified, noncoercive civil disobedience. He had himself loftily and rightly defined the only true patriotism as one of magnanimity happily leading men and women to contribute their "peculiar and legitimate advantages" to the benefit of all mankind, no longer parochial and with boyish egotism zealous to get "all the hurrahs on our side." Nationalism, however, was like party spirit, narrowly, fanatically partisan. Yet in identifying himself with the cause of the North, Emerson was susceptible to the virus of self-exalting sectionalism, and in praising the virtues of northerners, during and after the Civil War, he was occasionally guilty of chauvinism, cheering for one side. "The invasion of Northern farmers, mechanics, engineers, tradesmen, lawyers and students [in the ranks of the Army of the Union] did more than forty years of peace had done to educate the South" (W, XI, 355). He applauded the report that the reason why northern forces made slow progress through southern lands was in their having to stop and civilize the people as they went along. As for the war itself, instead of viewing it as a tragedy, at the very least as a colossally sorrowful necessity, jubilant over victory, his faith in the nation restored by the galvanization of spirit which had achieved the victory, he sang of it as a mighty means of redemption, a restoration of integrity to an immoral land ushering in "a new era, worth to mankind all the treasure and all the lives it has cost; yes, worth to the world the lives of all this generation of American men, if they had been demanded" (W, XI, 345). Curiously, after the war, in spite of his disillusionment over the settling back of the citizenry into their old ways, not spiritually regenerated after all, he apparently considered that the second revolution had run its course successfully, with the Negro, freed, fully a member of American society. The turbulence and poisonous prejudices of the Reconstruction seem not at all to have occupied his mind.

Involved as he was in the struggle to free the Negro, Emerson

knew himself to be a participant in the writing of a new chapter
of history. Yet history as a subject of study, he saw, continued
to be written with deplorable narrowness. Rightly looked at, it
was biography, for the effect of any historical work was only to
reveal the reader to himself, who discovered, in an account of
Alexander the Great or Leonidas the Spartan, or in a work by
Plato or Caesar, his own ideas. He identified himself with the
figures of antiquity, felt their feelings, and with his own eyes
enjoyed the features of the desert or the mountains where their
deeds had been done. What was this but to translate the past
into the present? All that had been was significant only because
it became the here-and-now and all other lives resuscitated became his life. But not enough from those once-lived lives was
transmitted to modern times; not enough had ever been recorded.
History, which should express the central and wide-related nature of man, was instead, with an ill-starred monotony, only an
"old chronology of selfishness and pride." What pretended to be
the narrative of all that had taken place on the globe had nothing to say of the relation of human beings to animals and vege-
tables—of the occult ties, for example, that bound Nebuchad-
nezzar at the banquet table to the rat gnawing the sacks of
wheat in his granary and to the lichen growing silently on his
garden wall. What should be the complete narrative of man was
altogether silent on his unconscious nature. Where was a treatise
written from the point of view of the intuition as well as the
understanding? History should be at once civil, metaphysical,
and scientific, but could any historical work be said to treat
what man had done as a social creature in relation to what he
had secretly thought and to what he had learned as a loving
inhabitant of the natural world? Art and religion; geology, chemistry, and astronomy; psychology and anthropology as we know
them today—all were indispensable to the writing of the only
history which Emerson believed worthy of man. The experience
of the single man needed to be shown in affinity to the experience of the race. He treasured the revelation by science, encountered in the 1840's in Robert Chambers' *Vestiges of Creation,*
that the human fetus in the course of its development passed
successively through stages relating it to the finally formed
fetuses of many lesser organisms, so that biologically man, part
containing whole, was the measure of all things. He believed no

less happily that each person during the arc of his growth lived psychologically through phases which were the counterparts to epochs in the growth of mankind. The experience of the race was, in effect, repeated in that of the individual; and to show this he adduced shadowy impulsions in the human psyche, similar to what are today called archetypes, leading one at various periods to be the pagan, the voyager, the rebel, and the believer. Every person underwent his Greek period, his period of the Middle Ages, and his Romantic period. Thus every "history should be written in a wisdom which divined the range of our affinities and looked at facts as symbols" (W, II, 40).

As for education in a new nation important in the future history of mankind, Emerson early recognized the problem of the elementary school, with its crowded classroom and wide diversity among pupils. Although he offered fine suggestions for improving classroom procedure, he refrained from prescribing how the problem was to be solved. "Our modes of Education aim to expedite, to save labor; to do for masses what cannot be done for masses, what must be done reverently, one by one; say rather, the whole world is needed for the tuition of each pupil" (W, X, 153-54).

At every level he believed too much emphasis was placed on the memorization of facts. What counted was that a teacher with his own delight in learning kindle a desire in those under him to cultivate the discipline necessary to the same satisfaction. Strictly speaking, no one could educate anyone else; he could only make him want to educate himself and help make the means of education available. Although respectful behavior was imperative, every teacher was to respect his students as well as truth: "if the boy stops you in your speech, cries out that you are wrong and sets you right, hug him!" (W, X, 158).

College students needed to be freer of burdensome rules and academic red tape, with a degree of freedom to choose studies to fit their aptitudes. Emerson not only favored the inauguration of an elective system but maintained that scholarships and special awards should be given solely for academic ability and achievement; the purpose of a college being to make scholars, scholarship should no longer be hamstrung by what was called deportment. As for professors, they ought to profess and inflame, but not give marks. They were inspirers, not judges; and Emerson advocated the abandonment of a grading system as a thing for boys, not men.

In seeking to live in the world of thought, to live by intellect, Emerson was not, on the face of it, doing anything different from what many seekers of the good life before him had done, his progenitors of the eighteenth century, for example. They too had sought to live by reason. So had More and Erasmus and the other humanists of the sixteenth century, and so had Socrates and kindred minds in ancient Greece. And when one finds that Emerson in prescribing a life conducted by reason meant largely a life according to nature, he again thinks automatically of those same progenitors for whom also enlightenment by reason was to bring man steadily closer to nature. He must remember, however, that Emerson's reason was a larger power than that of his predecessors, for it was the complete mind, unconscious as well as conscious, intuitive as well as ratiocinative. From the more comprehensive nature of his reason Emerson benefited in knowing a fuller relation to nature. With his intuition he was linked in profound, elemental ties to the invisible life of the universe; with his understanding he profited from his daylight observation of its external functions. Through the one agency the spirit of nature flowed spontaneously into him; through the other he deliberately imitated her behavior.

As for intuition, when Emerson looked into his mind, where his inner self was unfolding its activity, he saw a succession of images which startled him by their independence. "My will never gave the images in my mind the rank they now take." They occupied his mind spontaneously, through a kind of natural magnetism, which was sure to select what belonged to it. "What we do not call education is more precious than that which we call so" (W, II, 133). Will and determination blocked the intuitive flow of impulses and tried to substitute for them cluttering irrelevancies. It was not that choice should never enter life but that choice should be the choice of the whole man, not, partially, of his hands or eyes or appetites. The one important choice in life was of vocation, of calling, according to native constitution. Every person ought to discover the bent of his mind by ascertaining the persistent character of the pictures involuntarily entering it and then keep its channels open to them, letting them have their way, to grow in intensity, clarity, and consistency. His faculties he would exercise to the end that they would fulfill his bent and realize his vocation. One did not shape his moral nature any more than his intellectual, by voluntary effort. One's behavior and one's feeling about behavior, like what one thought at any given moment, were automatic:

There is less intention in history than we ascribe to it. We impute deep-laid far-sighted plans to Caesar and Napoleon; but the best of their power was in nature, not in them. Men of an extraordinary success, in their honest moments, have always sung "Not unto us." . . . Their success lay in their parallelism to the course of thought, which found in them an unobstructed channel; and the wonders of which they were the visible conductors seemed to the eye their deed. Did the wires generate the galvanism? . . . That which externally seemed will and immovableness was willingness and self-annihilation. (W, II, 134)

Life would be much happier and much more effectual if it were simpler, if people relied on their intuitions and ceased to interfere with the optimism of nature. The facts, words, and persons which dwelt in one's memory were never chosen or invited in but were self-selected and self-established. And the men and women one was impressed by or sought out in gatherings were never consciously decided on; they were stars radiating brighter light or superior planets exerting irresistible gravity. That one found himself speechless and blushing in the presence of a new acquaintance, whereas with another, met only two minutes later, he was fluent as a Shakespeare demonstrated how quickly our destinies were determined by affinity. Could not some lecturers talk for an hour without an iota of edification and others teach volumes before they had even begun to speak? The impression we make on people has nothing necessarily to do with the impression we want to make on them. At every moment nature in the individual—of him who reacts as well as him who acts—is seeking to direct him right; but its impulsions or correctives are too often suppressed out of deference to an academic inhibition, a social amenity, a conventional fear, or a religious duty. On every hand life is intent on expressing itself; on every hand life is thwarted or repressed. Affinity alone can transform our days and create atmosphere. And thought in its largest sense should be only "a pious reception."

Emerson's belief in intuition was not, however, an endorsement of random growth or impulsive, unintegrated personality. He disliked lopsided specimens of humanity and the narrow self-centeredness of false pretenders to self-reliance. The defense against both exaggeration and self-infatuation was culture, a development of all the faculties in a harmonious equilibrium which preserved a man from the ugliness of excess, "a range of affinities through which he can modulate the violence of any master-tones that have a droning preponderance in his scale, and succor him against himself" (W, VI, 137). A man of culture, benefiting from his large view of things, felt with his intuition and saw with the eye of common sense that if he was to live according to nature he must live joyously. Everywhere nature reveals exuberance and happiness in the multiplicity and multifariousness of her thrusts forward; activity and creation, therefore, are inconsistent with unhappiness. In joy—which is not loud hilarity, for Emerson defined serenity as sustained joy—one should do easily, strainlessly what one has to do. Nature does not sweat and labor, grind and groan, in the overnight shooting-up of a field of corn or in the opening of a rosebud in the morning. She gives the impression of achieving always in sport, and therefore the greater the intellect, the more the facility and play with which its human possessor accomplishes his ends. The great in history, always showing good humor and the sportiveness that was the bloom and glow of perfect health, had never condescended "to take anything seriously . . . [and] . . . would appear, could we see the human race assembled in vision, like little children frolicking together, though to the eyes of mankind at large they wear a stately and solemn garb of works and influences" (W, II, 256).

The man of culture was protected from the destructive clutches of an "organic egotism" by his comprehensive dispassionateness, by his knowledge that what counts is the "intellectual quality" we have in anything. "I must have children, I must have events, I must have a social state, and history, or my thinking and speaking want body or basis. But to give these accessories any value, I must know them as contingent and rather showy possessions, which pass for more to the people than to me" (W, VI, 158).

To have culture, in short, was to live with something of the large view of nature and of her disinterestedness, concerned over universal rather than partial aims. Nature moved always toward her full realization, never stopping to attach herself to any particular tree or animal but only favoring it in proportion as it contributed to the ultimate end of perfection. The man living by intellect, then, emulous of nature, his tutor, would be a man all of whose worldly relations hung very loosely about him, a man of detachment. He would be detached from time, from things, and from persons; yet he would be a lover, not a hater, of them. Detachment was not hostility nor was it indifference. Jesus, in his command to those who would follow him to forsake father and mother, and in his redefinition of those terms to his own parents, had illustrated its importance. A human being, like a plant, is created to grow, and growth means leaving yesterday perpetually behind and pushing forward into tomorrow. One must cut the ties binding him to the past, the ideas and feelings inexpressibly important to him last year, and be forever strengthening the relations all about him in the present. What he thinks or feels now he must on no account think or feel because he thought or felt it then. Yet insidiously the attractions of the past seek to keep us in their embrace. So also do those of things about us in the present—of material possessions, of business and duty, of reputation and ambition. So also do the lovely attributes and precious associations of persons close to us. We must heed Jesus' injunction, however, to cast off family—heed it in its widest sense. All that constitutes the world we must refrain from seeking to gain. We must use it cherishingly but with the constant recollection that we are no more than its stewards. If we strive to possess, we end up possessed, and possession is enslavement.

This same detachment underlay the elevated generosity which prompted Emerson to recommend that invalids find compensation for their suffering in a long view like his own:

So when a man is the victim of his fate, has sciatica in his loins and cramp in his mind; a club-foot and a club in his wit; . . . or is ground to powder by the vice of his race;—he is to rally on his relation to the Universe, which his ruin benefits. Leaving the daemon who suffers, he is to take sides with the Deity who secures universal benefit by his pain. (W, VI, 47)

What concerned Emerson was not so much whether he, a single person, was hurt but whether the universe was hurt by his hurt. And he rejoiced in the thought that it was not; whatever ills human beings suffer, which is to say inflict on themselves, their temporary discords do not at all affect the wondrous total harmony. Even so, it is difficult to defend the singular advice in the passage above, which leaves some readers in consternation. How does the ruin of a man through syphilis or cancer, for example, benefit the universe? Presumably, in removing an additional instance of the disease; as others like him drop away one by one, the disease will progress steadily toward extinction so that eventually humanity will no longer have to pay that specific penalty for vices indulged, or sins committed, by remote ancestors. The individual sufferer, attaining detachment, is happy that his particular suffering will be the means whereby someone still to be born will be exempt from it. And by so much the world of man will be approaching the health or perfection of the universe.

Emerson's disinterestedness may on occasion be carried to a height which seems to us unattainable or quixotic, but it must not be mistakenly labeled callous or inhuman. Nor must we conclude from a cursory contact with it, recalling his insistence on the primacy of individual reform, that his indifference to external organization would mean in effect opposition to efforts such as slum clearance, public health, and vocational rehabilitation. The evidence of his life as well as his books is against this. When he returned for a final time to England in 1872, although his admirers there through the years had included Carlyle and others equally conservative, it was the liberals among the political and religious thinkers of the island, middle-aged as well as young, who flocked to pay him homage.

The man of culture—who is at the same time the gentleman, the man of Self-Reliance, the American Scholar, the man of character, the hero, for Emerson has many names for him—is always the free man, growing from stage to stage, knowing and enjoying the right power and wealth because he is not enslaved and following lovingly from day to day the tendency to find his own soul. He will love those in his family and love those who are his friends, but love them for the qualities they embody— the interesting ideas they articulate, the pure affections they describe in gesture or expression, and the flashes of imagination which give color to the atmosphere. And out of his love he will want to do what he can to preserve their freedom inviolate for them and enrich it so that the growth of their souls too can proceed apace. He will even go to the gallows or to the stake for them if necessary. But in no respect will he sacrifice his own independence or tolerate encroachment on it. Imitating nature, he will somehow be able to love individuals without being fond of them, esteem their characters without doting on their persons, have affection for them untainted by sentimentality, be charitably aloof without becoming indifferently alienated, and remain devoted though never attached. People are too much together. In rare moments of magic the minds of friends ignite one another and the flames of quickened thought make heaven of the little space in which they sit—but only in moments. In the intervals of latency, when thought is gestating, they do better to stay apart.

In what he had to say about friendship and love Emerson wrote some of his most beautiful sentences and at the same time what may appear to some readers his ugliest—in their seeming reflection of callousness. "The moment we indulge our affections, the earth is metamorphosed," and this miracle is accompanied instantaneously with an increase in our intellectual and active powers. Our own thought is enlarged in company with a congenial mind, thinking on a higher level than ours; we rise to meet him and the ascent is exhilarating. To those, however, who cannot conceive of friendship except as continual physical presence and frequent embracing, Emerson addresses the question, "Are you the friend of your friends' buttons, or of his thought?" and the admonition, "Leave this touching and clawing" (W, II, 208 ff.).

If one's friend is despondent, doleful commiseration will not help. Often the best service that can be done him is through strong and forthright words to jolt him into a right sense of his qualities and his circumstance. If one visits one's friend after a long absence, one is not to spend time apologizing but offering the best of his mind and spirit at once in order to make the friend feel that the highest love has come to call, even though in the lowliest organ. Nature wastes no time in regret or self-recrimination; she replaces a faulty organism with a sound one at once. So a man, after a mistaken act, will atone for it immediately with another rightly performed, not futilely through words of extenuation. And as nature commends and assists those specimens which are already strong of their kind, so a man will realize the paradox that his fellows who are loved are those who do not need love, precisely *because* they do not need it, the human mind having a propensity always to go outward in admiration to that which is better than itself.

It is true that the doctrine of life according to nature lends itself to more than one interpretation. If one sets oneself to abstain from weeping over the loss of a loved one because nature never stops to weep, or from regret or contrition because nature never indulges herself in deploring a thing wrongly done, why does he not imitate nature and steal from lesser creatures about him, or crush out their paltry lives altogether, in the fashion of a hungry tiger in the jungle? How can he explain to another who questions him that, although the first two practices are consonant with the practice of nature, the third really is not? Falstaff justified his exploitation of gulls like Justice Shallow by an appeal to the predatoriness of nature's fish; and the Marquis de Sade felt himself constrained to adopt a philosophy of cruelty and destruction because cruelty and destruction were the everyday order in nature. Emerson's vindication of the first two acts as good and condemnation of the third as bad was based on his intuitive conviction that nature was at heart always beneficent. It was the moral sense allied to the intellect which preserved man from inhuman aberrations.

The only joy anyone can have in deifying encounter with his friend is that the *not his* is *his;* ideas from the Universal Mind discovered by his friend and communicated to him have now come to occupy his mind and the world anew has entered into him. Friends should remain to one another spirits, their encounters evanescent as lightning flashes. And every person should be disinterested and magnanimous enough when his merits of intellect are worn bare, to want his friend to leave him for another intelligence of finer strain and wider scope. Emerson was humanely, lovingly serious when he wrote the following verse:

> You shall not love me for what daily spends;
> You shall not know me in the noisy street,
> Where I, as others, follow petty ends;

Nor when in fair saloons we chance to meet;
Nor when I'm jaded, sick, anxious or mean.
But love me then and only, when you know
Me for the channel of the rivers of God
From deep ideal fontal heavens that flow. (W, IX, 352)

The same stricture was in order also for a man and woman in love. They were to give all to love, but if either was attracted to another mind of broader scope creating beauty on a higher level, he was to leave behind his former attachment and rise to a new alliance. Change and progression were the law of nature here as elsewhere in life. One loved ascendingly, from mind to mind-more-elevated, to gods from half gods.

The problem of sex in relation to love and marriage Emerson knew to be grievous and far from settlement. The common procedure was for a man blindly to rush into matrimony and beget children; then, tied to the treadmill in order to support his family, when asked for his ideas on the problem to reply that there was none or that it was too late in the day for him to have any opinion on it. Nature was ruthless in insuring through sexual attraction that species were reproduced. Although like that of some earlier European thinkers and of most American writers in the nineteenth century, the age of genteelism, his view of life had too little a place for sex, in our own that place may well be too large. Distrustful of the erotic impulse, he guarded against its incessant, deceptive claim to ultimate importance, its insidious, whispered promise that every act of intercourse would be the acme of excitement and gratification, whereas in actuality only a rare one was. In one of his poems, however, he touched surprisingly on the importance of instinctual, sexual vigor to right living. "The Romany Girl" contrasts "pale northern girls" who are captives of "air-tight halls" wearing out indoors their "sickly days" with a swarthy-tinted, passionate gypsy who makes love "below" the moon," whose wily tongue relates her to the birds, and in whose dances "the panther . . . flies."

Yet mankind needed a better view of the facts of sex—that, for example, of the young mother, who, at the time when his own children were being born, Emerson observed, contemplated all the chapters in the bearing of new life, from the act of conception through burdensome gestation, parturition, and suckling, with the purity of a nun in meditation. Where mind in marriage was concerned, at one point Emerson, very much like Milton in placing supreme importance on it, held the view that when two married persons had exhausted each other's intellectual possibilities, they ought to be able mutually and without violence to decide to end their relationship for the enjoyment of new society. Marriage "should be a temporary relation" (quoted from an MS Journal in G, p. 349). Yet he knew that with mankind in its present low state of development, not even saints and sages could be trusted to try such an ideal, for, sensual emotion being the delicious thing it was they, no less than ordinary folk, would confuse instinct with idea.

Where Emerson's attitude toward women as a sex is concerned, perhaps it is enough to cite his remark that all his points would sooner be carried in the state if women voted, or that women were not only wise but capable of making men feel so too. If women really wanted the vote, they should have it; if they wanted to own property they should be able to own it. He himself had not observed that the best women wanted those things, but he found it a very cheap wit that made jokes about their wanting them. Considering the many crass, animal-like creatures among male voters, it would be a gain for government if they were offset with the finest minds, the purest part, of the populace. Of course women should be educated; yet he did not see how it was possible to separate the interests and education of the sexes. If you improved and refined men, you did the same willy-nilly by women. Females were more intelligent readers and better scholars than males in grade school, and the only reason they did not continue so in after years was that men had occasion to use books in their professions and women did not. Yet women's intellectual life was deplorably handicapped by the burden imposed on them by nature, for at least twenty years, of reproducing their kind. And, irrespective of their material conditions, in the temperamental and physical relation in which they arbitrarily stood to man, they would continue to seek in him their guardian. It was in their private life, however, that the qualities of women were fully revealed—in their artistic sensibility, in their ability to create atmosphere, in their creation of the supreme art of conversation. They were, in short, the civilizers of mankind: "a masculine woman is not strong, but a lady is."

It is always a problem for the person who would live by the intellect to avoid misunderstanding by his fellows—and also to avoid the extremism to which his very inclinations may lead him. As for the intellect in an ideal sense—so Emerson once set it down in a couplet—"Gravely it broods apart on joy,/And, truth to tell, amused by pain" (W, IX, 375). How does one prevent considerate detachment, however, from becoming insensitive neutrality, compassionate rationality from desiccated intellectuality? Jonathan Swift, in the whole example of his life and works, is related more closely probably than any other figure of recent times to the issue. In *Gulliver's Travels* the bloodless Laputans, so engrossed in the perpetual contemplation of matters of pure mathematics that they moved trancelike, unaware of their surroundings, and needed to be shocked by a slap in the face into recognizing their acquaintances, reveal devastatingly the inhumanity of the exclusive cultivation of the abstracted cerebrum. In the same work the Houyhnhnms, horse creatures who lived according to reason, their principal virtues, friendship and benevolence, who treated their neighbors as themselves and strangers as their neighbors, and who had it that nature taught them to love the whole species, with reason making distinctions among persons only when there was a superior degree of virtue, more nearly represent the kind of detachment in which Emerson believed. A certain Houyhnhnm matron, arriving late for a social engagement, excused herself to her host by saying that she had been delayed by having to make arrangements for the burial of her husband, who had died that morning—after which she behaved as cheerfully as the rest of the guests. Correspondingly, one of Emerson's forebears was said to have been reproached by her daughter with want of feeling because on Sunday morning she had gone, "rapt in another world," to church although her husband lay dead on the matrimonial bed at home.

Emerson had known in his own family the repeated depredations of death. The losses of his beloved brothers, his first wife, and his first son Waldo were causes of suffering, and he suffered. He mourned most deeply and for the longest time, with his powers of creation seriously suspended, after the death of his little boy. Yet he sought to see even such desolating experiences in right perspective. Once when Boswell on the occasion of a parting from Johnson burst out passionately that it would be terrible if they were never to see one another again, he was reproved with the terse statement that it would not be terrible and with the admonition that he was not to use big words for little things. Emerson, as uncompromisingly a foe of cant as the great eighteenth-century figure he admired, looked unflinchingly into himself and saw that he was not prostrated by sorrow, his mind was not paralyzed, his body not spurning the day's animal comforts or doing without its animal needs, and his affections not eclipsed so that he took no pleasure in the scene or the friends about him. And so he said in his essay on "Experience" that the death of his son two years earlier no longer touched him, that something he had believed to be part of himself had been torn away without leaving any scar, and that the true grief in such an instance was that grief could teach him nothing.

What is one to do on the occasion of the death of a person beloved? To show his love and esteem of the person, which he best can do by thinking of him, not by weeping. To cherish the memory of his character means to refrain from sad self-abasement, to act in relation to it as though he were still alive. One pays tribute to the dead by the clarity of his memory of them, by the extent to which that memory colors his life thereafter, inspiring his speech, begetting poems or other works of art, and leading to generous deeds. Mourning is barren; only quickened thought is fruitful. After the death of his girlish Ellen, who had never been alone in her beauty like that of a tree in flower, Emerson had prayed briefly to God: "Oh help me to keep her memory always fresh and effectual to my comfort and salvation" (MS Autobiography, Houghton).

But it was not only the death of others that one needed to see in perspective with the intellect. One's own needed to be confronted and seen to be the trivial incident it was. Thomas More, for instance, who had exemplified all his life the sweetness of intellectual vision, unperturbed at the block, had smilingly sought to raise his executioner's spirits by advising him, since his victim's neck was very short, to strike true and sharp to save his honor. And Socrates, the noblest exemplar of humanity, who more than any other had confronted his end with equanimity, had joked with the Athenian Assembly condemning him to death and proposed that for his offense he be rewarded instead by a pension which would install him for the rest of his days in gentlemanly leisure in the State Hall for Heroes.

Such superb playfulness and lofty detachment were obviously signs of the highest courage, needed at every turn in life. Intolerant of the despondency and cowardice of contemporary religious and political theorists, which only bred despondency and cowardice in their readers, Emerson recommended to young people the works of Plutarch, the "Doctor and Historian of Heroism," whose pages were shining with "a wild courage, a Stoicism not of the schools but of the blood" (W, II, 248). Anticipating the thought of William James a half century later, he wished that forms of service for young men could be found which, in the absence of war, destined to disappear, would offset the tendency of increased civilization to soften character and preserve the martial virtues of courage, self-denial, and hardihood. Young men and women should know that they were born into a state of war but also that the means were available to them to take both reputation and life in their hands "and with perfect urbanity dare the gibbet and the mob by the absolute truth" of their speech and the rectitude of their behavior (W, II, 249-50).

That there was infrarational as well as suprarational power in human life, Emerson knew very well but the subconscious, or subliminal, part of man, in relation to the divinely unconscious, was indescribably inferior and although it had certain elements of interest, not worth study. He recognized two manifestations of the dark-flowing force—"spiritualist" happenings in séances and dreams; but both were contained in what he called "demonology." He did not deny extrasensory occurrences in table rappings and the like, but the results were too capriciously undependable and too paltry to be of value. A practitioner of occult rites was like a person stricken with amazement over the discovery of his thumbnail but blind to the miracle of his being a man. He had "mistaken flatulency for inspiration." No revelations by a medium had thrown any light on the big issues of life. Apart from the fact that they went dismayingly against the law-determined, daylight operation of the world, they were no more than "merely physiological, semi-medical [facts] related to the machinery of man, opening to our curiosity how we live, and no aid on the superior problems why we live, and what we do" (W, X, 24). If one read a page of Bacon, one was exhilarated and armed to manly duties; if he read instead a page of the latest report on demonology, he was "bewildered and perhaps a little besmirched." As for dreams, although he believed them much more significant than disclosures by sensitives and was often fascinated by his own, commenting on them in his *Journals*, Emerson feared the "dislocation," which seemed to be their principal trait. Almost always "the fairest forms, the most noble and excellent persons" were "deformed by some pitiful and insane circumstance." And the prevalence of violence in the action of dreams was no less disturbing. Yet the Proteus-like identity of the dreamer in his dreams was a fascinating thing; he was at once creator and producer, spectator and principal actor, and the whole phenomenon, having "a double consciousness, at once sub- and objective, was related to psychology and to art." It could not be denied that in dreams, no matter how grotesque or monstrous, there was a certain wisdom, although a man needed to be skillful in order to ascertain it; he must not be occupied with details but with the quality of the part he had played—courageous or timid, generous or selfish, eager or indifferent. In spite of the many shabby investigators of the hidden life of the mind, whose activities showed that they preferred "snores and gastric noises to the voice of any muse," Emerson would not invoke a law to put down all such research. "Willingly I too say, Hail! to the unknown awful powers which transcend the ken of the understanding" (W, X, 27). But it was significant that his verb was "transcend."

Emerson was taken to task again and again by adverse contemporaries for what they considered either the vapidity or the cloudy unintelligibility of his thought, the unjustifiable emphasis on unchecked intuition (often called by him impulse or instinct), and his view of the autonomous individual personality. A reviewer of the early "Nature" in *The Westminster Review* (London; March, 1840) reproved him for propounding the creed that although the single person was nothing, in his moments of mystical elevation he could see all and, with divine currents circulating through him, become part of God. It was dangerous to identify *Vox Populi* with *Vox Dei,* and if persons sought to live

only by Emersonian self-reliance, each believing he was not
speaking but was being spoken to, they would run amuck and
reduce the world to "a battlefield of enthusiasms" (Quoted in
Cn, I, 406-7). Yet Emerson did not retreat from his convictions.
It was true that his exhortations to cultivate spontaneous virtue
were susceptible of misunderstanding and might be taken to
justify sloth and sensuality, but he preferred to run such risks.
"If anyone imagines that this law is lax," he wrote in "Self-
Reliance," meaning the law of intuition and nature-dependent
intellect, "let him keep its commandment one day" (W, II, 74).

The importance of nature-dependent intellect to Emerson
cannot be too much emphasized. The relation between man and
nature was, as we have seen, for him the central and essential
relation, without a right understanding of which there could be
no true education. The consequences of the affinity between man
and nature were limitless and affected all departments of human
life. That every significant part of Emerson's thought was profoundly colored by his conviction of that affinity, the reader
has by now no doubt inferred. It can be additionally illustrated
and underscored by a consideration of his views on art.

Emerson, we must remember, had grown out of a soil with
little of the esthetic in it; furthermore, he had innate deficiencies
in taste. He was not only unresponsive to music and indifferent
to the theater; he also cared little about painting and he had
blind spots in literary taste. He scarcely knew the novel, although
he made some acute observations about its possibilities as a
form; and his taste in poetry was extremely erratic. Among fictionalists, although he could see psychological values in George
Sand, he had not grown beyond Sir Walter Scott; the power
and perception of Charles Dickens he was blind to; George Eliot
he apparently never even tried; and about Nathaniel Hawthorne
he was prompted to say only that he could not write dialogue
and that the man was worth more than the books. Among poets,
although he had translated his *La vita nuova*, he was not a lover
of Dante and could not read *The Divine Comedy*. Of his contemporaries he loved Felicia Hemans and Leigh Hunt, whose
"Abou Ben Adhem" he thought to be the one poem likely to
survive the age into futurity; he had no regard for Shelley, and

although he was a disinterested champion of Whitman when *Leaves of Grass* first appeared, he did not include him in *Parnassus,* the anthology of his old age. Yet in the face of these limitations of his sensibilities, what is astonishing is his intellectual grasp of the arts, so full, so lively, and so germinal.

Of the three members of the fecund Platonic triad, at the time of his lectures on literature in 1835-36 Emerson declared that Beauty and Goodness always faced each other, with each always tending to become the other. Beauty, which included Goodness as its highest form, was as a spiritual and eternal principle "a sufficient reason for the existence and publication of any word or work." In this, stated long before Poe's assertions of the autonomy of beauty in "The Poetic Principle," he was saying precisely what he had said in an early poem, "The Rhodora": "beauty is its own excuse for being." At that time he defined beauty as, in simplest terms, "an abstraction of the harmony and proportion that reigns in all Nature." Since, as we have seen, every man is organized like nature, he possesses the capacity to be pleased by beauty, and some men—Michelangelo, par excellence—are endowed with an abstracting power, by which they draw beauty from nature and re-create it in new forms.

Everywhere about him with distress Emerson saw separation, split, and divorce. Men thought one thing but openly said another, or they professed to believe one thing and did another. Created for health and efficiency, they made themselves diseased and lazy. They worked, reluctantly, at chores, and sought enjoyment in pursuits unrelated to them. Where oneness should prevail, twoness was the order of the day. Life for them was one thing; art, quite another. Unable to impart any beauty to their day's occupations, they invented *things* of beauty in which to find consolation for their ugliness or escape from it. In a sense, in everything he wrote or said Emerson sought to wake men up to this fact and to make them find it, as he did, abhorrent.

Beauty must come back to the useful arts, and the distinction between the fine and the useful arts be forgotten. If history were truly told, if life were nobly spent, it would be no longer easy or possible to distinguish the one from the other. In nature all is useful, all is beautiful. It is therefore beautiful because it is alive, moving, reproductive; it is therefore useful because it is symmetrical and fair. (W, II, 367-68)

Much is made of the adjective "organic" in connection with art. It has to do with oneness, with wholeness, but, in its highest sense with these qualities in something that is alive and growing, and this is the sense in which the mature Emerson used it. In his lectures of 1835-36 he had revealed a beginning preoccupation with the idea. He had exalted Shakespeare above all other poets, especially for his sonnets, which he felt to deserve the same rigorously penetrating analysis as had been given by Italian critics to the sonnets of Michelangelo, because they revealed a power to assimilate any element of the natural world and transmute it into an illuminating symbol of some element of our limitless emotional and spiritual life. Not only was the verse organically one with the mind that had created it; the mind itself was one with the cosmos from which it drew its materials.

Art, according to the mature Emerson, should imitate nature— and so should life. The tree before a man is a living, quietly powerful organism. It lives with dignity, with a form of symmetry, and every part of it subserves its function of living, of attaining and preserving its symmetry. It is impossible to distinguish between the leaf that is useful and the leaf that is beautiful. Man should imitate the tree, should live like it in such a way that everything he does contributes to the vitality and symmetry of his life. Thus, function and beauty would become one, inseparably. The use of fine art is, in representing nature in new and imaginative relations, to remind man of nature's organicism and inspire him to achieve it. Emerson defined organic art as classic, "the art of necessity," because the Greeks had first articulated the need of man to orient his growth to the standards that were nature's, but the idea of the classic did not necessarily involve historical time.

As a supreme illustration of the oneness of the useful and fine arts Emerson valued architecture. A building or a bridge was a creation of the human intellect and imagination on a big scale set in nature and made to be a part of the visible world, which assimilated it, if rightly made, as brother to the trees, the hillside, and the river. The architect, with his creation, was closer to nature than was the poet or painter or composer. His achievement, like the forms of nature, not only possessed beauty but housed function, to which its structure and organization were directly related and by which they were determined. In Emerson's poem "The Problem," the images confirming most tellingly the oneness of nature and art were majestic and architectural. It gave him pleasure to think on the readiness of nature to adopt into her family the pyramids, the Parthenon, Saint Peter's Cathedral, and the English abbeys along with the Alps and the Andes. Pleasure also to reflect on her equal hospitality toward the railroad, the steamboat, the woolen mill. Man was the thinking child of nature. Why, therefore, should not the creations of his brain designed for his use, industrial or commercial, and distinguished by form no matter how unprecedented, have equal place in the universe, alongside those of his parent?

In both the useful and fine arts the individual creator was abdicating his individuality and acting through the universal mind. It was only in proportion as he drew from it, was occupied by it, that he could succeed in what he was about. In the useful arts—in the operation of a loom, a water wheel, a steamboat— man supplanted his individual force by universal might, hydropower, gravity, or steam, whereas in the fine arts creation was not the replacement of his physical strength but the enlargement of that of his mind; yet, obviously, one must add, the mind of the inventor of a machine needed as much to be enlarged and illuminated as that of a painter, in both the conception and the execution of his idea.

About the so-called performing arts—drama, opera, ballet, concert music—Emerson had little to say. He rarely went to the theater, yet in spite of being indisposed to it by both constitution and upbringing, he did not deny its importance to others.

Although beauty could not be defined, its qualities could be listed: "We ascribe beauty to that which is simple; which has no superfluous parts; which exactly answers its end; which stands related to all things; which is the mean of many extremes" (W, VI, 289). Such in brief is the classical creed of America's classic Romantic. To follow, to imitate, nature in art is to create poems, paintings, sculptures, buildings which, like nature's own offspring, trees, plants, and animals, are organic—that is, are one, their form and function one; their structure one, with no extraneous decoration; their expression or tone one; their relation to their type consistent and therefore one. Every utterance by a poet, every gesture limned by a painter, every stance achieved by a sculptor must have the same cleanness, the same incisive but graceful force as is in the movement of a horse walking—must be "necessary," for the horse does not choose how it will lift its hoof or propel its leg, nor does it lift or propel to no end. "Hence our taste in building rejects paint, and all shifts, and shows the original grain of the wood: refuses pilasters and columns that support nothing, and allows the real supporters of the house honestly to show themselves" (W, VI, 291).

In Italy Emerson had been impressed everywhere by the domestic architecture, simple, dignified, eminently serviceable, and designed in such harmony with the landscape as to be integrally part of it and unforgettably beautiful. In Italy also he had made the acquaintance of Horatio Greenough, the American sculptor. Greenough's ideas, radically at variance with those of American architectural officialdom, were based on the equal importance of purpose and design, conspicuous in nature, as the key to right building, and they anticipated those which led at the end of the century to the resuscitating innovations of Richardson and Sullivan of the famous Chicago school, and in the twentieth century to the achievements of Frank Lloyd Wright. In such a passage as the following, from "Self Reliance," Emerson himself sounds like a precursor of Wright:

And why need we copy the Doric or the Gothic model? Beauty, convenience, grandeur of thought and quaint expression are as near to us as to any, and if the American artist will study with hope and love the precise thing to be done by him, considering the climate, the soil, the length of the day, the wants of the people, the habit and form of the government, he will create a house in which all these will find themselves fitted, and taste and sentiment will be satisfied also. (W, II, 82-83)

Emerson's insistence on the organic and functional qualities of art did not mean, however, that he rode simplicity into the ground. He hoped that in the future, as the nation began to build its homes in the expanding West, architects, not imitating but profiting by the example of Italian houses, would adapt their ideals and techniques to the American scene, populating the countryside without violating it. He wanted houses, however, not one-room huts or mean, stark barns, for in his mind simplicity went hand in hand with dignity and a certain grandeur. "The

wise man will prize and obtain the luxuries of baths, of venti-
lated houses, of gardens. . . . Is not thought freer and fairer in
a house with apartments that admit of easy solitude than in a
foul room where all miscellaneous persons are thrown together,
cheek by jowl, heads and points?" (J, V, 27). If you took the
roof off almost any house what, apart from unfulfilled, unthink-
ing, embittered men and women talking harshly to one another,
did you find? Clutter and tawdry gewgaws mistaken for embel-
lishment or, at best, reproductions of statues and paintings intended to bring art to domesticity. Persons should know that
the best taste lay in sparse decoration and that the right place
for reproductions was the museum; the genuine beauty of any
home would be realized in the harmony prevailing among members of the family and in the fineness of friends who graced it
with their presence.

To create works of art like the works of nature, however,
meant more than achieving simplicity, economy, functionality,
and dignity. It meant to endow them with spontaneity and to
render them capable of suggesting to the beholder the anima-
tion, the fertility, the perpetually evolving quality of nature.
Since nature, dynamic and never static, always seems to be on
the threshold of passing into something else and, never satisfied,
strives always toward the making of a better specimen of whatever it is we are looking at, so "Nothing interests us which is
stark or bounded, but only what streams with life. . . . Beauty
is the moment of transition, as if the form were just ready to
flow into other forms" (W, VI, 292). And a work of art ought also
be irradiated by "a certain cosmical quality, or a power to suggest relation to the whole world, and so lift the object out of a
pitiful individuality" (W, VI, 303). Everything in nature, pulsating with the same vitality, had this virtue, as did also certain
men and women, from whose faces, speech, and manners emanated a certain grandeur and who, even in the way they moved,
had "a largeness of suggestion."

In all of his recommendations of such an order, invoking the
essence of nature in relation to a progressive new art, Emerson
anticipates certain contemporary thinkers, dissatisfied with the
limitations of the art inherited by the twentieth century and
uninhibitedly experimenting with novel ways of depicting imaginatively their experience on a planet now for the first time

about to establish connections with other orbs in space. Such avant-gardists, convinced that neither the fine arts nor the performing arts as we have known them have been open to the streaming tendencies of the universe, or the continuous flux which is sensorily and intellectually every day's human lot, seek an enlargement of form and an indeterminacy or fluidity of procedure that will somehow put man in rapport with such phenomena. A composer, maintaining that the world does not discriminate derogatorily among sounds but assimilates them all—train whistles, cat wailings, dog barkings, door squeakings, factory clankings—into a harmonious symphony, not only abjures tonality himself but by whatever device introduces in his work sounds of the most disparate kind in imitation of the world. And since he is actuated by the same impulse that actuates animals, the same energy that propels machines and gives them voice, he yields to it, free of meddling intellect or presumptuous, idiosyncratic will, making sounds at random as impulse dictates. Furthermore, discovering that in nature what we know with our fallible and tiny minds as silence often is made up of sounds we are physiologically incapable of hearing, that is, of sounds not intended to be heard, he composes a work for the piano in which not a key is struck, not a tone made, during the several minutes of its duration, although the performer contemplates the keyboard and conscientiously turns pages of a "score" throughout. Painters, stung by the dead and static quality of a canvas fixed in dimension and bounded by a frame, its subject technically finished and frozen, passionately desiring to be creating with the unbroken incessantness with which nature creates, work endlessly at whatever it is they have chosen, drawing and erasing, putting on and taking away, building and unbuilding, unable through determination to complete, to conclude.

When Emerson, then, rhapsodically hymns art as "immense and universal," maintaining that it should "throw down the walls of circumstance on every side, awakening in the beholder the sense of universal relation and power," he seems to be addressing himself to such composers as the one already mentioned. And when he depreciates what is "stark or bounded" and exalts the "act or endeavor to reach somewhat beyond," when he flatly affirms all pictures and statues to be "cripples and monsters" and maintains that what counts in them is "what they aimed at and

promised, not . . . the actual results," he appears to be champion-
ing the no-subject, never-finish painters. In fact, lamenting that
the arts as he and his contemporaries knew them were but initial,
he may be taken by all those nowadays who also value the
kinetic rather than the static in expression and "the streaming
or flowing" of the circular movement of the universe rather than
the circumscribed topicality of localized place, to be their
eloquent spokesman.

The contemporary theatrical event known as the "happening,"
with its combining of as many arts as possible in as many concurrent activities on the stage as possible, governed by a mini-
mum of written plan and rehearsal, aiming to re-create something of the boundless spontaneity and simultaneity of act that
characterize the universe, might be considered an apt illustration
of Emerson's "feat of the imagination" as "showing the converti-
bility of every thing into every other thing." Yet, although no
one will ever know for certain whether Emerson, in writing as
he did, had in mind as desirable anything approaching a never-
finished-but-always-in-process painting, a musical composition
wholly of ineffable cosmic silences (not to speak of a self-con-
suming machine, which escapes the fate of fixity by being destroyed by its maker), or even a happening, it is unlikely that
he had. In greater or lesser degree all such modes of avant-
garde art rely on chance, whereas Emerson in all of his praise
of spontaneity never once considered the spontaneous to be the
aleatory.

All such modes also, though they seek to preserve (in the
hands of their serious practitioners) the name of art, in their
various ways of enlarging or "flexibilizing" form do away with
form. Art, by its very nature, depends on form, and form by its
very nature involves bound or definition. To seek to make form
as well as content kinetic is to involve one's self in contradictions.
A form that is in perpetual change never achieves form. To say
that art should be kinesis, or becoming, instead of being, and
then to occupy oneself in it in such a way as to be always tam-
pering with a form is to mistake the letter for the spirit of the
law and to be converting a principle into a foolish dogma. The
substance of what is painted, sung, or written, becoming a thing
by virtue of delineation, must somehow suggest that it is about
to progress, to transform itself; but it cannot be ceaselessly trans-

formed before the beholder. The true kinetic form would be an interminable extension of Duchamp's *Nude Descending the Staircase,* or, better, a cinematic rendition, in slow motion forever and ever protracted, of somebody walking.

Furthermore the desire of avant-gardistes to imitate the omnigenousness of nature by abjuring selectivity and substituting for it what is called plenitude, if followed strictly, cannot but run counter to Emerson's principles in promoting disorder, a thing he never countenanced. Actually, "plenitude," as a term for universe-imitating art is inappropriate. It means fullness, and fullness implies limit and boundary, within which is completion, a state at variance with the unconfinable dynamism to which such art aspires. Nevertheless, Emerson himself was on occasion not unwilling to leave it to nature somehow to establish order out of the lack of order in which, too much fragmented and discontinuously, he had projected his thoughts.

Emerson's imitation of nature, it is clear, was one in which the artist, like nature, created new forms, instead of sitting passively to make exact copies of her.

In landscapes the painter should give the suggestion of a fairer creation than we know. The details, the prose of nature he should omit and give us only the spirit and splendor. He should know that the landscape has beauty for his eye because it expresses a thought which is to him good; and this because the same power which sees through his eyes is seen in that spectacle; and he will come to value the expression of nature and not nature itself, and so exalt in his copy the features that please him. He will give the gloom of gloom and the sunshine of sunshine. In a portrait he must inscribe the character and not the features, and must esteem the man who sits to him as himself only an imperfect picture or likeness of the aspiring original within. (W, II, 351)

Obviously this passage is a plea for more freedom in landscape and portrait painting than any Emerson saw evidence of in his time—for more subjectivity and more abstraction. It might seem an endorsement a hundred years before its time of abstract expressionism. But it is not. The subjectivity here is of the special kind distinguished by him when he defined self-reliance as really unself- or God-reliance. When he says that the painter rightly dealing with a landscape will come to value the expression of nature and not nature itself, he means that he will intuitively discern that the Over-Soul in a given scene is expressing a special quality—tenderness or placidity or joy, or dislocation or turbulence, or whatever—and, then putting aside his own identity, will seek to reproduce that quality, using the trees, stones, and sky not so much as trees, stones, and sky but as its constituents. It is the spirit of the place that he must recapture, not his own mood that he must project, and, although he will employ considerable abstraction, he will still be treating the scene representationally (Emerson's word is "copy," unfortunately), so that its features are still recognizable as natural features. "He will give the gloom of gloom and the sunshine of sunshine" does not mean that he has license to fill a canvas with dark colors, in streaks or globs unrelated to nature, because psychically they mean gloom to him, or with vivid or hot tones in splashes because they express sunshine. It means, again, that the character of the scene, whether dark or light, is to take precedence over the exact rendering of all the details of topography and flora. And so also with portraiture; the subject is to remain recognizably a human subject, but it is the character lighting up his face which is important, and so the artist's concentration is to be on those facial elements which reveal it. Always in art, as in other intellectual work, for Emerson the aim was "to hinder our individuality from acting." Anticipating T. S. Eliot's dictum, "Poetry is not a turning loose of emotion, but an escape from emotion; it is not the expression of personality, but an escape from personality," again and again he deprecated the Romantic art of his day for its subjectivity and caprice. Unwholesome it was and overdecorated, the work of upholsterers rather than architects, unspeakably inferior to Classical art. A great mind introduces one to facts; a petty one to itself. In sculpture and in painting as in literature Emerson looked much less for the author than for what he called the author's author.

That for Emerson art existed to serve a religious end makes clear, if nothing else does, the difference between him and our contemporary extremist-speculators. It was wonder which he said art should evoke—awe and exhilaration in a "sense of universal relation and power." Yet an art exploiting plenitude and random association cannot stir anything in the spectator better than amused resignation to the absurdity of life. Works of nature

are organically reproductive; correspondingly, works of art were
for Emerson spiritually prolific by their "powerful action on the
intellects of men." Art was to bring men to a right view of
nature by making them aware of the beauty of the world; in
their renewed state they would open themselves to nature and
seek to shape their lives by its economy, symmetry, and wholeness. In a society of renewed men and women ugliness would
not be tolerated, nor would the conditions making slums and
delinquency ever arise. The Greeks had had great art because
in their civic life questions of religion and politics were para-
mount; but in a civilization where such issues were no longer
of moment, art would necessarily be no more than exhibition.

> Give to barrows, trays and pans
> Grace and glimmer of romance,
> Bring the moonlight into noon
> Hid in gleaming piles of stone;
> On the city's paved street
> Plant gardens lined with lilac sweet,
> Let spouting fountains cool the air,
> Singing in the sun-baked square;
> Let statue, picture, park and hall,
> Ballad, flag and festival
> The past restore, the day adorn
> And make to-morrow a new morn.
>   (W, IX, 277-78)

Yet whether the degree of tally between Emerson's ideas on a
revelatory and dynamic art and those of certain avant-garde
thinkers is as much or as little as some might have it be, and
irrespective of the precise worth of the experiments currently
going forward in the fine and performing arts, which are aimed
at opening domains heretofore uncharted, what is important is
that there is a correspondence between him and today's radical
theorists, of aspiration if not of execution, which additionally
illustrates the extensive applicability of his many-featured
thought.

Of the various arts that of which Emerson was himself practitioner was, of course, poetry; and so no account of his stature
as thinker can be valid or complete without an examination of
his character and accomplishment as poet. He was artist as well

as philosopher. He not only believed life itself, when successfully lived, to be poetry; he also declared the one supreme, verbal account of it to be formal poetry. He defined himself as essentially poet:

I am born a poet, of a low class without doubt yet a poet. That is my nature & vocation. My singing be sure is very "husky," & is for the most part in prose. Still am I a poet in the sense of a perceiver & dear lover of the harmonies that are in the soul & in matter. (L, I, 435)

In his old age he still maintained that the poet's way of dealing with reality was superior to that of the philosopher: "The poet sees wholes and avoids analysis. . . . The poet is in the natural attitude; he is believing; the philosopher, after some struggle, having only reasons for believing" (W, XII, 14). In large part, Emerson's ideas about the poet and poetry were what they were because of his devotion to nature and his affinity with her. The nature-dependent intellect alone was the means not only to a genuinely poetic utterance but also to a right understanding of poetry.

To consider the work of a Transcendentalist poet is necessarily to consider the relation of art to life. In this connection, ideas inherited from the remote past link themselves to ideas sprung from the soil of the new age. But to view the relation from the Transcendental point of view may be, for a modern, uncongenial —at once to say of art too little and to demand of it too much. For the Transcendentalist, art, although subordinate to it, had much to do with life, its function being to improve it by making the person living morally better. He considered art a by-product, valuable only as it enhanced the thing it commented on. In a sense, no Transcendentalist would spend time writing a sonnet if he could live it instead. The one work of art worth giving one's life to was life. Real color, proportion, harmony, and rhythm—real unity and sense of completeness—could be found only in the way one thought and felt, gestured and looked, loved and talked, moved and acted from day to day. "To affect the quality of the day," wrote Thoreau—to give its inchoate grayness and chill the warmth and order of one's own joy—"that is the highest of the arts." And again,

My life has been the poem
I would have writ;
But I could not both live
And utter it.

As for Emerson,

We parade our nobilities in poems and orations, instead of working
them up into happiness. . . . There is some reason to believe that when
a man does not write his poetry it escapes by other vents through him,
instead of the one vent of writing; clings to his form and manners,
whilst poets have often nothing poetical about them except their verses.
(W, VI, 191)

Every Transcendentalist was a Unitarian in the sense that he
strove to make his life a unified thing, a single and whole work of
art with no disparities and unresolved discords. He was kin to
poets who through the centuries all the way back to Greece had
sought to relate literature didactically to life. Although with him
as with Ben Jonson to write was a great act, it was always "lesser
than to do." Good writing was valuable because it could lead
to better doing.

That book is good
Which puts me in a working mood.
Unless to Thought is added Will,
Apollo is an imbecile.
(W, IX, 331)

So Emerson took pleasure in his attachment to the Horatian tradition of improving men through delighting them, which had
recently given to the world the grandeur of Milton, and in a few
works, the nobility of Wordsworth. Since the principal reason for
the universe was the formation of human character, it followed
for him that the purpose of art was the elevation of life through
the education of the perception of beauty. "There is higher work
for Art than the arts" (W, II, 363).

The Platonic cast of Emerson's mind in its devotion to Truth,
Goodness, and Beauty and its propensity for seeing the objects of
the world as shadows of Ideal Forms, is responsible for much of
what he had to say about poetry. Unitarian though he was, he
considered man by nature to be trinitarian, at once knower, doer,

and sayer; and of these three the poet was the sayer. He himself in his roles as essayist, preacher, and poet had embodied all three identities, never, one suspects, with strict separateness.

In the essay "The Poet" Emerson gave a full statement of his ideas on the art as a practitioner of which he would have most liked to win fame. It was not meters but a meter-making argument which made a poem, "a thought so passionate and alive that like the spirit of a plant or an animal it has an architecture of its own and adorns nature with a new thing" (W, III, 9-10). In this definition he revealed his kinship with other Romantic poets. Like them, he valued passion in poetry and ascribed a miraculous potency to the shaping faculties of the unconscious mind in its creation; once the artist was warmed to his task of composition, he could no more control the form his work would take than an animal in growth could prescribe its own shape. Correspondingly, Shelley had said that the poet was as helpless in determining the form of his offspring as a mother bearing a child in her womb, and Whitman was to declare that perfect poems grew autonomously into form like pears or melons. This did not mean for Emerson, however, that poems burst spontaneously and full-blown into life; the poet assisted the parturition of his brain-child and, once aware of the identity it was assuming, sought with every conscious means to help it realize itself perfectly. If his inspiration was genuine it would insure that his mind found the right words for expressing it.

Emerson's emphasis on the primacy of thought in poetry distinguishes him from most other poets of his era, yet it is hardly unexpected in an admirer of the seventeenth and eighteenth centuries and of ancient Greece. Thought meant not cerebrality or syllogistic intellection, however, but illuminating idea—some intuitive discovery about the world or man's destiny in it just made by the poet and still pulsating in his mental veins—in the truest sense vital. Hence his phrase "passionate and alive." He was fusing the best of the Neoclassic with the best of the Romantic tradition. If a poet started with such an idea, in his working of it large vistas would open in his mind, and the context in which it was seen would be universal. Indeed the truer it was and the more significant, the more it revealed the universe or the system of things as harmonious and beautiful; and the more this sense of harmony and beauty resided in the poet's mind, the more impelled he felt himself to be toward goodness because the more moved by love. And the exaltation of the poet, in a realized poem, was re-created in his readers.

So much for poetry. What of the poet? Like other Romantics, Emerson viewed him in the antique fashion, as a seer, endowed with vision deeper and broader than that of ordinary persons. Workaday, family man is a god in ruins, a creature of high potentiality but so bound in creaturely routine, surrounded by partial persons, and ensnared by illusory things that he never fulfills himself. Living a life of false starts, of abortive aspirations, he is a bundle of fragments. The poet, however, is a liberating god, freeing him from mobbing minutiae and restoring him to wholeness; out of a handful of shards he shapes again a complete vessel. The poet with his comprehensive and penetrating view turns the world to glass; he sees all things in their proper relation to one another and to the totality of life. He understands the unity that underlies the marvelous multiplicity of the universe. He knows that "it is dislocation and detachment from the life of God that makes things ugly" and therefore, "reattaching even artificial things and violations of nature, to nature, by a deeper insight" he reveals their essential beauty and significance. He makes us see how mistaken we have been about the facts of industrialization, politics, even physiology. Railroads, for instance, with their clatter and smoke; factories with their relentless throbbing and heat; and sex, in conception, gestation, and birth, when seen in relation to elemental forces of the universe and the creative impetus of man's mind, are purged of their grossness. The poet, rightly omniscient, can show us everywhere trifles animated by a tendency, the ceaseless effort of nature to evolve ever higher forms of life in species better adapted to ends of harmony and refined consciousness. He can therefore use with impunity words that are ordinarily proscribed from polite speech as obscene.

Where does the poet get his power—how does he come by his omniscience? He draws it from the same source tapped by the American Scholar or any representative of Man Thinking—from the Over-Soul, from the limitless reservoir of the Universal Mind, circumambient as the air or sea. Again and again in moments of meditation in nature he opens his mind to its flooding influences, and large measures of truth are imprinted on it. As a result, when he speaks he apprises us not of his wealth but of the commonwealth. But in order to be a sensitive and generous receptacle, he must show an affinity with nature, which means that he must live by natural discipline—simply, frugally, healthfully. All persons through history who would speak to their kind with the accent of eternity have known the need of intellectual reinforcement—of an enlargement of mind through a strength not their own—to raise them to the requisite perspective. Hence the ancient doctrines of inspiration and enthusiasm, according to which superhuman beings breathed, or entered, into poets and allowed them to think grandly. The Hebrew prophets, however, with their recurrent withdrawal into the solitude, poverty, and fasting of the desert mountains, were more right than the Roman poets, who sought stimulation in alcohol and persuaded others to believe that in wine was truth. Emerson's poet was to live on a plane so low that "the common influences should delight him. His cheerfulness should be the gift of the sunlight, the air should suffice for his inspiration, and he should be tipsy with water" (W, III, 29). With Milton he maintained that no one could write poetry who was not himself a true poem, that is, "a composition and pattern of the best and honourablest things."

What language should the poet use? Living language—living language always—not words from books, not attenuated words from metaphysical speculation, but words that were flesh. Emerson loved to talk with farmers, to overhear workmen in conversation with one another, to listen to teamsters as they unloaded their wagons at the warehouse; every word such men spoke was alive and if you cut it, would bleed. The air of most New England parlors was so thin and stale, since the persons who lived in them were wraiths of decorum and pale gentility, that he often could not breathe. He deplored the fact that one could on no account say "stink" or "damn" for fear of raising an alarm among all the old grannies from Bangor to Mobile. He had various terms for describing the right vocabulary—vascular, spermatic, man-making, prophesying. It should be always simple—at once of the earth, earthy and of the fire, fiery. It had pulse and sinew because it was related directly to things. In fact, teamsters, carpenters, farmers, fishermen, when they talked, could be said to be talking things, not about things. They lived what they uttered; what came from their lips was the deeds of their days. It was white hot with the flame of vitality. The figure of fire to indicate the intensity of idea,

the passionate thought which actuated the poet, was a favorite
with Emerson. A poem was for him what he had said in his piece
on the Lord's Supper a sermon should be—"life passed through
the fire of thought." What had early attracted him in the religious
lyrics of George Herbert, which seemed to him formed for the
devotion of angels, was "the power of exalted thought to melt
and bend language to its fit expression"; the temperature of
Herbert's mind had actually fused word and idea (EL, I, 350).
In a fine quatrain to set down the essence of the poet's métier
Emerson had written:

> To clothe the fiery thought
> In simple words succeeds,
> For still the craft of genius is
> To mask a king in weeds. (W, IX, 292)

What subjects should the poet treat, and what forms should he
use? No less than the scholar and the clergyman he should remember that it is only life which avails, not the having lived,
and that God *is,* not *was.* It was his own experience here and
now which should occupy him—the ideas and feelings burning
within from day to day and the multitudinous sights and sounds of
such immediacy in his own environment. Dante had shown the
way in modern times, recording his own pilgrimage and exploring
his own times; his greatness was that he had dared to write his
autobiography in colossal cipher. So American poets should sing
their American selves and their American day, should use the
present tense not the past.

We have yet had no genius in America, with tyrannous eye, which
knew the value of our incomparable materials, and saw, in the barbarism and materialism of the times, another carnival of the same gods
whose picture he so much admires in Homer; then in the Middle Ages;
then in Calvinism. Banks and tariffs, the newspapers and caucus,
Methodism and Unitarianism, are flat and dull to dull people, but
rest on the same foundations of wonder as the town of Troy and the
temple of Delphi, and are as swiftly passing away. Our log-rolling,
our stumps and their politics, our fisheries, our Negroes and Indians,
our boats and repudiations, the wrath of rogues and the pusillanimity
of honest men, the northern trade, the southern planting, the western
clearing, Oregon and Texas, are yet unsung. Yet America is a poem
in our eyes; its ample geography dazzles the imagination, and it will
not wait long for metres. (W, III, 37-38)

As for forms, new ones would organically disclose themselves, depending on the nature of the experience treated and the personality treating it. Pindar had shaped his odes to his own utterance, Petrarch the sonnet, Spenser his stanza. Such forms now seemed natural but only because they had originally been fashioned with rightness. Anything man-made which served its ends perfectly achieved inevitability and was assimilated by nature. Yet rhyme was one feature of form perennially the same, for it was a manifestation of the principle of undulation or alternation, or compensation, in the system or things. Inhalation is balanced by exhalation, maleness by femaleness, right by wrong, and so the answering of one line by another can only be fundamental.

In all of this Emerson reveals himself a child of his times, which were, as he had known ever since attaining the age of awareness, still those of the democratic revolution. What he aimed to do in poetry in the United States was therefore, in large measure, what Wordsworth, invaluable innovator intent on literature as democratized as politics, had said he wanted to do a generation earlier in England—to treat situations and incidents out of common life in a selection of language really used by men but to throw over them a certain coloring of imagination so that ordinary things would appear to the mind in an unusual aspect.

The literature of the poor, the feelings of the child, the philosophy of the street, the meaning of household life, are the topics of the time. . . . I ask not for the great, the remote, the romantic; what is doing in Italy or Arabia; what is Greek art, or Provençal minstrelsy; I embrace the common, I explore and sit at the feet of the familiar, the low. . . . The meal in the firkin; the milk in the pan; the ballad in the street; the news of the boat; the glance of the eye; the form and the gait of the body;—show me the ultimate reason of these matters. . . . (W, I, 111)

To create a poetry emancipated from the conventions in force during so many preceding nondemocratic generations was not easy. Literature recurrently has had to struggle to attain new forms of utterance at once faithful to life and appropriate to art. In the middle of the twentieth century an Arthur Miller feels it necessary to write a manifesto vindicating his conviction that tragedy can befall a common man as well as a titled nobleman—a traveling salesman as well as a prince of Denmark. Like

Wordsworth, Emerson believed poetry to be the breath and finer
spirit of all knowledge, capable, in spite of what had silently
gone out of mind or been violently destroyed, of binding together the vast empire of mankind, because the poet was the
man of all men who looked on the world with love and had
insight into the meaning of things.

Show me the sublime presence of the highest spiritual cause lurking,
as always it does lurk, in these suburbs and extremities of nature; . . .
and the shop, the plough, and the ledger referred to the like cause
by which light undulates and poets sing;—and the world lies no longer
a dull miscellany and lumber-room . . . but one design unites and
animates the farthest pinnacle and the lowest trench. (W, I, 111-12)

He recognized his kinship with all of the Romantic celebrants
of humble life—with Robert Burns, for instance, affirming a man
as a man in spite of circumstance, and with his own contemporary, Whittier, whose verse, inspired by a boyish love of Burns,
was dedicated to revealing "the unsung beauty hid life's common
things below."

Lest his advocacy of a poetry treating the milk in the pan in
an American way should seem a step not worth considering, we
ought to notice that Poe, the greatest American practitioner of
poetry among Emerson's contemporaries before the advent of
Whitman, was writing only verses of a highly contrived and
restricted verbal musicality to illustrate a conviction that the
loftiest poetic theme was the death of a beautiful woman la-
mented by her bereaved lover—verses as unrelated to America
as were his tales of terror about hermetically isolated, disinte-
grating aristocrats, male and female, compulsively driven to
destroy one another in some dim, decaying city of the Rhine or
its equivalent. And in England, while Wordsworth had anticipated Emerson in finding poetry in the familiar and low rather
than the remote and exotic, his creed did not postulate that they
should be the English familiar and the English low treated in
such a way as to illuminate and transfigure the national life of
England. An idealized and spiritualized nationalism seems to
have had no place in his esthetic.

Emerson was, of course, not the first American poet to write
verses on native themes—on native flora and fauna, on native

places, or on figures or events out of native history. Not only
was he not the first to advocate an epic for Americans; he did
not even advocate it, and he seems to have been not at all interested in the epic as a form. He left us nothing like Joel Bar-
low's *Columbiad*. But he seems to have been the first to believe
in the indispensability to the formation of a national consciousness of a poet who would immerse himself in the daily life of the
land, its issues as well as its places and persons, its habits and
occupations, and out of its multitudinous minutiae create a revelation—of a poet who would take the trivia of the life lived by
ordinary folk here and now, not by nobles generations ago, and
transmute them into art. Whether this would be in a single long
poem or in many small poems he did not say. What counted
was that the essence in everything in America that made it
America, be revealed; and furthermore that the essence be related to the invisible life of the spirit and the human craving
for the ideal, to something of universal import in the nature of
man and his future destiny on the globe. It was not enough to
depict, no matter how vividly, lumber camps, political rallies,
Negro slaves and displaced Indians, church pieties and street
factionalisms, farm pastorals and household routine. Poetry must
help its readers to take a step along the way leading to an original relation with the universe. Emerson's poet, in order to discern such things and light up such a way, would indeed need
to have what he called a tyrannous eye.

Yet it was not only to the poets of the Romantic age that
Emerson, in whatever pieces of a manifesto-kind he wrote,
showed himself to belong. It was to all genuine poets anywhere,
in any time, for they have all been inspired to cleanse the
clogged senses of their readers and lay bare the preciousness
of life, in which "Each moment crieth/As it flieth,/Seize me ere
I die." From time to time, poetry has a way of growing remote
and irrelevant and needing to be brought back to earth. Themes
of significance to one generation may be meaningless to the next,
even their language having become no longer intelligible. Poetry
has forever to be newly related to life. Emerson and Wordsworth had abjured the personifications, the apostrophes, the
circumlocutions, and the archaic contractions as well as the
overwrought intellections of the eighteenth century because they
constituted a falsely embellished and empty diction, as irrelevant

to the needs of modern man as were the outmoded ideas and institutions, social and political, which had characterized the pseudoaristocracy of that century. But similarly, vis-à-vis their predecessors, had Dante and the practitioners of the *dolce stil nuovo* done in Italy. So had the founders of the Pléiade done in France; so had Milton done in England, and so were later to do the members of the Pre-Raphaelite brotherhood and the Imagists. "It was one of our tenets that verse should have the virtues of prose, that diction should become assimilated to cultivated contemporary speech, before aspiring to the elevation of poetry," said T. S. Eliot about the young poets preparing themselves to write the New Poetry in 1919.

Another tenet was that the subject-matter and the imagery of poetry should be extended to topics and objects related to the life of a modern man or woman; that we were to seek the non-poetic, to seek even material refractory to transmutation into poetry, and words and phrases which had not been used in poetry before. (TSE, 160)

Today's gaudiness and inanity—that is, ornateness and hollowness—were alas, yesterday's beauty and pith. Each generation must discover and define such qualities anew.

It is not enough, however, to consider only Emerson's ideas on poetry. One must consider also a few of the representative poems that grew from them. In a book about an architect or a sculptor it would not suffice to discuss his principles alone; one would need to reveal them to the reader through photographic illustrations of specimen pieces. The mind of an artist reveals itself no less in his art than in what he says about his art.

Emerson never considered himself to be the poet he had described. Conceding that most of what he had uttered was conventional, he nevertheless believed that occasionally he had said something original and beautiful. Of the five hundred verses from his pen, he wrote amusedly, five might survive—but did any of his readers have eyes to know which they were?

The best Emerson poems are, as one would suspect, those in which he best realized his aims. They are at the same time those which are most modern; that is, those which are timeless, in which thought and passion are fused and communicated in a language always fresh and evocative, those which make a revelation in re-creating an experience important to Emerson himself.

His instant thought a poet spoke,
And filled the age his fame;
An inch of ground the lightning strook
But lit the sky with flame.

(W, IX, 334)

He tried his hand at strophic lyrics, at couplets, and at blank verse; and he felt a special affinity for the four-stressed iambic line and for the 4-3-4-3 quatrain, whose compression pleased him with its possibilities for gnomic utterance—both, he believed, instinctive in man and related elementally to the human pulse-beat.

Emerson's poetry is one with his prose, in that it treats the same issues of life, the same themes of mind. The ideas of self-reliance, the Over-Soul, the whole in the part, the universality of inspiration, nature as ceaselessly flowing and evolving, the fatality of the divorce between man and nature are all to be found, along with many others equally representative, in his best work. They are given different expression, however, and set in different context, so that to some extent they themselves emerge as different. In a sense, the way a thing is said *is* the thing said, insofar as form determines substance. The beautiful dive a diver executes is nothing but form; what he does is only the way he does it. A hand or leg out of line, a torso not arched means a botched dive. To see how in his best work Emerson the poet executes one of his characteristic convictions is to see an important additional evidence of the performing power of his mind, of the fertility of its invention.

In one of his best known poems, "The Problem," Emerson deals with the idea of the oneness of inspiration in life. As he sits in his study contemplating the portrait of the Elizabethan divine, Jeremy Taylor, whose sermons with accustomed admiration he has been rereading, he asks himself why, in spite of that admiration, he could never trade places with him and be a "cowled churchman." In something less than sixty dense lines he provides the answer, powerfully implicit, never explicit—because Christianity, with its pretensions to total truth, is painfully parochial. Its narrowness is revealed in its separation of spirituality from nature and often from art and in its exclusion of pagan nations—Greece and Egypt, for example—from access to the fountain of divine inspiration.

> Not from a vain or shallow thought
> His awful Jove young Phidias brought;
> Never from lips of cunning fell
> The thrilling Delphic oracle;
>
> .   .   .   .
>
> The litanies of nations came,
> Like the volcano's tongue of flame,
> Up from the burning core below,—
> The canticles of love and woe.

For Emerson, creative force is one and the same, whether in the thrusting up of a mountain, the formation of a seashell, the framing of a mathematical law, the designing of a great building, or the enunciation of a religious principle. Now it inhabits the upheaving, generative earth, now the silent sap of a pine tree, now the cells of the brain of a man; now it manifests itself in the Mediterranean world two thousand years before Christ; now in England one thousand years after. But wherever and whenever, in big things or little, in whatever has grown and has form and life, material or immaterial, it is eternally the same. Plato and Jesus, then, were equally inspired and by the same source; the architects of the pyramids, the Parthenon, and Saint Peter's in Rome were fraternal geniuses begotten by a common father, all related, in their conceiving power, to fructifying nature itself; and the impulse leading worshipers inside such edifices to prayer and song is no different from, no holier than, that which originally actuated their builders. There is only "one accent of the Holy Ghost" and the world can never lose it, no matter how doctrinally indifferent to it human beings become. Buddhist, Mohammedan, Jew, Protestant, and Catholic will all continue to be products of the one universal procreative force, which is eternally the sole spring of the waters of illumination.

But all of this is put by Emerson sententiously, in language of intensity and revelation which pregnantly combines figure and statement. His canvas is large—the whole earth—and the perspective he evokes is deep; yet the details are few and purposely discontinuous. They are all significant and vivid, however, and are introduced with telling incisiveness and force; like abrupt shafts of light from many angles, they make clear the subject in its magnitude, and we are moved by our exposure to some-

thing piercing and of grandeur. It is indeed an argument to
make meter, passionate and alive throughout.

Another characteristic poem, so brief as to be hardly more
than an exhalation, is "Days." Emerson was himself rightly fond
of it and thought it perhaps the best thing he had ever done.

> Daughters of Time, the hypocritic Days,
> Muffled and dumb like barefoot dervishes,
> And marching single in an endless file,
> Bring diadems and fagots in their hands.
> To each they offer gifts after his will,
> Bread, kingdoms, stars, and sky that holds them all.
> I, in my pleached garden, watched the pomp,
> Forgot my morning wishes, hastily
> Took a few herbs and apples, and the Day
> Turned and departed silent. I, too late,
> Under her solemn fillet saw the scorn.
>
> (W, IX, 228)

Here there may seem to be no thought passionate and alive. As
one sees it alongside "The Problem," he perhaps finds it tame
and polite. Intensity there was in "The Problem" in such things as

> Ever the fiery Pentecost
> Girds with one flame the countless host,
> Trances the heart through chanting choirs,
> And through the priest the mind inspires.

In "Days," however, what one has is the coolness of a morning,
with at most a thin ray or two of early sunlight filtered by the
leaves and trellises of a garden. In the first poem, surveying
the globe, one was dealing with a universal issue involving mankind in relation to art, religion, and nature; in the second, in an
intimate, domestic setting, he observes the deportment of the
poet, a single person, as he does what he knows he ought not
do. But in that "what he knows he ought not do" is contained
the crux of the matter. Self-betrayal in the desertion of one's
aspirations is a theme no less important than the universality of
inspiration. But for its exhibition it needs only a single moment
in a place no matter how small. The scale of its treatment is
necessarily reduced. One's life is not 24 hours multiplied by 365
days multiplied again by 75 years. One's life is not what one

has lived; it is what one is living. It is not quantitative; it is qualitative. It is one day: it is the nature of what one is thinking and feeling at a given instant.

In "Days" Emerson never uses "betrayal" or any word like it. He simply lets us see the betrayal taking place and lets us infer its consequences on the conscience of the poet by the concluding statement: "I, too late,/Under her solemn fillet saw the scorn." Like every good poem it re-creates its experience, instead of talking about it. It conforms to the canon enunciated succinctly years ago by Archibald MacLeish, that a poem should not mean but be. Or, better, it illustrates a conviction on Emerson's part that a poem should both be and mean. A poem should evoke an indefinable emotional and spiritual state in the reader through its depiction of a scene or through its re-creation of an experience or a quality of being in the life of a poet, but it cannot do this only. Music alone has that sole task for its province, being a thing of nothing but sounds. One cannot go up to a pianist, for instance, after the performance of a Mozart sonata or a Chopin nocturne to ask him what it means. Poetry, however, is an art whose sounds, being words, are more than sounds. It re-creates a situation or a mood and in doing so, is; but it also says something inescapably about the situation or mood in re-creating it. It relates its subject matter, if only implicitly, to life, and in doing this, it means. We are led to think piercingly, as well as to feel profoundly, by a good poem—even by MacLeish's "Ars Poetica"—and this thought, which willy-nilly takes the form of generalization, is meaning. "Days" does what it does with almost oriental economy, with sustained softness of tone, and with extraordinary understatement. The acuteness of its relevancy, its poignancy, may escape one at first reading, like the cut of a knife so sharp it is not felt until it is withdrawn from the flesh.

"Hamatreya," which contrasts the ephemerality of man with the permanence of the earth and reveals the vanity of the illusion of ownership, is also, in its first half, admirable in exemplifying Emerson's poetic ideal.

> Bulkeley, Hunt, Willard, Hosmer, Meriam, Flint,
> Possessed the land which rendered to their toil
> Hay, corn, roots, hemp, flax, apples, wool and wood.

Each of these landlords walked amidst his farm,
Saying, " 'Tis mine, my children's and my name's.
How sweet the west wind sounds in my own trees!
How graceful climb those shadows on my hill!
I fancy these pure waters and the flags
Know me, as does my dog: we sympathize;
And, I affirm, my actions smack of the soil."

Where are these men? Asleep beneath their grounds:
And strangers, fond as they, their furrows plough.
Earth laughs in flowers, to see her boastful boys
Earth-proud, proud of the earth which is not theirs;
Who steer the plough, but cannot steer their feet
Clear of the grave.
They added ridge to valley, brook to pond,
And sighed for all that bounded their domain;
"This suits me for a pasture; that's my park;
We must have clay, lime, gravel, granite-ledge,
And misty lowland, where to go for peat.
The land is well,—lies fairly to the south.
'Tis good, when you have crossed the sea and back,
To find the sitfast acres where you left them."

                                        (W, IX, 35-36)

The blank verse here contracts or expands accentually, grows
smooth or harsh, light or heavy as its substance determines. The
meter *is* the substance. The thought, if not passionate, is finely
compassionate and alive at every turn as it informs the utterance.
The language is vascular and tough, altogether free of the "rotten
diction" of the eighteenth century, which Emerson had set himself to pierce. The names in the first line happen to be those of
the first settlers of Concord, Bulkeley in fact having been one of
Emerson's ancestors, who led the little expedition in 1635 from
Boston into the wilderness to found the community. What a
mouthful each is, thick and earthy, stubbornly detached from
every other, its strong stress falling portentously at its beginning.
From the start the thick-muscled, slow-striding, weighty farmers,
with their practical, no-nonsense minds, are evoked for us.

In this poem Emerson sings not so much hoarsely as throatily,
even gutturally. Forswearing euphony, he does not embrace
cacophony but writes a music in which there is a large place for

dissonance and melodic continuity gives way to rhythmical variation. It had precedent in the blank verse of Milton but was the
furthest thing from the rich, flowing music of Poe, with its exploitation of sibilants, liquids, and nasals, and the smooth, conventionally tuneful verse of Longfellow. In its staccato elements
and "low" vocabulary it is nonpoetic poetry and seems to look
forward to the percussive dissonances of a Stravinsky.

When Emerson's first son Waldo died in 1842 at the age of
five, the sun went out for him. The boy was beautiful and highly
sensitive and intelligent, and his loss, though Emerson did not
cease to sleep or eat, was irreparable. To the end he remembered
the lad's sweetness and rich promise. His devotion and his grief
at the time both found eloquent expression in "Threnody," a
poem of almost three hundred lines, in which he aimed to adapt
to the lamentation of an American poet in the nineteenth century
some of the features of the conventional Greek pastoral elegy,
as Whitman, profiting from his example, afterward would do in
"When Lilacs Last in the Dooryard Bloom'd." It was a bold and
ambitious effort, at once paying his respects to tradition and
emancipating himself from it. It opens, in proper elegiac fashion,
in the minor key but moves through its anguish and hurt inter-
rogation to a conclusion, in the major, of exalted acceptance.
The early sections recollect the child in his homely pursuits and
intimate associations; a middle section expresses the father's
desolation in the wake of his departure and his bitterness in
trying to define it; and then an extended final part, a consolatory
and explanatory speech by "the deep Heart," or Over-Soul, recon-
ciles him to his state.

The language of "Threnody" is often distinguished by soaring
passion, by irresistible vitality, and by intense coloring. About
the inveterate impulse to stay death, to suspend or reorder nature
according to human desires, it asks:

> Wilt thou freeze love's tidal flow,
> Whose streams through Nature circling go?
> Nail the wild star to its track
> On the half-climbed zodiac?
> Light is light which radiates,
> Blood is blood which circulates,
> Life is life which generates,
> And many seeming life is one,—

> Wilt thou transfix and make it none?
> Its onward force too starkly pent
> In figure, bone and lineament?
>
> (W, IX, 156)

And its concluding lines, at once evolutionistic, Platonic, and Christian in the divine force whose activity it celebrates, affirm, with a reference to the growth of benefit from vicissitude, the eventual happy outcome of all:

> Silent rushes the swift Lord
> Through ruined systems still restored,
> Broadsowing, bleak and void to bless,
> Plants with worlds the wilderness;
> Waters with tears of ancient sorrow
> Apples of Eden ripe to-morrow.
> House and tenant go to ground,
> Lost in God, in Godhead found.
>
> (W, IX, 158)

For Emerson, as we have seen, the eternal riddle of the sphinx was the right relation of man to nature. Each generation must answer it as best it could. As in his prose one finds vast the range of his treatment of the theme, so also in his poetry. In many pieces he is the conventional "nature poet"—in the early "Rhodora," for example, written out of love of that "rival of the rose"—and simply sings the beauty of some flower or bird or the charms of some sylvan or rural scene, with a brief didactic association of himself, or of divinity, with the subject. In others, such as "The Snow Storm," he is content only to paint a picture, eschewing all comment. These are idyls, canvases of diminutive scope of more or less attraction to us. In others, however, he goes far beyond flora and fauna to the cosmos itself, his imagination excited by the long and endless sweep of elemental forces through all that is. He loved to see in the tiniest elements of domesticated nature close about his house the evidences of the influence of universal powers—to reflect that the mute white blossom beside his garden path was the product of geological cataclysms, no less than the grandest mountain, and owed its fragile life equally to the operation of the laws of gravity and terrestrial rotation. Yet, no matter how awingly grand the dimensions of nature in the uni-

verse, no matter how indifferent to the individual—and even to
some species—in her inexhaustible fecundity and her zeal to
achieve her own realization, she showed herself to be, she was
necessary to man, who, deprived of contact with her, suffered
psychically as well as physically. That this was for Emerson a
meter-making argument is shown by many poems but in particular by two in blank verse which are noteworthy for their passion and strength, "Blight" and "Musketaquid."

In "Blight" he explores the increasing alienation of man from
nature. In a civilization which is urban, science-dominated, and
industrialized most persons can be said rarely to set foot on the
earth, never touch plants that they have helped to grow from the
earth, and do not know the names of those that grow wild from
it. Even technical specialists who know their Latin names, have,
no less than engineers who seek natural resources for industry, a
contact with the woods which is only commercial and exploitative.
Men have no longer any organic tie with nature, such as allowed
their forebears to call all green and flowering things by their
common names and to use them, lovingly, for food and medicine,
applying their chemistry "by sweet affinities to human flesh." We
are only

> ... thieves
> And pirates of the universe, shut out
> Daily to a more thin and outward rind, [who]
> Turn pale and starve.
>
> (W, IX, 141)

In such a situation Emerson can only cry out to be given truths
for he is weary of the surfaces and dying of inanition.

> ... life, shorn of its venerable length,
> Even at its greatest space is a defeat,
> And dies in anger that it was a dupe;
> And, in its highest noon and wantonness,
> Is early frugal, like a beggar's child;
> Even in the hot pursuit of the best aims
> And prizes of ambition, checks its hand,
> Like Alpine cataracts frozen as they leaped,
> Chilled with a miserly comparison
> Of the toy's purchase with the length of life.
>
> (W, IX, 141)

The poem is prophetic of the grim situation confronting man, A.D. 1972, his very existence threatened by continued spoliation and contamination of the natural environment.

"Musketaquid," its title the Indian name for the small Concord River which flowed indolently past the back property of the Old Manse, perhaps more fully than any other Emerson poem treats the relation between small and large in the universe. Emerson, admiring the large landowning farmers who in the midst of forests are exposed to the rigors of climate and stake their whole lives on a continuing big-scale struggle with the forces of the air and earth, seeking to enlist their cooperation, however, as often as to oppose or check them, feels ashamed of the timidity and parsimony of his own efforts in his small garden.

> They fight the elements with elements
> (That one would say, meadow and forest walked,
> Transmuted in these men to rule their like),
> And by the order in the field disclose
> The order regnant in the yeoman's brain.
>
> (W, IX, 143)

Yet he is not altogether to be disparaged. Nature is nature, irrespective of bound.

> What these strong masters wrote at large in miles,
> I followed in small copy in my acre;
> For there's no rood has not a star above it;
> The cordial quality of pear or plum
> Ascends as gladly in a single tree
> As in broad orchards resonant with bees;
> And every atom poises for itself,
> And for the whole.
>
> (W, IX, 143)

And, no less than the "strong masters," he has the opportunity of observing nature and cultivating, Stoic-like, her manners—her wonderful equanimity, her patience, her adaptability to change:

> . . . Canst thou silent lie?
> Canst thou, thy pride forgot, like Nature pass
> Into the winter night's extinguished mood?
> Canst thou shine now, then darkle,

> And being latent, feel thyself no less?
> As, when the all-worshipped moon attracts the eye,
> The river, hill, stems, foliage are obscure,
> Yet envies none, none are unenviable.
>
> (W, IX, 144)

Frequently Emerson rises to a Lucretian exaltation in his contemplation of the whirling, endlessly begetting stream of nature, of the blinding miracle of beauty as everywhere transmutative embodiments of energy. He loved to consider Pan a symbol of this mysterious urgency, as in a fragment entitled by his name.

> O what are heroes, prophets, men,
> But pipes through which the breath of Pan doth blow
> A momentary music. Being's tide
> Swells hitherward, and myriads of forms
> Live, robed with beauty, painted by the sun;
> Their dust, pervaded by the nerves of God,
> Throbs with an overmastering energy
> Knowing and doing. Ebbs the tide, they lie
> White hollow shells upon the desert shore,
> But not the less the eternal wave rolls on
> To animate new millions, and exhale
> Races and planets, its enchanted foam.
>
> (W, IX, 360)

The theme appears in various poems. In "Woodnotes," for instance, in the revelation by a pine tree to the poet of the truth about nature:

> Ever fresh the broad creation,
> A divine improvisation,
> From the heart of God proceeds,
> A single will, a million deeds.
> Once slept the world an egg of stone,
> And pulse, and sound, and light was none;
> And God said, "Throb!" and there was motion
> And the vast mass became vast ocean.
> Onward and on, the eternal Pan,
> Who layeth the world's incessant plan,
> Halteth never in one shape,
> But forever doth escape,

Like wave or flame, into new forms
Of gem, and air, of plants, and worms.
(W, IX, 57-58)

Those who complain of roughness and irregularity as a fault in
Emerson do so largely without justice. He purposely used half
rhymes and false rhymes and often left his meter irregular in
order to deviate from the palling correctness of conventional
verse. This is not to say that every irregularity, like the slight
disorder in dress praised by Herrick, kindles a delicious poetic
wantonness in the beholder—or even that it was craftily intentional. Emerson, though he had a degree of response to music,
knew he ought to like it and talked often about it as a great art
and the essence of poetry, had a rather bad ear and occasionally
left a line maimed, so that it reflects ignorance or willfulness
more than ingenuity. In two important poems in 1845, "Bacchus"
and "Merlin," he exulted in his awareness of the grand music
of the cosmos—something like the music of the spheres in which
the ancients had joyed but far more deeply interfused, relating at
once to the infinite variations of living forms prodigally produced
(as though creation itself were a gloriously interminable rondo),
to the flexible tempo of progress, now in augmentation and now
in diminution, and to the subtleties of oscillation and transformation in the moral realm uniting the True, the Good, and the
Beautiful and requiting each quality with its polarizing opposite
or its compensatory complement. The ineffable harmony of the
spiritual universe manifesting itself elusively in the physical world
was what he was sensitive to and aspired to re-create as a poetic
hymnodist—strains perhaps resembling Keats' songs unheard,
that excite the inner rather than the outer ear. In his essay on
"The Poet" he had said that all the music that could ever be had
already been created by the universe and was forever being sung
by it in its operation. The poet, then, in singing his music was
not discovering it but mystically rediscovering it. It was not a
"trivial harp" he aimed to smite with "strokes of fate," but one
whose "chords should ring as blows the breeze,/Free, peremp-
tory, clear," able to ". . . make the wild blood start/In its mystic
springs" (W, IX, 120). Such music was the supreme intoxicant, the
wine of the one true Bacchus because it was the blood of the
world,

                    . . . shed
                    Like the torrents of the sun
                    Up the horizon walls,
                    Or like the Atlantic streams, which run
                    When the South Sea calls.
                              (W, IX, 126)

In a sense, Emerson, irrespective of what he means now or may some day mean to twentieth-century readers, has been for our age a poet's poet. He has been of importance or shown a surprising relatedness to three of our major figures—Robert Frost, Robinson Jeffers, and Wallace Stevens. Of these, Frost was most indebted to him and most explicit in voicing his indebtedness as well as his admiration. Unlike personally though they were in many respects, the two were bound by an affinity of mind which Frost knew to be germinal. Perhaps it was only a way of seeing New Englandly—a need to live in a climate where men thought well and constructed well—but that they both shared it with preeminent force is significant. Frost early encountered Emerson's preoccupation with vascular language, with man-making words, and was set by it on his own quest for the right simple speech. He loved the toughness of Emerson's mind and his demands on the reader's intelligence. Having himself defined a poem as something that begins in delight and ends in wisdom, he naturally took to a predecessor who had declared it to be thought, passionate and alive. In 1959, still praising "Brahma" for its oracular concentration and its power to stretch his mind, he said that after several decades of admiration he had almost mastered its meaning, only one or two lines still baffling him. In his "Masque of Reason" he referred to "Uriel" as "the greatest Western poem yet." Like Emerson, but much more successfully, he wedded his life to the New England farm and forest, lived with the wood god, made his vocation one with his avocation, even to the point of splitting his own logs for the fire and laying his own rail fences. Like him, he was unsentimental about nature, no mewling, puking runaway from its diurnal severities, but reconciled to the buffetings of its outer as well as inner weather, at once accepting man's insignificance and unimportance in the scheme of things and praising his independent will and ingenious brain. Like him, he valued short poems—tight, metered, and rhymed—each a tennis court with the net always up, imitating nature, in which "Perfect-paired as eagles' wings,/Justice is the rhyme of things." Like him in his love of his country he returned again and again in mind to the venerable Founding Fathers of the eighteenth century, whose hope and courage and will had shaped a new era for mankind. When someone observed that Washington, Jefferson, and Franklin had believed in the future, he corrected him—they had rather believed the future *in*. Frost, hard-headed, valuing qualities more than persons, tersely rephrasing the Emersonian ideal of friendship-in-absence with his "keep off each other and keep each other off," had similarly disbelieved in organizations and been averse to joining—enough, to join a family and the nation and maybe a college in between. Suspicious of parties and society's claims to improvement, he was Emerson's self-reliant man, a true representative of Man Thinking: "I bid you to a one-man revolution,/The only revolution that is coming." And, like Emerson, always a lover of power, in his late years he drew closer to the national government, considering himself a sort of paternal adviser and even appearing as a bestower of blessings in a ceremony inaugurating a new president, whom he exhorted to become a new Augustus for the Western world.

Emerson can be seen to have been the "only begetter" of two important strains in twentieth-century American poetry. He bequeathed to New England posterity the tightly structured, terse, philosophical nature lyric but at the same time, paradoxically, having "fathered" Whitman in his advocacy of libertarian or autonomous form, of stink-or-damn spermatic language, and of the tyrannous eye which would focus on the spectacle of America, through him he is responsible for the equally dithyrambic Sandburg and, more recently, for the "Beat" poet Allen Ginsberg.

Perhaps what most impresses one in a survey of Emerson's poetry is the evidence of mind at work everywhere in it. And this is as it should be. The hardest of all things, he had once laconically stated in his journal, was to think, and he was fond of the figure of the opening of the iron lids of reason to indicate its difficulty. It is mind, in his case, addressing itself at once to small matters and to big, but always in a perspective that is universal. Even when he deals with love he makes clear that it is love of the general good and ideas, not of individuals and things, which is valuable—in its broadest sense, a happy acceptance of things as they are and a serene disposition to unfold one's abilities within the inexorable limitations imposed by that system. Perhaps in the work of no other American poet is nature as a cosmic force so often the protagonist, directly or indirectly fulfilling herself through the operation of unswerving law, not tutorially mindful of individual man yet not hostile to him, and even disposed to lend him her force and succor, to the extent of his capacities, if he opens himself to rely rightly upon her. One is tempted to say that from the start of his writing career Emerson's poems stress, as the essays do not, the magnitude and disinterested might of nature and in relation to it the puniness and dependence of man, whose freedom was a drastically quali- fied freedom. In his disposition to find a tie between human affec- tion, thought, and will and the power that moves the seas, shrinks and replenishes them, wheels constellations and universes through incomprehensible immensities of space, draining and rebuilding them, and frames millions of creatures in thousands of species, from gnat to whale, to be the feeding, acting, repro- ducing inhabitants of its illimitable domain, Emerson was an enraptured seeker combining the aspirations of Romantic or religious spirit with the claims of scientific fact. He was a dith- yrambist of the atom seeking to chant ". . . the cadence of the whirling world/Which dances round the sun." Although he does not turn the world to glass and show us all things in their right series and procession, as he said in his essay the poet should do, he does more often than not show us the trifle animated by a tendency—some feature of man's situation or behavior related to the vast, meliorative function of nature.

For many years some difference in character between the Emerson of the 1830's and the early 1840's and the Emerson of the 1850's and 1860's has been acknowledged. The older Emerson has seemed to be different from the younger by being less ab- stract, less anarchically individualistic, less given to solitude, and less "impractical." And the later essays, as well as the acts of his life, show that this is so—that he was less metaphysical, that having largely given his theory of life he became more occupied with illustrating its application, and that he was more willing to recognize the practices of society for their merits and its institutions for their validity. He became for a period a member of the board of examiners of the United States Military Academy at West Point and served also as an overseer of Harvard College. His most comprehensive and scholarly biographer distinguishes the Emerson of 1860 from the Emerson of 1841 by his disposition, merchantlike, to rearrange his window, and, for a change, display his "cheaper wares" to advantage, a procedure in which, however, although he allowed certain dark ideas to be seen in prominence, he did not at all abandon familiar bright ideas, only lent them new guise (see R, p. 407).

However, since the mid-1950's, various students, through assiduous attention to the published works, relating them as closely as possible to the *Journals* and the *Correspondence* and to manuscript materials, have disclosed what is for them, in degree if not in kind, a more arresting change—from an Emerson who championed illimitable individualism to an Emerson who endorsed indefinable universalism, from one who embodied ardent free will to one who embraced determinism, and from one who chanted the consummation of the single person to one whose preoccupation was the destiny of the race.

Change being a universal fact of nature, Emerson gauged the vitality of his mind by the degree to which it was not static. The truest state of mind rested in, he found, became false. At the same time, he was very much like nature in exhibiting the one in the many; no matter what the seeming newness of his variation, in a sense he was always singing the same old tune. He once said that all his teachings contained only the doctrine of the infinitude of the private man, which, so long as it was termed society or politics or the times, pleased people, but, if discussed as religion, caused them to chafe. What is interesting, then, in the later essays, along with signs of difference, is the evidence of thought unchanged.

Emerson never departed from his belief in the value of intuition, even though he took the pains to illustrate more clearly that what he had all along meant by individual growth, with instinct becoming opinion and finally, knowledge, "as the plant has root, bud, and fruit," was a consummation that could only be wrought by "a vigilance which brings the intellect in its greatness and best state to operate every moment" (W, II, 340). In later years, for example, when he lectured on character or power or wealth, although he made it clear that these were qualities that attached to the very self-reliant person he had from the start been prophesying, he also added that they were the fruit of discipline. Power is one's native endowment, his bias or bent or genius, what he has come by intuitively, but unless it is concentrated and developed through controlled exercise, it is wasted and brings its possessor to nothing.

One feature of the later Emerson is his larger attraction to oriental thought, an attraction which was, sooner or later, inevitable. The lad who at eight or nine sitting in church had found himself bewildered at the realization that the simplest words he had been silently repeating to himself—"black," "white," "door," or "tree"—no longer meant anything but were empty sounds, undistinguishable and only arbitrarily attachable to things external, was naturally the young man excited at Harvard by the discovery of Berkeleyan idealism and the mature poet of "Nature" in 1836 meditating on the elusive and symbolic character of the features of the landscape which embellished his days. He was naturally the Heraclitean believing in all things as flux and the Platonist treating with the phenomena of every day as provisional and promissory. He was, in short, a thinker to whom the illusory character of human experience came by right of birth. And, this being so, certain features of the thought of the Far East could not but deeply engage him.

Before he was twenty years old, already with his curiosity about "Hindu mythologies" stirred by a brief verse which urged the rejection of the world as a theater of unsubstantial shows in favor of the absorption of the soul in the one Being who was source of all perceptions, he could deplore his ignorance of the Eastern half of the globe and admit the possible rightness in the argument that "all the books of knowledge and all the wisdom of Europe twice told, lie hidden in the treasures of the Bramins & the volumes of Zoroaster" (L, I, 116-17). It was years before he made the acquaintance of those riches, but when he did, his way appropriately prepared by his beloved Neoplatonists, it was with such satisfaction that he returned to them, as to other favorite spiritual works, through the rest of his life. He did not read the *Bhagavad Gita* in its entirety until 1845, but in the decade of the 1850's, in which his explorations of Eastern religious wisdom were most intensive and his interest in German

thought declined, he began a separate journal, *The Orientalist*.
Thoreau's interest in orientalism spurred his own, and his in-
heriting of certain oriental volumes from the disbanded library
of the ill-fated community of Fruitlands added materially to his
means of extending his knowledge.

The age-old preoccupations of the oriental, with the hidden
unity of all Being as distinct from its seeming multiplicity, with
the transcendent reality of spiritual life as distinct from the
illusion of the life of the senses, with the inevitability of fate
governing all forms and modes of life, and with the transmigration of souls in relation to fate, appealed strongly to Emerson's
mind, and in the degree to which he accommodated such doctrines to his own beliefs, his thought could be said perhaps to
have become more universally appealing. No people, in his sight,
had surpassed the Hindus in the grandeur of their ethical statement. He has in turn been praised by Indian scholars for the
extent to which he harmonized "the modern spirit with the
noblest teachings of ancient times" (Car, 158). And the idea
of the absolute oneness of Being, according to some of them, has
nowhere been presented with more beauty, accuracy, or force
than in his poem "Brahma," which was a paraphrase of certain
sacred passages in Sanskrit (Car, 247).

> If the red slayer think he slays,
>   Or if the slain think he is slain,
> They know not well the subtle ways
>   I keep, and pass, and turn again.
>
> Far or forgot to me is near;
>   Shadow and sunlight are the same;
> The vanished gods to me appear;
>   And one to me are shame and fame.
>
> They reckon ill who leave me out;
>   When me they fly, I am the wings;
> I am the doubter and the doubt,
>   And I the hymn the Brahmin sings.
>
> The strong gods pine for my abode,
>   And pine in vain the sacred Seven;
> But thou, meek lover of the good!
>   Find me, and turn thy back on heaven.
>   (W, IX, 195)

From time to time in Emerson's later lectures and essays, notes of coarseness obtrude. It is not only that from the writing at its best—taut, straight, and vivid—a certain poetic exquisiteness or delicate felicity has disappeared; the rose, after all, cannot keep the lustrous down of its opening. It is that a degree of endorsement of society's standards has found its way into his mind. Concerned as strongly in 1860 and 1870 as in 1835 or 1845 over the failure of so many young men of promise to realize themselves in America, Emerson became more and more a spokesman for success. Not forsaking integrity and spiritual aspiration, he nevertheless strove to link those virtues to abilities and practices which made leaders in business, industry, and politics. His aim was still to "speak with the vulgar, think with the wise"; yet in effect he was frequently, as he had once described Walter Savage Landor to be, rather a man full of thoughts than of ideas.

A disconcerting, baffling portrait sometimes emerges from the later addresses, as though a subtle metamorphosis had taken place. The American Scholar, limned in various ways on diverse occasions years before, now seems, to one's astonishment, to want to appear in the joint identity of Tennyson's Sir Galahad and an antecedent of Theodore Roosevelt—a Goliath after he has been to elocution school and learned how to bear himself and how to talk.

I wish to see that Mirabeau who knows how to seize the heart-strings of the people and drive their hands and feet in the way he wishes them to go, to fill them with himself, to enchant men so that their will and purpose is in abeyance and they serve him with a million hands just as implicitly as his own members obey. (W, XII, 119)

Socrates, Plotinus, George Fox, and the wise mystics of the East—noble minds and spirits all—figure less in what is said, as if, holy unveilers and illuminators of life, they are less relevant. In the later years the idea of self-fulfillment, of individualistic consummation, has become the idea of success, and success means prevailing over others. In 1841 he had written:

real action is in silent moments. The epochs of our life are not in the visible facts of our choice of a calling, our marriage, our acquisition of an office, and the like, but in a silent thought by the wayside as we walk; in a thought which revises our entire manner of life. . . . (W, II, 161)

But now he reminds audiences that every man, on meeting a newcomer, sizes him up to ascertain the extent of his powers, just as every new bull, on being let into a pen, scrutinizes the ring of beasts facing him to see which of them can first be the object of challenge.

The way to conquer the foreign artisan is, not to kill him, but to beat his work. . . . The American workman who strikes ten blows with his hammer whilst the foreign workman only strikes one, is as really vanquishing that foreigner as if the blows were aimed at and told on his person. (W, VI, 225)

I do not wish you to surpass others in any narrow or professional or monkish way. We like the natural greatness of health and wild power. I confess that I am as much taken by it in boys, and sometimes in people not normal . . . even in persons open to the suspicion of irregular and immoral living. (W, VIII, 316)

Yet one must remember that all his life Emerson had been fascinated by power, in human beings as well as in nature. Although he sought, in spiritual as well as physical matters, to adjudicate the claims of the two kinds of power, temperate and eruptive, clement and aggressive, he often found it hard to keep within bounds his admiration for its more spectacular manifestations. In an early lecture on the genius of the English nation he had defined human power as "great activity of mind united with a strong will." Martin Luther had attracted him precisely because he had possessed both to an extreme degree, was in fact demonic, an "enraged Poet," providentially kept from insanity by his earthy, affectional nature, an achiever of "a spiritual revolution by spiritual means alone," yes, but of such militancy that he had shaken the bastions of tyranny to the very ends of the earth. And in spite of what he had said about love and the religious sentiment as the greatest principle—renewing man and hindering the degeneracy of the human race—Emerson was powerfully drawn to military conquerors, to Napoleon particularly, from whose works he quoted through the years more frequently than from Plato and almost as much as from Shakespeare. At the time of his lectures on biography Napoleon's image had loomed peremptorily in his mind as claimant for each of the first four attributes essential to greatness—

rightness of aim, sincerity, healthiness of mind, and strength of mind—so that before any other could be considered he had first to be disqualified with such a verdict as "Napoleon a very bully of the common" or "no intellectual action on others in any generous sense."

To throw this aspect of Emerson's thought into sharper relief in his later years, several circumstances had combined. Something of the cast of Carlyle's thought during the long epistolary friendship had perhaps rubbed off on him; the fact of struggle in the adaptation and survival of earthly organisms had been increasingly emphasized with the spread through the century of the dogma of biological evolution; and the Civil War had erupted as the violent, and seeming inevitable, means of ending slavery in the United States. It is not surprising that his mind became tinged with a degree of severity it had not known earlier. In his young manhood he had thought, so to speak, privately, having personal problems of vocation to resolve; in his full maturity, anguished by the spectacle of iniquity flourishing in the timorousness and corruption of government and by the engulfment of his nation in a cataclysm, he was caused to think publicly. What was important in the early days was that an individual come of age capable of making the right decisions about himself on grounds at once religious and natural; in the later, what was imperative was that there be many able to make the right decisions about the entire country and to cause the whole populace to adopt and act on them. In the early days, the ideal was the self-governing individual; in the later, often, the leader who could govern others. To exert influence on another was less important than to have power over him.

Similarly it can be said that there was a change in Emerson's thought about freedom and necessity, even though it is one of degree and tone rather than of kind. In 1860 and 1870 he does talk more than in 1845 of nations and races than of the single person, does emphasize more the destiny of the species than the salvation of the individual, and does remind his readers less frequently of the capacities of man as instrument than of the grandeur and might of the fate which uses him. But these duple features had characterized his view of life from the start, and it would be a gross error to state that in his early days, believing in a form of Christianity, he was an advocate of libertarian in-

dividualism, whereas in his old age, subscribing to the evolutionary doctrines of science, he became an apostle of stern causal
collectivism.

It was not at all difficult for Emerson to assimilate the ideas
of science in his time. God (or the Over-Soul) simply became
nature; His will became nature's tendency; and His plan became
nature's law. For Emerson, grown up in an atmosphere still
colored by Calvinism, the universe had always been ordered and
controlled, with man, the principal animal actor thus far, destined for an end unforeseeable but sublime and altogether beyond his power to affect. Man had always been endowed with
will, but one insignificant in relation to the might which created
and guided the universe; and paradoxically his proper will was
at its greatest only when it was coincident with the larger will.
Man achieved most, then, not when he was acting but being acted
through. His freedom—and therefore his happiness—consisted (as
it had consisted for centuries for orthodox Christians) in choosing to do what an overruling Necessity (He or It) had created
him to do. Freedom was the acceptance of voluntary service
required. In a verse fragment entitled "Insight" he once put it
characteristically:

> Power that by obedience grows,
> Knowledge which its source not knows,
> Wave which severs whom it bears
> From the things which he compares,
> Adding wings through things to range,
> To his own blood harsh and strange. (W, IX, 360)

It is true that the exuberant note of "Nature" of 1836—"Who
can set bounds to the possibilities of man?"—is not sounded in
1860 and that Emerson is not ardently singing the infinitude of
the private man, his power of being enlarged during ecstasy
into God Himself. In such a letter as the following, written in
1859, although not at all repudiating the idea that each man
can become better than he is, he seems to have settled for allegiance to the universal forces which shape masses of man, and in
this vision single persons are not distinguished:

I think, as we grow older, we decrease as individuals, and, as if in an
immense audience who hear stirring music, none essays to offer a new

stave, but we only join emphatically in the chorus. We volunteer no opinion, we despair of guiding people, but are confirmed in our perception that Nature is all right, and that we have a good understanding with it. We must shine to a few brothers, . . . not from greater absolute value, but from a more convenient nature. But 'tis almost   chemistry at last, though a meta-chemistry. (Ho 226-27)

Yet to the power of the metachemistry he had always subscribed. The joyful embracing of the sublime order was what all along he had been advocating for the fulfillment of man. In 1835 he had affirmed the rightness and goodness of the what is, one with what must be and what ought to be:

there is an inextinguishable conviction in the human mind that in the great Universe which bears us as its fruit and by which we are subdued and subordinated, the best is always done; the good of the whole is evolved, the discordant volitions of men are rounded in by a great and beautiful necessity, so as to fetch about results accordant with the whole of nature, peaceful as the deep heaven which envelopes . . . [man], and cheerful as the green fields on which the sun finds him. Over men the purposes of Providence are thrown like enormous nets enclosing masses without restraining individuals. (EL, I, 225)

Never had he counseled a course of conduct or described a benefit inconsistent with the attitude he had set himself as a youth to cultivate—"loving resignation." His men of the future, knowing clearly their relation to the cosmos, would constitute ". . . a majestic race,/Who, having more absorbed, more largely yield/And walk on earth as the sun walks in the sphere" (W, IX, 339).

CHAPTER 4

Emerson's Significance in His Day and His Relevancy to Our Own Age

THE importance of a thinker or man of letters in his own age can be shown in many ways: by adducing the extent of his fame and the number of distinctions he achieved; by revealing significant evidences of his influence on numbers of ordinary literate men and women; by showing the connection between his thought and that of distinguished predecessors; and by citing other thinkers or writers of stature among his contemporaries to whose ideas his own bear a relation or for which they are, in part at least, responsible. A great thinker, of course, can be either original or eclectic. If he is original, his ideas, no matter how distant from those generally accepted in his own time, must ultimately be seen to have such radical truth as to become recognized if not accepted by the best minds. The new in the case of the great cannot be the bizarre. If he is eclectic, his ideas must in their assemblage together make up a body of thought of dimension and of illuminating relevancy to the life currently lived around him. Eclecticism is not mediocrity or commonplaceness. Out of his fusion of materials from disparate sources, the eclectic thinker achieves an utterance which strikes with the force of the new. Emerson was great in the latter sense.

Emerson's fame during his lifetime, particular official evidences of which have been pointed out on an earlier page, was widespread. In addition to enjoying formal honors from institutions and organizations, he was the recipient of affectionate homage from many individuals of note, abroad as well as at home.

Theodore Parker, one of the earliest thinkers of stature in America to try to estimate the peculiar nature and value of his genius, in *The Massachusetts Quarterly Review* in 1850 saw Emerson unexampled in the extent of his influence in forming the opinions and character of young men and women, revealing always the "superiority of a man to the accidents of a man." He was at once the most American and the most cosmopolitan of native writers—deficient, yes, in logic and in the historical sense, not scholarly enough and too dependent on intuition—but, in the singular consistency of his imaginative vision and his life, a genius of the first order, such as the world rarely produces, and in some features of his idealism and his prose fit to rank with Milton. He had taken a position as thinker far ahead of his time. "Eminently a child of Christianity and of the American idea," he was yet "out of the church and out of the state."

Henry James, Sr., a Swedenborgian and long-time friend, in spite of his own preoccupation with the reality of sin and evil, which made him intellectually his opposite, admired Emerson's special potency. Of a mind and spirit extraordinarily universalized, Emerson was to him fascinating, always "full of living inspiration," for he was a "show-figure of almighty power in our nature": "he recognized no God outside of himself and his interlocutor, and recognized him only as the *liaison* between the two, taking care that all their intercourse should be holy with a holiness undreamed of before by man or angel" (Mat, 437-38).

Henry James, the novelist, for whom he was a unique American spirit in letters, loved to open Emerson for the same benefit he sought in Goethe, "the sense of moving in large intellectual space" and the frequent gushing from the rock "of the crystalline cupful, in wisdom and poetry" (Mat, 431). In his essay in *Partial Portraits,* although he regretted that in spite of his exquisite style Emerson had never found a form for his thought, he lauded his "genius for seeing character as a real and supreme thing;" "no one has had so steady and constant, and above all so natural, a vision of what we require and what we are capable of in the way of aspiration and independence" (HJ, 9).

Emerson's influence abroad has been notable and pervasive. In England from about the middle of the century onward he affected fine minds with the same beautifying, inspiriting, liberating force as gave meaning to life for seekers in his own country. The young Oxford poet Arthur Hugh Clough venerated him and, according to legend, upon Emerson's departure from the island in 1848, pleaded with him in the final moments to stay to lead his generation out of the desert in which Carlyle had left them. Clough later came over to the United States to make his home for several months near Emerson in Concord. Matthew Arnold, elated after his reading of a volume of the *Essays,* inscribed on its flyleaf in 1849 a sonnet commemorating the experience and the oracular voice of its writer; he wrote years later to Emerson to tell him of what importance the work had been in a crucial period of his manhood. And in a lecture tour of the United States in 1884, in spite of the fact that Emerson, in his opinion, was not a great poet or a great philosopher, he pronounced his *Essays* the most important body of work in prose of the century and described him as the friend to all who would live in the spirit. Carlyle through the years had proclaimed Emerson's special qualities, in public pronouncements as well as in private letters. He was especially struck by the elevation of thought of the early *Essays,* which was that of "a *Soliloquizer* on the eternal mountain tops only, in vast solitudes where men and their affairs lie all hushed in a very dim remoteness; and only *the man* and the stars and the earth are visible . . ." (W, III, 290, notes). Although they had no system, the *Essays* pointed far beyond any system. The scientific thinkers Thomas Huxley and John Tyndall paid tribute as well. And in the 1870's the distinguished philosophical and religious theorist Max Müller dedicated to him his *Science of Religion,* for his having been a constant refreshment of head and heart over twenty-five years.

In Paris, Emerson, discovered in the late 1830's, was figuring conspicuously by 1844 in lectures on philosophical thinkers in the Collège de France and was shortly afterward the subject of substantial essays in *La Revue Indépendante* and *La Revue des Deux Mondes.* Charles Baudelaire found him in the 1860's a needle-sharp spur to meditation, and Maurice Maeterlinck in 1920 hymned his sensitivity to the symphonic eloquence of silence and his evocation of wonder. Interest in France continues, with the publication only recently of a big volume examining the evolution of his thought about the individual and society.

In Germany shortly after the middle of the century Emerson seems to have been first devotedly read by Herman Grimm, son of one of the famous Brothers Grimm, and his friend Joseph Joachim, the celebrated violinist. Grimm, a professor of art history at the University of Berlin, especially prized Emerson's faculty for making every reader feel that he alone had been written for and his genius for transfiguring the present: "When I read your words the course of years and events appears to me like the rhythm of a beautiful poem, and even the most commonplace is dissolved into necessary beauty through your observation" (Cor, Gr, 51). Nietzsche also encountered Emerson with admiration—and with the feeling that they were brothers in thought. He deplored Emerson's lack of discipline and his repetitiveness but in 1863 listed him first among his most read authors and later classified him as the most pregnant of American thinkers, superior to Carlyle in England, and one of the four masterful prose writers of the century (see R, p. 502).

Few people in most eras undergo Pauline conversions, which reroute their lives from materialistic Damascus to spiritual Jerusalem, but many young men of undistinguished circumstance in America experienced the sudden illumination of the point of no return as they heard or read Emerson's words. In 1852 John Albee, a poor youth from a narrow New England Puritan community, one day in a bookstore accidentally coming across a volume by an author of whom he had never heard and opening it out of curiosity, after the first few pages was so agitated by *Representative Men* that he had to put it down. No longer the same being who had entered the shop, he had had a revelation for which, it seemed, without knowing it he had all along been waiting. It was "the message that made education possible," with talismanic power enabling him to read other books and without shaping it, wondrously laying a foundation for his life. A perhaps even more spectacular conversion occurred when another young man in the middle of the century, Moncure Conway of Virginia, as he lay in a field one afternoon, idly turning the pages of a magazine, happened by mere chance to cast his eye on a single sentence by Emerson; from that instant he dated the whole future course of his life.

These may have been the most dramatic cases of their kind, but both Albee and Conway, who sought out Emerson and later became close acquaintances, considered themselves representative. Speaking for the generation which came of age in the decade before the Civil War, Albee declared that its spiritual bondage was dissolved and its negations were turned into affirmations by Emerson's word preached from his "tabernacle by the Concord wayside."

Young men came from all parts of the world and those who could not come wrote! We who were nearer made frequent pilgrimages alone or in companies. He received us each and all with his unfailing suavity and deference. His manner toward young men was wonderfully flattering; it was a manner I know no word for but expectancy; as if the world-problem was now finally to be solved and we were the beardless Oedipuses for whom he had been faithfully waiting. (Albee, 56-57)

Emerson was to innumerable minds precisely the liberating force he had aspired to be. He had long believed that, in spite of the tyranny exercised for centuries by famous names in the domain of intellect (Aristotle and Saint Thomas—even Jesus—for example) and in spite of the propensity of mankind to deify individuals of singular intellectual attainment, the great mind was one whose works freed the persons who read them, lifting them to such elevation that they saw the limitations of his highest achievement and, excited by the sense of what human powers, fully exercised, might do in surpassing it, could go on to mine their own wealth. He did not want his own book to startle readers or impel them to seek him out and hug him; its influence ought to be quietly and affectionately pervasive, like the odor of a flower, leading them to self-respect and manful independence. He never laid down the law; he only proposed new law, always with the proviso that it be continually reexamined. At his best he was, as he said, an experimenter, living by a conviction that life was a series of approximations:

Do not set the least value on what I do, or the least discredit on what I do not, as if I pretended to settle any thing as true or false. I unsettle all things. No facts are to me sacred; none are profane; I simply experiment, an endless seeker with no Past at my back. (W, II, 318)

In his later years he compared younger men doing brilliant and important things to gymnasts performing feats of derring-do, of which he was incapable but which, in effect, he had earlier conceived and for which he had sketched the plans.

Yet famous as he became and revered as he was by many, he was also jeered at, when not feared and hated, by others. Albee says that those "who followed him suffered contempt from some, reproach and suspicion from nearly all." He was considered either an apostle of license or a mouther of flowery unintelligi-

bilities by older persons given to "plain talk" and no longer trust-
ful (if they ever had been) of the impulses on which Emerson
urged young idealists to rely. As late as 1868, according to Henry
James, Sr., "many half-witted people in church and state" still
thought that Emerson counseled "a dangerous degree of self-
conceit, and intellectual license generally, to callow youth"
(Letter, *The Republican*, Houghton 195). But Albee among his
acquaintance observed Emerson's effect to be only salutary.
Young males at the crisis stage, "surcharged with the exaggera-
tions of self-importance," in reading the *Essays* were brought
out of disorder to order, given a self-reliance which was not
egotism but a desire for a higher life.

As one sees Emerson in perspective against the American past,
what strikes with force is his relation to certain figures who had
enunciated or epitomized an idea since become a dominant
thread in the fabric of the American character, namely individualism. Andrew Jackson and Thomas Jefferson, for example,
earlier representatives of the idea, the one empirical and the
other philosophical, find in their descendant Ralph Waldo Emerson its culminating, idealizing embodiment.

Among the Greeks, of course, from the Hellenic period on,
individual achievements by athletes and artists as well as by
warriors and statesmen were celebrated, although not many
names of pugilists and track stars, painters, sculptors, and architects have come down to us. In the performing arts, although
poet-playwrights were distinguished by public laudation, their
actors, choreographers, and composers of music have not survived by name. Essentially the same situation seems to have
prevailed in ancient Rome. Individual performance of an exceptional kind was highly regarded in sport and in art, and anonymity was not the order of the day; yet no great pains were taken
to insure the passing on to posterity of the identity of the per-
formers. In the time of the Renaissance, however, painters,
composers, sculptors, and architects took pride in their work
and, departing radically from the practice of the centuries intervening between their time and that of the ancients, revealed
an intent as strong as that traditionally shown by writers to
perpetuate their names to future generations.

Yet in all of this there is nothing like the individualism to which we are accustomed. In the Italian Renaissance, true, it seems to have been possible for individuals of less than noble birth, by virtue of extraordinary aptitude and training, to rise to the top as painters or musicians (a situation by so much anticipating that of the early nineteenth-century revolutionary period, in which in disregard of birth, careers became for the first time opened to talents—*carrières ouvertes aux talents*), but it was a life of merciless competition in which, as such a work as Benvenuto Cellini's *Autobiography* makes clear, ascent on the part of a few was accomplished at the cost of descent in a great many. In a society which was wide open, the qualities necessary for spectacular rise were those of the exploiter-adventurer, not deterred by tender conscience from treading on creatures lesser in will and force as well as in skill when they stood in his way. Individualism among us, however, is not the freedom of exceptional beings to take whatever means can be found to develop to the utmost their special abilities so that they can glorify themselves to posterity. It is the belief that every individual, irrespective of his natural endowments, is important—to his state in its functioning as well as to his Maker—and has the right to develop as fully as he can his particular if nonspecial abilities, using means, however, which do not impinge upon the equal right of his neighbor so to do.

Certainly the view of the single human being taught by Jesus and early advanced by Christianity was of a kind ultimately to foster the growth of individualism. To the humblest man or woman, in the Creator's view of them, was attached an ineradicable significance. Jesus reminded his followers that inasmuch as they had done anything to the least of their brethren they had done it unto him; and in the Parable of the Shepherd, concerned over the state of the hundredth sheep outside the fold in which the other ninety-nine are safe, he showed beyond any doubt the preciousness of the single person. Yet through the Middle Ages, when, presumably, the influence of Christianity in Europe was at its height, individual men and women not nobly born, which is to say the mass of mankind, were valueless and often elicited less concern from their betters than the sheep they tended and slaughtered. It needed the improvement in material living conditions made possible by the rise of capitalistic cities in modern times, in which masses could live as persons of self-respect, to restore to the forefront of the religious consciousness the importance of the individual, which, then, building on the idea of the equality of all in the sight of God, eventually developed into the idea of the equality of all before the law.

The idea of individualism, as an idea consciously held and acted upon, seems not to be very old. Among American thinkers, for example, it meant little if anything to the distinguished metaphysician Jonathan Edwards. According to the Calvinist theology, given such belated but eloquent summary utterance by Edwards, the individual person was of no importance. A man and a woman were of value only insofar as they were instruments through which the will of God could be enacted. They were not separate persons with sharply differentiated abilities and aspirations, whose realization and fulfillment here on earth was a precious thing, the end of life. They were objects created by a creator to the end that through them he could cause his inscrutable sovereignty to be always manifest, his omnipotence to be ceaselessly operative. The sole relation which counted was between each man and the Creator; it was a relation which had been determined in advance by the Creator, and it was one of only two possible kinds: salvation or damnation. What identity— better, what meaning—a man or a woman had was solely in connection with the impersonal working out of the divine plan. In his own natural person every human being was worthless and fit only for destruction: "the natural state of the mind of man, is attended with a *propensity of nature,* which is prevalent and effectual, to . . . [sin]; and . . . therefore their nature is corrupt and depraved with a moral depravity that amounts to and implies their utter undoing" ("Christian Doctrine of Original Sin Defended").

With Benjamin Franklin, a contemporary of Edwards but a breather of the new as against the old intellectual atmosphere, one encounters explicit statements of the significance of single persons as single persons and of the rightness of their making as much as they can of their powers while they live. Franklin took pleasure in contemplating the effectuality of the life of the individual citizen, the earthly success he might achieve.

I have always thought that one man of tolerable abilities may work great changes, and accomplish great affairs among mankind, if he first forms a good plan, and, cutting off all amusements or other employ-ments that would divert his attention, makes the execution of that same plan his sole study and business. *(Autobiography)*

And for Franklin, as for other large-minded eighteenth-century rationalists, the important relation was not that between creature and creator but that between man and man. When the English religious reformer George Whitefield, invited to stay at his house on his next evangelizing mission to Philadelphia, replied that for Christ's sake he would be glad to accept, Franklin rejoined that the offer was not for Christ's sake but for his own. The relation between a man and his fellows needed to be developed with tact: "a benevolent man should allow a few faults in himself, to keep his friends in countenance." One's efforts should go into developing pleasurable ties with one's colleagues, not into avert-ing the displeasure of God. The great theist Edwards, heeding the biblical injunction that we be perfect even as our Father in heaven is perfect, had sought perfection, maintaining that to lie out of Christ—to tolerate, that is, any persistent form or quality of imperfection—was sin. Franklin counseled the deliberate culti-vation of a gentlemanly amount of imperfection, of the opinion that human nature found its opposite intolerable.

Franklin's pleasure in the unfolding of the potential of the individual becomes Jefferson's, but Jefferson related the unfolding more fully and systematically to his ideas for the organization and growth of life in the states of the new nation. It is true that the individual must be informed and sturdy simply if the repre-sentative government which depends upon him is to endure. But the individual exists before the government, and it is solely for the betterment of his condition that the government is formed. In Calvinism the single person was made only for the scheme of the deity. In Jeffersonianism the scheme of government is in-vented only for the single person. "The equal rights of man, and the happiness of every individual, are now acknowledged to be the only legitimate objects of government" (to A. Coray, 1823). The end of government is to enable man to achieve earthly happiness in a state of liberty—as much liberty as the fact of his coexistence with many other single persons in society will allow. In this land men live as individuals; in the Old World they survive as anonymities in masses.

Before the establishment of the American States, nothing was known to history but the man of the old world, crowded within limits either small or overcharged, and steeped in the vices which that situation generates. . . . Here everyone may have land to labor for himself, if he chooses; or, preferring the exercise of any other industry, may exact for it such compensation as not only to afford a comfortable subsistence, but wherewith to provide for a cessation from labor in old age. Every one, by his property or by his satisfactory situation, is interested in the support of law and order. And such men may safely and advantageously reserve to themselves a wholesome control over their public affairs, and a degree of freedom which, in the hands of the canaille of the cities of Europe, would be instantly perverted to the demolition and destruction of everything public and private. (Letter to Adams, 1813)

This ideal, inherited by him, Emerson subscribed to. Emerson's Man Thinking is Jefferson's virtuous citizen, originally a tiller of the soil although now not necessarily so, living frugally, removed from the rabble of big-city slums, educated to an acquaintance with literature and history, sturdily thinking for himself and making up his own mind on vexatious issues. In his religion there is neither bigotry nor superstition; in his patriotism, no zealotry. He is Jefferson's virtuous citizen, but he is that citizen spiritualized. He has his progenitor's enlightened brain and his stock of knowledge, but he adds intuition to intellection and his mystical identification of himself with the eternal in nature enables him to comprehend as well as to understand. He is inspired by the vision of the whole as more than the sum of its ostensible parts.

Knowing the delusiveness of action for action's sake and the error of holding one man equal to another simply because he has the same shape and organs and fills the same amount of space, Emerson could not rest easily with the incarnation of the Jacksonian individual. A man was indeed "a man for a' that and a' that," but the satisfaction of his creaturely needs was only an elementary thing, simply putting him in a position where he could begin to become a human being. Emerson followed Jefferson in believing the value of democracy to be in its production of a true aristocracy, in its being a way of life, that is, which allowed single persons, developing their powers, to become veritable *aristoi*. "The aim of aristocracy is to secure the ends of good sense and beauty without vulgarity or deformity of any kind" (J, VI, 93). But, to repeat, he went beyond Jefferson in maintaining that individuals, who were the veritable *aristoi*, would result only if their powers included the spiritual and their rationality was illuminated by suprarationality. For Emerson, although he never allowed himself the gently self-depreciating irony of Franklin in talking about it, the cultivation of right relations between benevolent individuals was indispensable to the fruition of the nation, but he restored as a *sine qua non* to that cultivation the establishment of a relation between the human being and the divine. Nor could he have advocated, like Franklin, the purposeful nurturing of a degree of imperfection. He was, although without their sternness and abnegation, as much a pursuer of perfection as any of the Puritan divines. He could not remain content with a life only occasionally lit by lightning flashes but sought to show how it could be led under the full splendor of the sun. He thus embraced in this regard both the position of a Franklin or a Jefferson and that of an Edwards; he fused the benefits of the seventeenth-century theistic and the eighteenth-century rationalistic points of view. His divine power, however, was not the same as that of Edwards.

Described in somewhat different terms, Emerson's journey in this whole connection can be seen to have been not unlike that of Socrates. Socrates, in the midst of a society which subscribed to a particular type of revelation relating to a hierarchy of Olympian gods, had begun his thinking life not subscribing to polytheistic religion but to investigative science, hoping that in rational inquiry into nature he would discover truth. Disillusioned by that path as a dead-end street, however, he rejected natural, for pure, philosophy. In this, turning the mind in upon itself and its own conceptions rather than outward upon phenomena, he was convinced that he could make discoveries of principles to enlighten man about his own nature and destiny. Not abjuring rational activity, he was readmitting revelation to the life of his mind, although of a different stamp from that of his fellow Athenians who were polytheists. "The Apology," "The Crito," and "The Phaedo" among the dialogues bear testimony to the special brand of that revelation.

Similarly, although born into a New England society largely distinguished by belief in revelation inseparable from biblical myth and from a God still anthropomorphic, Emerson was early a subscriber to another faith, more advanced and more credible because more largely justifying itself with human reason, through which it squared itself with the facts of life and of the natural universe. Yet its rationalistic nature ultimately proving bleak and incapable of satisfying his deepest spiritual need, Emerson developed his own faith, which, without forswearing rational inquiry, was based on the primacy of intuition and was distinguished by its restoration of the experience of revelation. It was a revelation, however, internal rather than external, mystical not prescriptive, peculiar to each individual worshiper and not codified by system for all.

In Emerson's times, which were those of an expanding frontier and of an aggressive sense of nationality, expressing itself in the slogan "Manifest Destiny," lawless persons in newer sections of the land took advantage of the idea of individualism in the air, of individualism as something indefinably "American," to live anarchically, preying upon docile, convention-abiding citizens. They were rampant exploiters, sometimes downright ruffians, for whom feuds, vigilantism, or horseback-raid thuggery were assertions of their "inalienable right" to trample on the rights of others. In older states, as the century wore on, other exploiters equally predatory or exploitative although not visibly so, amassed colossal fortunes, shaping monopolistic empires for themselves in the fur trade or railroads or banking or oil or steel, their deeds often justified by their admirers with an appeal to the Darwinian "law," wrongly construed, that in nature only the fittest survived. To all manifestations of the doctrine that might made right, Emerson's individualism was intransigently opposed. His ideas of the importance of the individual were a counteragent to all the crassly if not fiercely materialistic motives in the air, deriving from the truculence of a young nation suddenly aware of its muscle and of the might of the incalculable riches of its soil to supplement it. Whatever put individual apart from individual, staunchly independent yet sensitive and sympathetic, enabling each to become fully an individual and to fill his head rather than his pocket, he was for. Whatever pitted individual against individual, sowing exclusion and money pride, he was against.

The statement that from a political point of view Emerson-ianism was spiritualized Jeffersonianism is not unrelated to a description of what from a theological point of view Emerson is seen to have achieved. His sermons, although the fruit of a young man in his late twenties, standing midway between the rationalist Unitarianism of the eighteenth century and the sepa-rationist intuitionism of the nineteenth, were said by their first editor (1938), a member of the faculty of the Chicago Theolog-ical School, with their rudimentary doctrine of divine immanence to have "ushered in a new era in the history of religious thinking in this country" (YES, xxviii). And in a similar vein, although with larger scope, one of his first biographers in an admirably comprehensive and beautifully written volume, summing up the whole of his thought, essentially religious no matter what the subject it was addressing, declared (1907) that Emerson's arrival on the scene occurred at the moment when it was inevitable that theology give way to philosophy as the substance of a modern religious view and a mythological explanation of things be re-placed by one metaphysical, in which the universe could be "contemplated not as being in the order of time, of history, but in the present . . . an eternal NOW." "This step out of the past into the present, out of theology . . . into metaphysics was taken by Emerson. He is the sole important representative of this stage in American literature; that is his true significance. He was the in-carnator of the moment of change . . ." (Wo, 62).

The philosopher John Dewey, on the occasion of the centenary celebration, praised Emerson for having demonstrated, as no other thinker had, "the identity of Being, unqualified and im-mutable, with Character." In this respect he had been par excel-lence the philosopher of democracy, who, even if he could be shown to have had no system, would at the last be seen to have laid the foundations for the only set of beliefs that could become one fit for democracy. In his conviction that "perception was more potent than reasoning; the deliverances of intercourse more to be desired than the chains of discourse," and in his enlarge-ment of philosophic activity beyond the restricted bounds of an exclusive, aristocratic class, maintaining always that the value of ideas, no matter how transcendent, was not in their attachment to "an overweening Beyond and Away" but in their relation to an urgent here and now, Emerson had done more than any other thinker to point the way to the only kind of democracy worth achieving—spiritual democracy (D, 68-77). In this appraisal Dewey struck the theme sounded a half century earlier by Theodore Parker. Emerson indeed believed in democracy as spiritual democracy. He fused the best of the democratic ideal enunciated by the Founding Fathers (the right to life, liberty, and the pursuit of happiness) with the essence of Christianity ("Whoso would save his soul must lose it" and "Thy kingdom come on earth as it is in Heaven") as well as with the finest strands of Platonic intellectuality.

But in embodying as he did each of these things, Emerson had made himself an anomaly. Believing that Jesus Christ was not, in the ancient doctrinal sense, of the same substance as God the Father, he was technically a heretic, an Arian, for whom there could be no membership in the Christian congregation. Believing furthermore that each individual worshiper could emulate Jesus and absorb God directly without a mediator, he was in the most immediate practical sense a radical deviant. In his valuation of nature he was also heretical. Traditionally, Christianity, along with this life in the flesh as opposed to the afterlife in the spirit, had disvalued nature. Indeed for centuries, teaching that it was the domain of Satan and his powers, to whom it had been turned over by God as contemptible spoils of war, so to speak, after Satan's triumph over Adam and Eve, the Church had forbidden the investigation of nature and sought to prevent the development of what we know as science. During the Renaissance it had tried to stamp out promulgators of new natural law, through its persecution of such figures as Giordano Bruno and Galileo. No wonder that Faust, in order to penetrate to the operation of forces underlying natural objects, had to make a pact with the powers of darkness; science was, in effect, necromancy. This is not to say that Emerson, or any of the other Romantic thinkers who viewed nature more or less as he did, deified nature. They did not say that the leaf was God; they said that in the leaf—inherent in it, underlying it—God was. As for patriotic allegiance, or membership in the national community— although his devotion to America was as strong as that of Paine and Jefferson, for whom it was the "asylum for mankind" and a "beacon to the world"—Emerson's idea that patriotism was something international rather than national and his advocacy that, until states became moral, good men not obey the laws too well, disqualified him from being numbered among those who belonged. This is the meaning of Theodore Parker's astute judgment, that although he was both Christian and democrat he was outside both the church and the state. Like him today in this respect is the Italian writer Ignazio Silone, self-styled Christian without church and Socialist without party.

Emerson came on the stage at a time when, because of severe strains imposed on the nation by its rapid growth—a rampant materialism, a nationalist arrogance, and a vicious racial belligerency—sensitive spirits needed precisely the restorative of the vision which only he could offer. What kept them from inner death was his ideal of a country beautiful and vigorous because it was healthy and whole. And it was healthy and whole because its citizens were healthy and whole. Indeed it was the wholeness, the oneness of life which he was most intent on opening people's eyes to—whole and one because the source of inspiration for transmuting the quality of daily life was one, divine and inexhaustible, yet accessible to all alike. He not only democratized religion; he "religionized" democracy.

For us, mistakenly, religion is a branch of study, like history, mathematics, or sociology, or it is a department of life, along with politics, education, manufacturing, or recreation. It is a thing in itself, compartmentalized, distinct from other things which make up the classification of the features of our existence. Accordingly, one day of the week is separated for it out of seven, whose effects are supposed to extend themselves over the other six. We insist, rightly, on separating church and state, church and school, but what really happens is that we divorce religion from government and religion from education.

Religion is not piety, nor is it whisper-hush church awe. Religion is a creative quality of being; it underlies every deed we do, every occupation we enter. It should infuse every particular of our lives every day. The bread a housewife bakes will be better bread if in her baking of it she is religious; the act of planting a field will be better if religiously entered into; so will the act of teaching a class, painting a picture, writing a book— even the act of sexual intercourse. All of which is to say that there is a single source of inspiration for the improvement of all that we aspire to—in thought, imaginative vision, or deed. The illumination of the painter's mind, of the composer's mind, of the author's mind, of the architect's or horticulturist's or carpenter's or housewife's, is the same illumination as that of the priest. This is the meaning of Emerson's "One accent of the Holy Ghost/This heedless world hath never lost." The painter does not paint a better picture on Wednesday because he went to a "holy" edifice on Sunday and in a service there acquired something called "spirituality," which, added to his native powers, will enhance the quality of every effort he chooses to make through the rest of the week, as the perfume a woman adds in the afternoon will enhance the attractiveness of her person through an entire evening. He paints a better picture because he is more immersed in his subject, more concentrated in aim and determined in will. This combination of immersion, concentration, and determination, according to its thoroughness, we call inspiration. It is a heightening and intensification of intellectual and imaginative power, and it has the same origin as the lofty, self-effacing charity of a Saint Francis. The church has no monopoly on illumination—no more claim on it, in fact, than the courthouse, assembly hall, studio, or household kitchen. In our pursuit of the true and the beautiful, no matter on how humble a scale, we have as much access to the fount of the ideal and the perfect, as in our pursuit of the good. It is no wonder that Emerson wrote as he did, under the title, "The Informing Spirit":

> There is no great and no small
> To the Soul that maketh all:
> And where it cometh, all things are;
> And it cometh everywhere.
>
> I am owner of the sphere,
> Of the seven stars and the solar year,
> Of Caesar's hand, and Plato's brain,
> Of Lord Christ's heart, and Shakespeare's strain. (W, IX, 282)

In simple terms religion consists in realizing the pricelessness of each moment and in living it fully—with joy when we can and with intensity when that is impossible. To do so requires a

certain abandonment, a giving of oneself to the experience at
hand, which cannot take place unless one has trust or faith that
it is worth giving oneself to—in broader terms, that life itself,
of which the experience is an infinitesimal part, is good and
justifies such a continued surrender. We must shed our self-
consciousness along with our apprehension of society. To respond
with complete response is to be like Jesus' lilies of the field. It
is devotion, for devotion does not mean devoutness but self-
giving. Yet we take so much thought of the morrow that we never
enjoy today.

A contemporary word for such devotion is commitment or
engagement. We need to commit ourselves to life, to engage ourselves in it. Any of the commonest acts we are called on to perform, or undertake voluntarily, or find ourselves by accident
doing, contain elements that make them immemorial. We ourselves are only temporary participants but the movements and
the rhythms they generate, and the desires, the needs, the aspirations they bespeak are timeless. The bodily attitude now of the
woman washing clothes or washing dishes or sweeping the floor
is what it was three thousand years ago and what it will be three
thousand years from now, and her hands and arms are used in
the same way. The impulse toward order and the love of clean-
liness by which she is actuated have inhabited the minds of
millions of women before her time and will lead millions after
her to execute the same gestures in their work at once homely
utilitarian and beautiful. Similarly the violinist practicing his
scales, the father giving his child its first lesson in reading, the
athlete practicing his hurdle-jumping, the young girl making
her first dress, the politician making his speech to his constituency
or casting his vote in the assembly—all are actors in scenes which
perpetually commemorate impulses imperishable in mankind.
Each person hospitably gives them residence during his brief
life, but he does not originate them nor with his death does he
extinguish them. They have an indestructible life of their own.
The urge to grow, to enjoy well-being and rhythmical activity,
to learn and know truth, to execute with mind or body cleanly
and well, to create things of beauty, to feel harmony and kinship with one's fellows—such things are divine and must characterize the all-embracing divine that it has been the custom to
call God. They manifest themselves instant after instant in form

after form, and insofar as we give ourselves to them we are living in eternity. Eternity is participation in the endless present. This is what Emerson exulted in as miracle and never tired of revealing to his readers:

In how many churches, by how many prophets, tell me, is man made sensible that he is an infinite Soul; that the earth and heavens are passing into his mind; that he is drinking forever the soul of God? (W, I, 136)

And this is what Reinhold Niebuhr today seeks to reveal:

Eternity . . . is not a separate order of existence. The eternal is the ground and source of the temporal. The divine consciousness gives meaning to the mere succession of natural events by comprehending them simultaneously, even as human consciousness gives meaning to segments of natural sequence by comprehending them simultaneously in memory and foresight. (RN, 299)

A contemporary student chaplain on a large university campus expresses himself in terms essentially Emersonian:

The [church] edifice symbolizes all that's wrong with religion: the idea of God in his place. God in a box locked up in archaic language and serving archaic people. I don't think religion . . . is symbolized by this. Instead, I see it as a cup of coffee and doughnut crumbs left in the student center where one of us has been talking to one of you. (PAL 5/16/67, 4)

For many, Emerson is great because he was a singular combination of the practical and the speculative, the homely and the ethereal. This duality was early recognized and cited, most aptly perhaps by James Russell Lowell, who depicted him in now famous lines as a singular composite of a Greek head on Yankee shoulders. He was simultaneously as attentive to the worldly as to the otherworldly—intent always, however, on making the one approximate as closely as possible to the other— the real object to the invisible ideal after which it was drawn. He amphibiously occupied two worlds, earthly and supraearthly, but strove to translate the first into the second. He was not a dualist accepting the irreconcilability of opposites, affirming

sadly that East was East and West was West and never the
twain should meet. For him, East and West were indeed separate
but each, so to speak, would be more beautiful when the two
had met and become one. Oliver Wendell Holmes, emphasizing
at bottom the same duality of character, later praised Emerson's
phrase about hitching one's wagon to a star as his most characteristic figure. A wagon was a good thing, solid and useful;
but, hitched only to a horse, mean.

A perhaps more arresting manifestation of his duality is in
the fact that Emerson at once accepted his country and rejected
it. He loved the principles on which it was founded but hated
the desecration of those principles by the shoddy practices of its
daily life. Unlike such a contemptuous reactionary aristocrat as
Poe, for whom democracy was an "admirable form of government—for dogs," he revered the ideal to which the nation was
pledged. He was the first great affirmer-denier among American
poets, the first given at once to hymning the potentialities of
America and decrying its performances which betrayed them.
There is nothing in Longfellow, his more illustrious contemporary
versifier, for instance, to compare with his

> But who is he that prates
> Of the culture of mankind,
> Of better arts and life?
> Go, blindworm, go,
> Behold the famous States
> Harrying Mexico
> With rifle and knife! (W, IX, 76)

> United States! the ages plead,—
> Present and Past in under-song,—
> Go put your creed into your deed,
> Nor speak with double tongue. (W, IX, 199)

Nor is there in William Cullen Bryant nor in any of his predecessors. Whittier alone among his contemporaries matches him
in this vein.

One distinguishing characteristic of American literature is its
nearness through the generations to the pulse of national life.
The founding of the American nation occurred late enough in
human history that the founders felt obliged to set down the

convictions on which they were acting and to broadcast them to the world: "When . . . it becomes necessary for one people to dissolve the political bands which have connected them with another, . . . a decent respect to the opinions of mankind requires that they should declare the causes which impel them to the separation." The founding, moreover, occurred near enough to us in time that even today, less than two hundred years after the event, writers and artists continue to work, conscious of those actuating principles and, one is tempted to say, with an instinct from month to month to assess, watchdoglike, the extent to which they have been fulfilled. It was Emerson who first planted such a theme—national character and national destiny— as a preoccupation in the artistic mind of America: "We do not with sufficient plainness or sufficient profoundness address ourselves to life, nor dare we chaunt our own times and social circumstance. If we filled the day with bravery, we should not shrink from celebrating it" (W, III, 37).

A Sinclair Lewis, in 1920, hardly more than a generation after Emerson's death, in exposing the blighting effect of standardized mediocrity on the American conscience and American sensibilities—"dullness made God"—deplored the waste of his countrymen's value in sarcastic terms strongly Emersonian: "A savorless people, gulping tasteless food, and sitting afterward, coatless, and thoughtless, in rocking-chairs prickly with inane decorations, listening to mechanical music, saying mechanical things about the excellence of Ford automobiles, and viewing themselves as the greatest race in the world" *(Main Street)*. William Faulkner, wrestling anguishedly with the issue of slavery as an evil which had blackened and poisoned the national soil, showed no less deep-rooted a devotion than Emerson's to the originally envisioned America.

He . . . looked about for one last time, for one time more since He had created them, upon this land this South for which He had done so much with woods for game and streams for fish and deep rich soil for seed . . . and saw no hope anywhere and looked beyond it where hope should have been, where to East North and West lay illimitable that whole hopeful continent dedicated as a refuge and sanctuary of liberty and freedom from what you called the world's worthless evening. . . . ("The Bear")

Ernest Hemingway in 1938, although not like Emerson in his language, revealed the depth of his attachment to the American ideal in setting down his bitterness over the failure to realize it.

Our people went to America because that was the place to go then. It had been a good country, and we had made a bloody mess of it and I would go, now, somewhere else as we had always had the right to go somewhere else and as we had always gone. You could always come back. Let the others come to America who did not know that they had come too late. (*The Green Hills of Africa*)

There is nothing comparable to this in the literatures of, say, England and France, although each has its characteristic, distinguishing features. England, to be sure, can show a Shakespeare, who glorified Henry the Fifth as the star of England; a Milton, who wrote triumphantly, before his disillusionment, of the English as the people through whom God preferred to reveal His truth to mankind and therefore through whose Puritan Revolution the millennium would come to pass on earth; and a Wordsworth, who, inspired by hatred of Napoleon, boasted that the English were born of earth's first blood and had titles manifold. But there is no thread of preoccupation with a national destiny running through English poetry comparable, say, to the thread of nature lyricism which sets it off from French poetry. Shakespeare was not, after all, a sixteenth-century Eugene O'Neill; Milton in *Paradise Lost* was not writing an English "Song of Myself"; and Wordsworth was not a nineteenth-century Robert Frost.

In Emerson, then, a tradition of idealistic affirmation-dissent had its inception. Hardly a day passes but that a new evidence of the power of the national ideal over the creative conscience of the contemporary artist is revealed. A reviewer upon the appearance of the first volume in eighteen years from the pen of our most distinguished man of letters, Thornton Wilder, finds it flawed by its author's zeal to depict his central characters as American—authentically, compellingly, consummatingly American. Another critic, reviewing a retrospective exhibition of paintings by one of the most perturbed spirits among native creators of canvases of the last fifty years, Jackson Pollock, observes that in the very strength and originality of the works which gained him his reputation lies his deficiency—excessive strain; the strength and originality are too strong and too original, betraying only a consuming desire to be different at any cost, to paint as no one before had ever painted, to paint as only an American could paint.

Emerson's relation to the thought of his own period can be evidenced in parallels between his ideas and similar ideas of certain artist-contemporaries in America and in explicit signs in the work of other writers of his influence on them. In the first instance, we see him simply to be representative of certain views which were held in common by a number of minds; in the second, we find him to be germinal.

The ideas of Romanticism being widespread, all men breathed the atmosphere they colored. Mark Twain had breathed it fertilizingly. In his waking, tough-talking, workaday hours, he was a realist, prone to disparage man's efforts in ways that ranged from bitter determinism to sardonic, not altogether unsympathetic, caricature. His off-the-job self, however, was a dreamer and idealist. Huckleberry Finn, perhaps his supreme creation, is really an Emersonian hero. Huck says no to the seedy society in conspiracy against his manhood and shows that spiritual self-reliance can flower in the Mississippi world of rattlesnakes and shotgun feuders as well as in the pine woods and huckleberry-covered fields of New England. The "Whim" written by Emerson on the door of his study when he would flee to escape from the claims of his household, finding it, however, in the woods to be more than "Whim," was precisely what actuated Huck. In his youth, Emerson said in "Self-Reliance," he reached a point where he could not go on "with the dear old doctrines of the church" and remonstrated with a valued spiritual adviser importuning him with them. He would have nothing to do with sacred traditions but seek to "live wholly from within." "But these impulses may be from below, not from above," he was told. He replied, "They do not seem to me to be such; but if I am the Devil's child, I will live then from the Devil" (W, II, 50).

This, we can see, is the same decision made by Huck in his crisis over turning in Jim, when he tears up the letter he has already written to Miss Watson and, setting his teeth, ejaculates, "All right then, I'll go to hell." It is these same impulses which have awakened his sense of human solidarity and brought him to a love of Jim, so that the Negro is for him what a friend was to Emerson, a person to whom by all spiritual affinity he was bought and sold and for whom he would go to prison if need be. And these impulses were nourished and matured by Huck's blissful, reverential giving of himself to nature—to the enveloping maternal vastness of the starlit night over the river as well as to the delicious mist-tinted beauty of morning. He let himself (in Emerson's phrases) "lie in the lap of immense intelligence," which made him a receiver of "its trust and [organ] of its activity." This was the kindly Over-Soul, and it was precisely because under its power the axis of his vision became coincident with the axis of things that he attained to brotherhood. Open as he was to its humanizing influences, he was in religious communion; and that he was never conscious of his worship only underscores Emerson's point that its operation was suprarational and its best effects involuntary. Whether he ever realized it or not, Twain had written a very Transcendental book.

As a novelist, whether or not he personally believed in the Over-Soul or compensation or fate or circles, Henry James thought transcendentally insofar as the protagonists of his great works were individuals of fine intellect and active conscience for whom the ideas they entertained of those they loved were more important than their persons. James himself was as Platonist as Emerson; the only true human beings were those who were good, and for the same reason they alone were beautiful. At the age of twenty-three Emerson had imaginatively stated in his *Journal* that his real friends seemed to be "not men, but certain phantoms clothed in the form and face and apparel of men by whom they were suggested and to whom they bear a resemblance" (J, II, 96). To James no less than to Emerson friendships were precious, and the intellectual atmosphere created by a contemplation of the singular qualities of a loved one was heavenly. The protracted, wonderfully spun, and exquisitely tenuous analyses to which his characters subject their relationships reveal that to them as to their creator the essential life is that of the mind. Beautiful manners begotten of beautiful intelligences, transmuting brief encounters into moments of revelation, for James as for Emerson made heaven on earth; and men and women must approach one another with the devotion and awe of a hierophant approaching his altar in order not to desecrate the quality of their moments together. A spoken word, a glance, a tone of voice could be at any instant a celestial evocation, and so, in the very late James novels, what is spoken is usually much less important than what is not. The extreme attraction to his mind of psychological reasons, "adorably pictorial," resulted in his making the stuff of his novels of the most delicate and elusive of mental phenomena—velleity, suggestion, surmise, allusion, intimation, intuition. For neither him nor Emerson was experience ever limited or ever complete; it remained "the very atmosphere of the mind," pregnant with pulsations of infinity.

Among Emerson's contemporaries who achieved fame as writers in the middle of the century and on whom his impact directly was of consequence, the three most important were Thoreau, Whitman, and Melville.

Emerson and Thoreau were at once too much and too little kindred spirits. Influence worked reciprocally between them. But what Emerson learned of Thoreau was mostly of a personal, not an intellectual kind; his mind was made up, his outlook on life formed, before they ever met. His acquaintance with figures of oriental thought was certainly enlarged as a result of the friendship, but there is no idea in *Walden*, for example, which he had not already thought or was not perfectly able to think on his own. And while it may be true, as the scholar-editor of a popular anthology of Transcendentalist pieces a few years ago maintained, in an effort to bring Emerson down a notch for what he considered his smug high priestliness and his injustice to Thoreau, that in spite of his greater reputation at the time, the one real masterpiece of Transcendental literature has turned out to be the work of Thoreau, it is also true that without the *Essays*, or the man who had written the *Essays*, a *Walden* is utterly unthinkable. This is as true for its style as for its content. Whatever it was in Emerson that affected Thoreau's manner of walking, talking, and gesturing in such a way as to cause various persons to discredit him for imitating Emerson, it left its mark also in the way he used his pen. There are, it is true, passages in *Walden* that are sharper, tangier, cockier than they would have been had Emerson written them, but this is a difference of degree, not of kind; and at the same time there are innumerable passages which in their peculiar point of view, acuteness of thought, turn of phrase, and "flavor" could have been written by either.

Whitman had no hesitation at all in admitting his debt to Emerson. "I simmered, simmered. Emerson brought me to a boil." And later in "Specimen Days" he appraised Emersonianism accurately and generously, saying that its greatest virtue was in breeding "the giant that destroys itself," leaving a young man unable to worship or believe in anything but himself. And so in his astounding *Leaves of Grass*—in that part of it later named "Song of Myself"—Whitman revealed, as his "Master" never could, the very "infinitude of the private man" which it was the "Master's" lifelong aim to teach. Almost everywhere in the poem (as in the famous Preface accompanying its first edition), one sees ideas drawn from Emerson but treated in un-Emersonian fashion. Just as Theodore Parker had said in founding the *Massachusetts Quarterly Review* in 1847, that it would be "The Dial with a beard," so one could say about the "Song of Myself," that it was the man of self-reliance with sex.

The whole idea of "Song of Myself" as a "transcendent poem" would have been impossible without the Transcendentalists and without Emerson as the exemplar of their peculiar spiritual exaltation. The new poem was utterly different from all epics that had preceded it, though in some traits it paid its respects to their pattern. It was transcendent in that it rose above localized place and sought, with terrific and giddying sweep, to encompass the physical and spiritual life of the entire nation—more, to survey the evolutional activity of the whole globe, the illimitable cosmos. Where the coverage of the nation was concerned, Whitman was obviously aiming to show himself the bard whose imminent advent Emerson in his essay "The Poet," had predicted— the "genius in America, with tyrannous eye, which knew the value of our incomparable materials." The poem was transcendent in another sense, for the narrator of the poem, the "I," was not an individual but every individual—a myriad of individuals, mankind itself. In this respect, in the identification at once protean and Christlike with all men and women from the moment when human life first arose, Whitman derived from, but had gone beyond, the infinitude of Emerson, whose perfectly self-reliant man was unselfish, his private will disappeared in its dilation into the universal soul. It was Emerson who looked for such magnitude of mind in persons that when in conversation they said, " I think" or "I feel" or "I hope" one knew it was the universe thinking or feeling or hoping, so much was their loftily public ego always distinct from their biographical ego, which spoke only in such statements as "I had breakfast late this morning" or "I knew the flower bed was on the other side of the house." And finally the poem was transcendent in that the experience of mystical revelation which was its substance, simultaneously befalling the reader and the narrator, it was altogether beyond the power of the poet to describe. This being so, the end was not really an end at all but a beginning—a launching of all readers, men and women, into the adventure of infinity still to unfold. The experience of the poem was a becoming, an endless progression. For years Emerson had been hymning rapturously the propensity of life ceaselessly, prodigally to evolve in new forms, defining it not as achievement but as tendency.

We give to this generalization the name of Being, and thereby confess that we have arrived as far as we can go. Suffice it for the joy of the universe that we have not arrived at a wall, but at interminable oceans. Our life seems not present so much as prospective; not for the affairs on which it is wasted, but as a hint of this vast-flowing vigor. (W, III, 73)

As the bard chanting "Song of Myself" can only open vistas for us, to show us the way we should go to fulfillment, so Emerson had repeatedly said that the effects of art could not surpass the lifting of the veil and the pointing of the finger to what lay beyond.

When I converse with a profound mind . . . I do not at once arrive at satisfactions, as when, being thirsty, I drink water . . . no! but I am at first apprised of my vicinity to a new and excellent region of life. By persisting to read or to think, this region gives further sign of itself, as it were in flashes of light, in sudden discoveries of its profound beauty and repose. . . . But every insight from this realm of thoughts is felt as initial, and promises a sequel. (W, III, 71)

That impact can be creative in either an affirmative or a negative sense is illustrated by the old definition of a pessimist as a person just come from talking with an optimist. Emerson was a

sayer of no to many temporal things but to the eternal cosmic
order a sayer of yes. Whitman in his reading of the Concord
essayist found his own affirmative disposition enlarged and invigorated. Herman Melville, however, disinclined to flatter the
universe with any sign of assent, was repelled by Emerson's
happy, sometimes rhapsodic, subscription to its rightness and his
celebration of the infinitude of the private man. Although ready
at one time to defend Emerson as "more than a brilliant fellow,"
at another in *Pierre,* he dismissed him as a preposterous Muggle-
tonian with Greek and German Neoplatonic originals. He did
not propose to let himself be hanged in a halter of Transcendental
rainbows and praised instead the reading of life by Hawthorne,
which, like Shakespeare's, was truer because it was blacker.
Hawthorne, he said, knew how to say "No in thunder" to the
slings and arrows of outrageous fortune.

In his own right Melville went on to create the supremely
no-saying figure of American prose fiction in Captain Ahab, the
monomaniacal protagonist of his great *Moby Dick.* In titanic
luster hurling his harpoon at his monster enemy or intransigently
defying the universe with his "in the midst of the personified
impersonal, a personality stands here," Ahab can be seen as
a portrait to illustrate the self-destroying nature of Emersonian
self-reliance carried to what some might consider its logical extreme. Ahab is altogether motivated by the conviction that nothing is sacred but the integrity of his own will. In prolonged
periods of seclusion, unlike Starbuck, who knows the disastrous-
ness of isolated brooding, he consults only the voice within his
own breast; but that voice is not the same to which Emerson
listened, for the nature of Melville's universe, although no less
symbolic, is different from Emerson's. The system of things inhabited by Ahab may be monistic—in fact, Ahab in certain
moments supposes it to be—but the great intelligential force
animating its entirety, the Melvillean "Over-Soul," to which Ahab
opens his mind in his broodings, is, if not maleficent, at best
inscrutable and unknowable. In his perverse dilations, then,
while he does attain as private man to a certain infinitude, and
while his eloquence certainly begets a power, wished by Emerson for his man of character, to melt the will of listeners into his
own, with every emergence from his cabin into the world of his
fellows he grows perversely further away from them, sowing

fearful obedience at best instead of love and destruction instead of harmony. In his solitude either he has projected the shapes of his retributive fantasies, magnified, on the screen of his deepest psyche and mistaken them for revelations of the universal spirit, or, if in any sense a transparent eyeball, he has been bewildered and wildly disoriented by the currents of the capricious, delusive cosmic being circulating through him, whose sense is man's insanity. In either case, he becomes mad—madness maddened, as he himself says. Whereas for Emerson the consummating element of life was joy, he finds his topmost greatness in his topmost grief. The lofty independence of Emersonian self-reliance, the portrait of Ahab may signify, is an impossibility; given the world as it is, what results for anyone who pursues it in earnest is only chaotic, suicidal solipsism. Emerson's ever widening and ascending circles of liberation from the ego through wholesome communion were for Melville only steadily narrowing involutions downward into the dark imprisonment of the self. Where Emerson had written good angel on the Devil's horns, he had printed DIABOLUS on the wings of the angel.

To ask whether Emerson is relevant to the twentieth century is itself in a sense irrelevant. The big problems of his age—government (socialism or democratic capitalism), industrialism and labor, materialism, education, feminism, nationalism and war, religion and science—continue to be the big problems of our own; and two epochs, sharing the same preoccupations, must certainly be said to be relevant to one another. Thus, spokesmen from one generation should automatically be significant to inquirers of the next. But this is not necessarily so. What makes relevancy is exceedingly hard to define. Certainly no writer not interested in politics or religion can be relevant to readers who are. Yet that he *is* interested in such matters does not make him relevant either. More important than that he writes on those issues is what he says in writing on them and the tone in which he says it.

In 1901, when he published his little *Remembrances of Emerson,* John Albee observed that for two generations Emerson had been read by young people. Where once they had been drawn to him by necessity, however, the attraction now, he feared, was one of fashion. By 1931 the fashion seemed to have waned, for in that year, in his commemorative *Emerson Today,*

Professor Bliss Perry recognized that for some time Emerson
had been unread, although it seemed that, with the winds of
scientific and philosophic thought blowing as they then were,
emphasizing the universe not as matter but as energy and idea,
an interest in him might be revived. The interval between Albee
and Perry had seen the breakup of Victorianism, the first emerg-
ings of the reaction against the cruelties of colonialism, the
horrors of World War I, and the dizzying vacuities of the inflated
years which were its aftermath. The disillusionment bred by
such things had no doubt made Emerson seem as removed from
the demands of modern life as a cowbell from an airplane. That
this was so had been made clear by the appearance in *The
Atlantic Monthly*, shortly before Professor Perry's book, of an
article entitled "Emerson Re-read" by the historian James Trus-
low Adams. Adams, then about fifty, had had occasion to go
back over several Emerson volumes which he had valued on
his entrance into young manhood years before, at the turn of
the century. His reacquaintance was a mortifying disillusionment.
He found the *Essays* to advocate a dangerous and unjustifiable
reliance on intuition and spontaneity (in effect, "we are all wise"
simply because we are walking animals) and also, reflecting no
sense of evil, of sin, of suffering, to parade a trumpeting optimism which he could only deplore as callow, in keeping with the
immaturity and shallowness of our nation. Emerson might still
be good for boys, but he was unthinkable for men. Adams' attitude seems to have remained the "standard" attitude.

The charge of optimism, however, as has already been shown,
must be carefully qualified when it is leveled against Emerson.
The indictment that he did not know suffering is, of course,
untenable, since he had been at various times, as excruciatingly
as any human being could be, an inhabitant of the house of
pain. What is true is that through an effort of will and mind he
transcended its devastations to live in a high region of thought
beyond tragedy, among those ideas and emotions he had described early as more intimate and more awful than friendship
and love. That by nature he was equipped to make such an effort
does not in the least detract from his success in realizing it. As
for evil, in his earlier days even when he was the ecstatic spokesman for the infinitude of the private man, he did not believe in
any easy instantaneous transformation of ugly actuality but

maintained only that the best could be achieved by a clarification of vision and a sustained effort of will. The impetus of his high character and the ardor of his imaginative intellect, it is true, led him to talk about this possibility in terms that made it seem imminent and effortless, but it was a feasibility always and not an inevitability, and its simplicity not its easiness was what excited him.

That the ultimate end of the universal pageant, whatever and whenever it might be, was good, was a belief in which, stated in evolutionary terms, he rested during at least the last forty years of his life and which therefore, for those who like to distinguish between the younger and the older Emerson, can be said to have constituted his later optimism. Everything that happened was for the best, and, like Pope, Emerson loved the thought that all partial evil was universal good. All the adversities of a single life, all the wasted single lives, all the obliterated civilizations and swallowed peoples, all that constituted misery and all that fed oblivion contributed to a final outcome whose rightness it was beyond the power of any human mind to define. From this perhaps persons recoil. That evil will be shown to have led to good and to have turned into good is to them totally unacceptable; and that the individual, after having done his best to prevail against them, should submit to whatever calamities surpass his forces and destroy him, serene in the knowledge that his destruction will assist the advent billions of years from now of an indescribably glorious consummation of the limitless cosmos, may seem to them abhorrent counsel. If this is what is meant by seeing things under the aspect of eternity, they may say, it is better to be without sight. They will probably find reassurance in the observation of one of Emerson's biographers that, where such ideas are concerned, his "constitution acted as a safety valve for what was dubious in the doctrine" (Wo, 155).

It is an error to dismiss as untenable, because disproved, Emerson's belief in progress. Because in this century we have known an unspeakable regression to depravity on the part of what had been considered one of the most enlightened nations of the world and because we now see ourselves, under the stimulus of continued violence, the possessor of the most potent product of our ingenuity, a bomb with which to annihilate the human race, we conclude that the evidence confronting us is irrevocable and final, whereas that by which our grandfathers judged was provisional and illusory. They may not have proved anything absolute about human nature, but neither have we. Emerson never said that the line of man's achievement was continuously, unbrokenly upward. He knew there were reversals in the long graph of the story—appalling errors to offset and abominable crimes to be compensated—but he also believed that all in all, if seen from a perspective sufficiently deep, it would show ascent, improvement. Thomas Jefferson before him, representative rationalist of his age, had believed in progress too, yet his eyes were hardly closed to the recurrent backslidings of humanity. He viewed with alarm the deep tears in the fabric of civilization made by the wars of his day and stated that the nineteenth century had dawned with a return to the vandalism of the fifth. But he had confidence that with reason and renewed strength mankind could repair the damage to the fabric and go on to extend and further embellish the pattern. Every age believes, apparently, that its progenitors have been capriciously playing the game of "Wolf!" but that its own lot is to shout the word in earnest.

Any person who does not live blindly or unconsciously from day to day must believe or hope that in some way good will prevail, at least that retrogression is not the law of life, or commit suicide. "Because thou must not hope/thou needs't not then despair," said Matthew Arnold's Empedocles, and where many things as the possible objects of hope are concerned—personal immortality, for example—this is true. But where other things are concerned, despair is the only alternative to absence of hope, and despair leads straight to suicide. Sensual gratification is much, often indescribably much, but without intellectual discrimination and reflection, in the long run it is hardly enough. The knowledge that the truth one has attained to, for instance, can be communicated to another and sympathetically received by him because the faculty of reason by which truth is truth, by which indeed anything is *known,* is possessed in common, is inestimable and finally sustains us. There are things not us which endure—the ideas of justice, of truth, of equality and brotherhood, of love—and, as Emerson said, insofar as we live in them, we inhabit eternity and know immortality. True, we may feel constrained to add, if these qualities have existed from time immemorial, so also have their opposites. What, then, is to insure that injustice, dishonesty, tyranny, slavery, and hatred do not prevail in their stead? Nothing but the conviction that the human mind, coadjuted by the human heart, when addressed by these negative counterparts, sniggering alongside their positive orig-inals, will in the long run reject them. Nothing, then, but the feeling that good does come to pass. Surely the least experienced civil-rights worker, demonstrating at risk before the eyes of a brutal southern sheriff, is actuated not only by the knowledge that justice for a fellow human being is an idea which transcends all human beings but also by the belief that, when brought dra-matically to the consciousness of his fellow human beings, it will be accepted by them as right and sooner or later translated by legislation into actuality. The human mind, then, has an in-nate susceptibility to being addressed by ideas of both right and wrong, but ideas of right seem naturally to possess qualities which recommend them to it more strongly. This recommenda-tion, however, is not instantaneous or automatic; it does not occur at the same instant with the same force to all persons. It is often slowly, arduously, perilously achieved.

Is not some such belief, although approximating a travesty when set down so baldly, what most sensitive people go by, whether they have admitted it to themselves or not? If not of optimism, the point to be remarked is that it is one of hope, of confidence, of affirmation, unfashionable as these words may be. And this being so, persons harboring it are much nearer Emerson than they would have said they were. Their pessimism is much less thoroughgoing than they had imagined. We have all been born into an atmosphere of despair which we have drunk like the gin said by Shaw's Eliza Doolittle to have been mother's milk to her mama. Our own Holden Caulfield as juvenile in his self-pity as Goethe's Werther five generations earlier, we have not seen through the sentimentalism of much antisocial art, false in its simplistic division of humanity into good guys and bad guys—that is, the young and the old, children and parents, who are the honest and the phony, the exploited and the exploiters. We are blind to the factitiousness of the black view of life which, equally simplistic and pernicious, casts all of mankind in the role of the antihero, deplorably corrupt yet pitiably forlorn, the *victim*, in short, of invisible and nameless victimizers masquerading under the collective name of life.

What may be indications of a clearing of the general intellectual atmosphere do not have to be sought. Reviewers of books (as well as writers of books) reveal themselves from time to time quite ready to question the vogue of despair. In *The New Yorker* not long ago the review of a new edition of Bernard Shaw's *Collected Letters, 1874-1897,* observed that "Today, what seems newest in these letters—more than contemporary, they read as if they were written tomorrow—is their mood," triumphant and energetic even when reflective, a mood which makes "alienation appear old hat." About Shaw's pride in his instinct, which was "to turn Failure into success, not to expose success as failure," the writer of the piece with no embarrassment admitted, "It is doubtful . . . that our contemporary emphasis on human limitations is more accurate or more profound than Shaw's emphasis on human possibilities." Another journalist, in the course of the day's work reporting in *The New York Times* on a new musical drawn from Cervantes' *Don Quixote,* stated that the most interesting thing about its success was that it was "against the prevailing current of philosophy in the theater," of alienation, moral anarchy, and despair, which, apart from a few bona fide works of art, had produced (and continues to produce) only pieces which are "insulting to the intelligence, debilitating to one's morale, and worst of all tedious and a bore." Don Quixote, for whom "facts are the enemy of truth," touches people "at some deep, instinctual level." Saul Bellow, one of our most distinguished novelists, on the occasion of receiving a well-deserved award some years ago, aligned himself unabashedly on the side of the angels, repudiating dreary negativism and alienated artiness as worn-out and mistaken fads. Other fictionalists—John Updike, John Cheever, and Bernard Malamud—irrespective of whatever statements about their work they may have made, disclose occasionally in it their sense that human life in spite of betrayals, or of its purposelessness, when shot through with affection and colored by imagination, can become a thing of magic.

Twentieth-century philosophers have found Emerson relevant. William James, in praising him in Concord during the Centenary Celebration in 1903 quoted many passages to illustrate his essential importance as residing in the doctrine that "the commonest person's act, if genuinely actuated, can lay hold on eternity" (KW, 23). Privately he stated that in rereading Emerson, he had felt his "real greatness" as never before; he benefitted not only personally from the "incorruptible way" in which the "divine" and "beloved master" had lived his life in the rural setting of Concord but also professionally from an exposure to the thought of the *Essays,* which helped him reconcile the scientist to the philosopher in America, both as incarnations of Man Thinking (Mat, 431-33).

John Dewey, also on the occasion of the centenary, described Emerson as "the one citizen of the New World fit to have his name uttered in the same breath with that of Plato," whose whole work could be regarded as "a hymn to intelligence, a paean to the all-creating, all-disturbing power of thought."

Negative voices among philosophers and scholars, however, have also occasionally been raised. George Santayana, although as ready as anybody else to admit Emerson's personal uniqueness, maintained that his admirers confused high character and linguistic skill with power of thought; Emerson had not been original and germinal in his ideas but potent and efflorescent in his imagination, and the most that could be said of him was that, related at once to Calvinist Puritanism and European humanism, with his special brand of mysticism he had given extraordinarily beautiful and original expression "to thoughts that are old and imperishable" (KW, 38). Professor Perry Miller was led to his detractions by the conviction that neither as artist nor as thinker was Emerson really of the first rank and that in character he suffered from arrogance, which objectionably stamped his relations with others of high ability by snobbishness and condescension.

As one surveys the contemporary scene he finds Emerson relevant in three respects: in the extent to which his body of thought continues to be a stimulation to literary and philosophical scholars, drawing them to make specialized studies of its various features, as well as the degree to which beliefs of his turn out to be congenial to the convictions of certain speculative thinkers in biology and theology; in the relation of certain of his ideas and of his example to various issues of moment affecting our public well-being and our national life; and in his perennial nearness to the needs and aspirations of ordinary men and women in their daily private life.

Since the mid-1940's scholars have continued to publish volumes which reveal that for them Emerson is still an audible voice. Most of their studies, however, do not seek to orient him historically or consider his influence as ethical inspirer on readers either past or present. Following in the wake of several earlier intellectual studies, they aim to treat one or another aspect of his thought as something interesting in itself—his esthetic as contained in ideas dispersed through his writings, his complexity and ambivalence in accommodating the concepts of freedom and necessity and of good and evil, his epistemology and ontology in his ideas about the soul, his illumination of the relation between psychology and art in his pioneering use of symbol in literary expression, his use of Montaigne and Plutarch, his views on history and race. When statements bordering on historical estimate or ethical judgment occur in such works, they are likely to be incidental or to be accompanied by an observation that, since Emerson did not consider that he had given the final word on anything, it is better for us not to respond to features of his thought according to whether they are true but whether they are imaginative or stimulating. It is not Emerson the teacher, as for their grandfathers and great-grandfathers, who attracts, but Emerson the thinker. One scholar-admirer, in his study of Emerson's assimilation of Asian thought, pronounced him a new Petrarch, "the great precursor of a new Renaissance, the American Renaissance of Orientalism" and "probably the founder of the modern school of Comparative Religion in America" (Car, 244-45, 247). More recently, for his belief that human history, already in a late stage, develops cyclically rather than linearly, or in continuous progress, and that civilizations all are destined to phases of growth, fruition, and decay, both ideas considered advanced, Emerson has been praised as a precursor, even if not an influencer, of the historians Spengler and Toynbee (see N, 255).

Whatever the degree of rapport to it of recent speculation among theorists in physics and astronomy, the optimism of Emerson's evolutionary view can be congenially related to the phi-

losophy of certain contemporary biological thinkers, no less teleological in outlook. Both Edmond W. Sinnott and Pierre Teilhard
de Chardin have seen the human race, because of spirit somehow
inhering in matter (the equivalent of what Emerson called meta-
chemistry), as destined to an inevitable end of fulfillment if
not of total perfection, although Teilhard de Chardin relies, as
Sinnott does not, on the dynamism of an ecumenicized Christianity to lead the race into higher stages of life characterized
by increased unity and love—through what he calls a Noosphere
to an ultimate Theosphere.

In recent years, particularly owing to the increasing influence
among college-educated persons of theologian-philosophers such
as Martin Buber, Sören Kierkegaard, and Reinhold Niebuhr and
the impact as well of the conquest of space, an intensive reex-
amination of the nature of God has occurred. The spread of
existentialist ideas and the revelation since World War II that
human beings can endure the conditions of space travel—which
means the possibility that creatures not altogether different from
ourselves enjoy life on other planets—have revolutionized the
attitude of certain sensitive individuals toward vital being, mortal
and immortal. Some Christians themselves have been constrained
to rejudge the elements of the great Christian narrative. A slight
book by the English churchman Bishop John Robinson, *Honest
to God,* which in the middle 1960's achieved an extraordinary
popularity, showed that the traditional concept of God as a per-
sonalized being in a somewhere beyond earth, in a "Heaven,"
was no longer valid. A Deity "up there" could no longer be
fitted into the facts of the universe as science had revealed them
to us. In a universe of curved space, infinite in extent and infinite as well in the number of solar systems like our own which
it contains, there is no "up there." God—the divine, that is to
say, or Being as well as being—is not a localized presence, remote; God is a force within us. God is truth and courage and
love in every man or woman; and to get to God we do not go far
out, we go deep within.

Such an idea is essentially that of Emerson in his doctrine of
the Over-Soul and the "original relation to the universe." Spiritual
elevation has nothing to do with spatial elevation, nor does
spirituality, in relation to the divine, have anything to do with
personality. Seeking to disabuse his readers of the ideas of an

anthropomorphic God, of a physical heaven and of a posttemporal immortality, Emerson taught God as eternal, immutable principle, omnipresent, as spirit within man as well as without, and he aimed to show that worship was not going out to God but opening oneself and bringing God in. Such a God-filled state was heaven. He hoped, like other thinkers before him intent on reconciling the growth of scientific knowledge with religious experience—Thomas Paine in the eighteenth century, for example—that Copernican astronomy with its revelation of a plurality of worlds had finally and forever destroyed the parochial myth of God's sending His Only Begotten Son to this globe because it was the apple of His eye. It is apparent that Copernican astronomy did not achieve any such end—nor did Laplace's speculations nor Newton's discoveries. Perhaps in the Einsteinian era, with man actually exploring other globes in the immensities of space, the irrelevancy of the church myth and the relevancy of Emerson's thought will simultaneously be made clear.

Among the events which can be designated upheavals in our national society since World War II, the rebellion of the younger generation against the ways of its elders—a rebellion of dimension also in other lands—figures significantly. It is true that in every epoch children, on attaining the age of expression and self-assertion, have fought against wearing the straitjacket of the customs and habits of their parents, but in the past half century their recurrent recalcitrance has become steadily bigger and more formidable, revolutionary in character. In the past decade under the threat of the annihilation of the species through the perpetual imminence of a nuclear holocaust, the revolt has become more widespread and passionate, more deep-rooted and determined than ever before. The unwillingness to continue in the ways of the old generation is not only the instinctive impulsion of the new creature to stand on its own feet but at bottom the uncompromisable aspiration of young men and women of conscience to try at the eleventh hour ways that will bring human being closer to human being in harmony, diminish poverty and suffering in the world, and replace ugliness and squalor with beauty. Shall humanity destroy itself without once having tried to save itself?

Shocked and angered by complacency and injustice—by the

disparity between what is known about the good life and what has been undertaken to achieve it for all, by the limitlessness of the means, financial and material, for transforming society and the pitiableness of the extent to which they have been employed —the idealistic young have determined at long last to make action more consistent with thought and deed with word. They refuse to acquiesce any longer in the dehumanization of life by machines and computers, in the untraversable gulf between the individual citizen and the governments which pretend to represent him, and in the inconsistency between the protestations of those governments in behalf of peace and plenty and their performances in service to war and annihilation. That their intransigence affects the survival of all the institutions of society, educational and religious as well as political, is obvious. That their search for new procedures and new patterns of relationship involves the relations between men and women, between white persons and persons of differing color, between this nation and other nations, is also obvious. The rebellion of youth is concurrent with upheavals in racialism, sex, and internationalism.

The youthful insurrectionists seem still to be mostly college students or persons who have been exposed to a college education. Overnight some years back the members of what had been known in the 1950's alternatively as the Cool Generation and the Apathetic Generation, disproved the diagnosis of moralistic college-surveying experts in leaping to the defense of sit-in-striking Negroes in the South with electrifying solidarity. And the impetus, if anything, only continued to grow; sit-ins led to bus rides to achieve integration on means of interstate transportation, and bus rides led to voter-registration campaigns among the impoverished and terror-ridden descendants of slaves in Mississippi. Every year by the thousands young men and women still volunteer for humanitarian service overseas in the Peace Corps or for work among the underprivileged at home in one or another of its domestic counterparts. Still wrongly represented by many conventional newspapers as spoiled, irresponsible exhibitionists, as troublemakers capable only of demonstrations *against* things—against the draft, against Negro subjection, against inadequate schools, a good part of the American public has yet to see them as affirmative, not negative, doers. There is a certain paradox in their behavior, since many of those who go out from academe to do good do so with copies of Kierkegaard or Sartre or Beckett or Genêt in their pockets. But this only illustrates the unpredictability and resiliency of human nature, because it shows that even when they have thought hopelessly they have not felt so. Certainly their determination to translate their particular word into flesh reveals a state of mind congenial with that of Emerson.

Emerson would support the cause of all who protest for the Negro. Had he not spoken passionately in praise of John Brown, who would free the Negro even with violence, and in condemnation of Daniel Webster, who had betrayed him through law? In words burningly apt for today he had described the moral plight of a country indifferent to the continued degradation of the Negro. Things had reached the point where the very air one breathed was poisoned by it, and the honest man found himself the first thing in the morning unmanned by the domination of his mind by its image, unable even to look his children in the face without asking miserably what he had done that they should begin life in dishonor. As for war, having himself denounced the war against Mexico as infamous aggression, he would be profoundly sympathetic with all who are moved to dissent from the policy of a government which conducts a repressive conflict on the opposite face of the globe against a revolutionary people it outnumbers ten to one in order to keep its word to a tiny military faction of an even lesser population which pretends to represent a nation that does not exist, while questions of tragic import lie unresolved at home and grow nearer disaster proportion by the moment.

Where the most advanced position among radical young thinkers today is concerned, among those who in their extreme contempt for the Establishment and their desire to secede from it are "way-out," one must consider it in relation to two recent events of astonishing magnitude and unforeseeable consequence on the character of our century. As in the Renaissance, when, thanks to the simultaneous discovery of the thought of the ancients and the Western Hemisphere of our globe, man's life underwent a tremendous expansion at once inner and outer, so human experience in the 1960's was suddenly revealed to have horizons unlimited, psychically as well as physically. What only a generation ago was pipedream and the wildest of fantasies, namely, the conquest of space, is today a reality; and to children of six and eight seated before their family television sets, the incredible facts of the moon's surface photographed by an instrument alighted there only minutes before and of the earth circumnavigated by an astronaut in less time than a housewife requires for washing and waxing her kitchen, are now commonplace. Coincident with the sudden projection of the human being beyond the terrestrial bounds which for millennia had confined him is his irruptive venturing across the threshold of consciously controlled, rational life into a domain of illimitable vision, the like of which hitherto it was reserved for only a few mystic souls to know. What science in the external universe has enabled man in space capsules to accomplish—transcendence of his daily, earthly self or flight from the conditions that are his daily, earthly existence—it has correspondingly given him the means for achieving through chemical pills in the universe that is internal.

There is no minimizing the importance of these two extensions of the universe. Speculation grows prolifically out of the discoveries accompanying each, new in the history of mankind. Ours is indeed a time of revolution, and one recalls Emerson's own satisfaction that he had been born in such a time since it allowed the new and the old to be so dramatically compared and stimulated the energies of men with both fear and hope. The rich possibilities of the future, he was excited by. The possibilities of our own future, we find it exhilarating but also perhaps bewildering to contemplate. The changes that will flow from them, affecting human values and habits, will be drastic, even though they may not be so absolute as some unrestrained speculators would have them be, who believe that since certain stupendous things have come to pass, anything can come to pass, even to the point of man's changing somatically and genetically in space so that he will reproduce himself monosexually and subsist by eating the air, like Hamlet, promise-crammed. But whether man's biology is destined to change, his psychology will do so—and his morality. Indeed, some of those who never harbor a thought of themselves going to the moon one day, who are utterly indifferent to the conquest of space and to the possibility of life being supported on other planets, have already broken with the morality inherited from previous generations and proclaimed the advent of a different set of relations among men contained in the "New Morality." Principal among these relations is the abandonment of sexual continence. To the aid of young men and women drawn to espouse sexual freedom by the early maturity, increased health, and increased leisure which are the products of contemporary affluence, has come science, furnishing reliable and easy means of contraception and, more important where the revolution of the inner world is concerned, hallucinogenic, or psychedelic, drugs. The most vocative and widely known propagandist for the drug-activitated life has described in detail the strange states of being, unexampled in conscious, volitional life, which the various phases of the operation of LSD induce on the human psyche as it is swept on, in a man and woman together, toward an indefinable ecstatic consummation. The supreme stage is one of union. The subjects know a sense of harmonious identification with themselves (with the very molecules of their blood stream and of their viscera), with their race, with the universe blindingly clear to them in the immensity of its infinitude, and with all Being. Essentially the revelation seems to be one of love as the adhesive force of the cosmic system of things. The height of religious aspiration has been attained without self-denial—in fact, seemingly only because of total self-abandonment.

In one respect this new brand of mystical idealism, of goodness inseparable from pleasure, of compassionate altruism together with passionate sensualism, can be said to have had precedent and on the same soil, that of the United States. Walt Whitman in his "Song of Myself," taking a tack different from that of other mystics before his time, in spite of the respects in which his account of the attainment of transcendent illumination can be seen to parallel that of a Buddhist, glorified rather than abjured the body and exalted rather than depreciated sex. In his emphasis on happiness as the end of all being, he was sure that gratification was a necessary part of happiness. Yet Whitman was an advocate also of the "great chastity of paternity to match the great chastity of maternity" and of a simple, nature-close way of life. Believing in the ability of the "divine aggregate" to transform itself, it is doubtful that when in "Democratic Vistas" he described a community in the west of a few ordinary men and women come together, organizing the machinery of their social lives in efficient fashion so that they had time left over for the important thing—the flowering of their spiritual selves—he had in mind anything like the psychedelic communities advocated by Timothy Leary, of forty persons, dropouts from society and non-cooperators with the government, who depend upon the taking of LSD for their motivating power.

The relation of Emerson to all of this is clear. Himself for years a foe of the Establishment—indeed it was a word he often used, with the same pejorative sense—he would understand the widespread fear of, and antipathy toward, it among young people. (He would understand also the relation of the young generation's rebelliousness to the permissiveness in which it had been raised, for he was sensitive to the same relation in his own day and liked to cite the observation of a contemporary, that his had been the misfortune to have been born in a time when children had not counted for anything and to have lived into a time when adults no longer did.) Accustomed himself to saying that no book written by anyone under forty should be judged by anyone over forty, he knew well the gap between generations and no doubt would smile at the disparaging slogan, "Never trust anyone over thirty." The growing disinclination among college graduates to enter business for their careers would surprise him not at all, since the aversion among young men of his own day to dedicating their lives to the profit motive, sometimes leading them to suicide, was one of his preoccupations. The intolerance of the past among young people he would understand as well; he would say now no less strongly than he said a century ago that every generation must write its own books. He would particularly rejoice in the conviction among many young that mystical elevation and enlargement are necessary to the attainment and fulfillment of the self; at last individuals by the hundred, by the thousand, are seeking an original relation to the universe.

Yet at the same time he could not approve of certain features of the contemporary phenomenon. His own intolerance of the past took the form of a refusal to submit to its tyranny, not a wholesale repudiation of it. One did not refuse to read Bacon or Plato because they belonged to the past and so to the perpetuators of the Establishment. One read their books as open-minded and impressible as possible, with the hope that they would raise him to the point where he could write an even better book. The past, in short, was indispensable to the present in enabling it to be a better present. By the depreciation of the conscious will and reason through a bypassing of it in the use of psychedelic drugs, potentially dangerous to body and mind, he could only be saddened.

Two medical authorities several years ago reported that the use of psychedelic drugs by students was directly related to the Transcendentalism of Emerson's time and judged it an indictment of contemporary American higher education, which they found not to contribute to an enrichment of life. They saw drug users as idealist-dissenters actuated by a deep concern over meaning and a need to attach the thinking, feeling, aspiring part of themselves to something not personal and not ephemeral. Not since the period of the Civil War, when Emerson's influence was at its height, did the doctors think there had been such a preoccupation with ethics and morality, such refusal to acquiesce in inhumanity, such determination not to be content with the values of a society which at a cost of billions of dollars could send ships into space, whose pilots could talk to one another only in locker-room banter (see *Nation,* January 31, 1966).

> It cannot conquer folly,—
> Time-and-space-conquering steam,—
> And the light-outspeeding telegraph
> Bears nothing on its beam.
>   (W, IX, 16)

That sensitive men and women, feeling themselves unable to belong to their nation, by whose daily practices at home and abroad they are repelled, should seek to belong to the universe and in spiritual flights have the ultimate experience of joy in transcendent unity ("grooving with the elements" was recently a phrase for it) Emerson, as has been said, would applaud, although he would urge them not to forsake their country but to use their new found sense of unity to purify its spirit. At the same time, given their medicinal nature and the absence of productive work in the wake of descent from them, he could only deplore those flights as spurious and their benefits as specious. The meditative isolation, genuinely creative, which he recommended for each individual—spiritual, not mechanical—he could only regret seeing exchanged for narcissistic, hermetic escape. He would, however, no doubt be heartened by the growing number of earnest, perceptive individuals who, disabused of a faith in drugs, have been led on by their experiments with them to explore the disciplines of oriental mysticism.

Artificially created spirituality and the sensuality attaching to it, Emerson could not but reprehend. Any emphasis on sudden goodness, not striven for and not even willed but occurring through the ingesting of a pharmaceutical grain, is at variance with the enlightened, vigilant personality, at once spontaneous and reflectively critical, which was his ideal. And a notion that quick and easy gratification is according to the way things are, as distinguished from the way things have in the past been "mistakenly" held to be, by any Emersonian criterion must be pronounced error. Inveighing always against the "vulgar prosperity that retrogrades ever to barbarism" as well as against the love that "pules and whines," maintaining always that goodness needed to have some edge to it in order to be goodness, he believed that in the ceaseless strife which was life not "flower power" but only love buttressed by the warrior's virtues would enable persons to triumph over themselves. Nevertheless, he could not but be moved by the earnestness of many young men and women who in their experimenting with sexual associations are impelled by the desire to put the man-woman relationship on a basis which will be one of equality, fairer to the woman.

How many unselfish, uncompromising Peace Corps students or how many uncompromising "way-out" dropouts read Emerson? When Bliss Perry a generation ago considered the problem of Emerson's relevancy to the age, he wisely remarked that he would not prescribe him as a tract for the times because tracts had a way of going out of fashion. Perhaps the hortatory mode of Emerson, along with his vocabulary, which with terms like "spirit," "soul," "reverence," and "God" may seem too close to the language of the religious establishment, makes it impossible for some youthful readers to respond to him. Yet the hortatory tone is never militant, never authoritarian, never duplicitous, and the terminology is soon seen to have no tie to anthropomorphically centered faith or to churchified piety. Emerson's very moderateness may also be an obstacle to his acceptance. Youth is passionate and absolutist; it demands action in the name of reform. Thoreau, absolutist in the simplest sense and with a program for action of the most elementary kind—"under a government which imprisons any unjustly, the true place for a just man is also a prison"—is perhaps more likely to invite emulation than Emerson, who had set himself the task of mediating between the ideal and the real community—of staying in the world but never belonging wholly to it. His middle position, in which in the midst of the crowd he aimed to preserve with perfect sweetness the independence of solitude, may seem to young people compromising in the kinds of tolerance it entails and self-contradictory in its desire to avoid downright hostility, to the point where the figure occupying it is all things to all persons but nothing to any.

The writer, a conscientious objector, can testify, however, to the inspiriting, bracing effect of Emerson's individualistic idealism in the formation of his own outlook and recalls the instance of a young man who only a few years ago after a consecutive reading of Emerson's early essays and Thoreau's *Walden* had to leave formal education altogether and commit himself to the hospitality of life untethered.

A decade ago by certain "Beatniks," along with Whitman as the apostle of a sexual revolution, Thoreau as an antimaterialistic, mystical contemplative seems to have been considered the bequeather of an evangel. By some of their number Emerson also was probably read, even though he no less than Thoreau would have found strange their idea that to the realization of a wholly free life the right to experiment sexually was indispensable. Such a circumstance only reminds us in salutary fashion that no writer can prescribe who is to read him, and how, in the generations to come. What he wants to be valued for and what he is valued for may sometimes be two radically different things. The commune in the Fort Hill ghetto of Boston, Massachusetts, may be only one of a number whose members, A.D. 1972, seek to live by the principles of Emerson alongside those of Thoreau and Jesus.

As for contemporary teachers for today's young seekers, there are always John the Baptists, some of lesser voice, some of greater, showing the path out of the wilderness. Whether any among them will manage to strike the peculiar chord of affinity with youth that distinguished Emerson's leadership a hundred years ago remains to be seen. In spite of the extent to which as

a collective anonymity they support it with their annual con-
sumer purchases of billions of dollars, there are thousands and
thousands of young men and women who in Emersonian fashion
want to resist the commercial tendency to put things in the
saddle so that they can ride mankind. Thirty years ago it was
the sociologist Pitirim Sorokin whose passionate indictments of
our sensate culture drew them to read his books. A decade and
a half later it was the cogently reasoned, convincingly documented *The Lonely Crowd* of David Riesman which pleaded
for autonomous individuals as distinct from persons other-di-
rected by social convention or inner-directed by early imbibed,
institutionalized faith.

A significant and influential force appeared not many years
back in the thought of Paul Goodman. Like the early Emerson,
skeptical (at least) of institutions, a disbeliever in association, an
ardent idealist wanting to see everywhere a fruition of personality, prevented by prevailing modes of life, Goodman addressed
himself to those he knew to be fellow searchers. Willingly be-
guiled by "the sirens of reason, animal joy, and lofty aims," he
was a dissenter from a system which "has sapped self-reliance
and therefore has dried up the spontaneous imagination of ends
and the capacity to invent ingenious expedients" and everywhere
sought to restore faith in "the possibility of a higher quality of
experience" (PG, 9, 10, 15). In poems, essays, novels, and plays
his reformist mind, appalled at how many young men and women
are compelled to grow up absurd, has touched their sympathies,
affirmed their doubts, strengthened their resolution. Aware,
though with no ostentation, of their interest in him, he has given
generously of himself in visits to college campuses, lecturing and
participating in discussions. His word has seemed to fall on their
ears at once with authority and humility, eliciting respect and
admiration. And the transparent oneness of his life—the anarch-
ism he preaches, he practices insofar as possible, even to the
freedom of his sexual habits—won their regard at the outset.
Like Emerson he believes that nothing is at last sacred but the
integrity of one's own mind, and, although without a style of
poetic distinction, he more than any other public figure seemed
at one stage to have made comparable rapport with the college
generation.

To cite such things as evidence of conditions propitious for a "rebirth" of Emerson is, although interesting, unrealistic. He cannot, reborn, be again the oracle he once was to youthful seekers, and the attempt on anybody's part to make him so would be absurd. He himself would be the first to disclaim it. But the writer who in his lifetime made it his aim to speak to nonprofessionals ought not now have his only existence as the property of specialists. What relevancy does he possess today to the ordinary person, the average literate reader, Man Thinking, the descendant of the individual to whom, with no condescension, he addressed himself in his lifetime?

No reader of the poems or the essays can forget their tone of celebration. With his joy of life Emerson removed the tarnish of familiarity and habit from the commonest objects and occurrences. He was a hierophant revealing with wonder the incredible nature of the things every day about us and the things we daily do. In releasing us from the tyranny of the dreary mechanicality of routine, in filling us with the exciting sense of the glory of the present scene, in which we seem by ourselves only to grope or turn round and round in confusion, he is invaluable.

With his respect for other creeds and other gods and for the achievements of other cultures, with his belief in the uniting power of love and his untiring counsel to cultivate it, and with his relish for an infinite diversity of human personality streaming from a single fountainhead of inspiration, Emerson stands relevantly as an advocate of world brotherhood. Transcending national and religious parochiality, he declared that truth and spirit know no boundaries of time and place in a voice which we need still to hear today.

Yet his supreme importance remains what it was a century ago—the power to help persons find and believe in themselves. It may be that in a strict logical sense no one can prove that he exists; yet everyone feels that he exists, and he furthermore knows periodically the desire to be the best self it is possible for him to be.

It is because we know how much is due from us that we are impatient to show some petty talent as a substitute for worth. We are haunted by a conscience of this right to grandeur of character, and are false to it. But each of us has some talent, can do somewhat useful, or graceful, or formidable, or amusing, or lucrative. That we do, as an apology to others and to ourselves for not reaching the mark of a good and equal life. But it does not satisfy *us*, whilst we thrust it on the notice of our companions. It may throw dust in their eyes, but does not smooth our own brow, or give us the tranquillity of the strong when we walk abroad. We do penance as we go. Our talent is a sort of expiation, and we are constrained to reflect on our splendid moment with a certain humiliation, as somewhat too fine, and not as one act of many acts, a fair expression of our permanent energy. Most persons of ability meet in society with a kind of tacit appeal. Each seems to say, "I am not all here." (W, III, 217-18)

In somehow identifying the reader to himself and strengthening his impulses to integrity, Emerson is still the magician of idealism. As no other writer has done, he makes us feel the fact of personality and stirs us with an ineffable expectancy of its possibilities.

Elated by the discovery of his own self, by the intensification of life resulting from it, he had declared that the fulfillment of a single individual was a revolution greater than that which brought a nation out of subjugation, to itself. This, we may say, is extravagance. Yet that nation is best which is made of individuals prepared to stand against it when it is wrong, whose allegiance is to the principles the parent should embody, not to his person. There will always be respects in which the quality of our corporate life in society suffers in comparison with that of our single selves with family and friends. The inducements of business, the blandishments of advertising, the claims and distortions of journalism, the contortions of politicians are often at odds with the ideals held up for us in the two ancient institutional repositories of truth, the school and the church. Plato and Jesus, if taken seriously, are indeed heady fare. But it is the nature of youth to take them seriously. And it is this disposition which Emerson reinforces. He imparts the strength to stand quietly against the meretriciousness of society and the distractions of the world, a sayer of no because he is a sayer of yes.

Selective Bibliography

I. Emerson's Works

The Complete Works of Ralph Waldo Emerson. Edited by Edward Waldo Emerson. 12 vols. Boston and New York: Houghton Mifflin, 1903-4. The Centenary Edition, standard. Invaluable for the abundant notes by the editor, which are of interest biographically and important critically for the light they throw on the relation of the published works to lectures and the Journals, as well as to events of the times.

The Journals of Ralph Waldo Emerson. Edited by Edward Waldo Emerson and Waldo Emerson Forbes. 10 vols. Boston and New York: Houghton Mifflin, 1909-14. Indispensable to any who would know Emerson.

Uncollected Writings (Essays, Addresses, Poems, Reviews, and Letters). New York: Lamb Publishing Company, 1912. 208 pages. A miscellany of pieces not available in any other source at the time.

Two Unpublished Essays. Edited by Edward Everett Hale. Boston and New York: Lanson Wolfe & Co., 1896. The undergraduate Bowdoin Prize essays on the character of Socrates and the contemporary state of ethical philosophy.

Dante's *Vita Nuova*. Translated by Emerson in the early 1840's. Edited and annotated by J. Chesley Mathews. Studies in Comparative Literature, Chapel Hill, North Carolina: University of North Carolina, 1960.

The Dial (4 volumes, for the years 1840-44), New York: Russell and Russell, 1961. Edited by Emerson from 1842 to 1844 and containing throughout various prose pieces and poems by him.

Memoirs of Margaret (Fuller) Ossoli. Edited by J. F. Clarke, W. H. Channing, and R. W. Emerson. 2 vols., 703 pp. Boston: Phillips, Sampson and Company, 1852. Of this work Emerson assumed sole responsibility for the last 151 pages of the first volume, those treating Margaret Fuller's life in Concord and Boston. He narrates and interprets, in addition to choosing the pages from her letters and journals in which Margaret Fuller speaks for herself.

SERMONS:

Young Emerson Speaks. Edited by A. M. McGiffert, Jr. Boston:
Houghton Mifflin, 1938. 275 pages. Contains 25 of the more than
170 sermons by Emerson, excellently annotated. Valuable volume.

CORRESPONDENCE:

The Letters of Ralph Waldo Emerson. Edited by Ralph L. Rusk. 6 vols.
New York: Columbia University Press, 1939. The definitive edition
to date of the voluminous correspondence, excluding, however,
the collections of letters to particular friends, already separately
in print.

The Correspondence of Emerson and Carlyle. Edited by Joseph Slater.
2 vols. New York and London: Columbia University Press, 1964.
A famous correspondence of almost half a century which reveals,
among other things, how much two minds, opposed to one another
on basic convictions, could still find in common, to their mutual
enrichment—in a sense illustrating Emerson's belief that character
teaches over our heads. A new edition of the work first published
by Charles Eliot Norton in 1883.

A Correspondence Between John Sterling and Ralph Waldo Emerson.
Edited by Edward Waldo Emerson. Boston and New York:
Houghton Mifflin, 1897. A slight correspondence between two
persons who never met but who over the space of a few years
humanely illustrated what fine minds in affinity and in mutual
admiration can be to one another.

Correspondence Between Ralph Waldo Emerson and Herman Grimm.
Edited by Frederick William Holls. Boston and New York: Houghton Mifflin, 1903. A brief series of letters revealing how much
Emerson's poetic teaching of the preciousness of personality and
the pricelessness of every day's promise could mean to a man
whose habits of thought and cultural accentuation were those of
system and tradition rather than of spontaneity and innovation.

Big projects of definitive reediting are under way, which seemingly,
when completed, will make available on the printed page, except for
intractable lectures, almost every word Emerson ever wrote. To date,
seven volumes of a new edition of the Journals and Notebooks, assembled complete from the manuscripts, have appeared under the
aegis of the Harvard University Press and the direction of various
Emerson scholars. *The Early Lectures of Ralph Waldo Emerson,*
begun under the editorship of Stephen Whicher and Robert Spiller
and published also by the Harvard University Press, have already in

their first two volumes (1959 and 1964) reached the year 1838. Beyond the year 1847 the editors think they will be unable to go because of excessive confusion in the manuscripts. As for the correspondence, the six volumes of Emerson Letters published by Ralph Leslie Rusk will be supplemented by additional volumes edited by Eleanor M. Tilton of Barnard College. The supplementary volumes (to be published by Columbia University Press) will gather all letters discovered since 1938 (ca. 1500) and all other letters not gathered in Rusk's volumes, exclusive of the Carlyle-Emerson Correspondence. The new volumes will provide such correction of the original Rusk work as the new materials have indicated is necessary.

The poetry will be edited by Professor Carl Strauch of Lehigh University, who has been assiduously studying its manuscript forms for years.

II *Works About Emerson*

ALBEE, JOHN. *Remembrances of Emerson.* New York: Robert G. Cooke, 1901. Indispensable in its revelation of the importance of Emerson in his heyday to a new generation seeking its own maturity, by a man the course of whose life was changed by his discovery.

BENTON, JOEL, *Emerson as a Poet.* New York: M. L. Holbrook & Company, 1883. 134 pages. A small volume issued in the year after Emerson's death to show that among all his American contemporaries there was no personality "at once so compact, so essence-like, so opulent, so strong." Praising Emerson for his virile vocabulary and even for his false rhymes, memory-haunting, the author compared him, in the condensation of his thought and his putative unintelligibility, with Browning. Better his "spinal system" than the "perfumery" of the many Longfellows.

BERRY, EDMUND G. *Emerson's Plutarch.* Cambridge: Harvard University Press, 1961. A very important book which reveals the extensive influence on Emerson of Plutarch, who not only gave him his first knowledge of the theories of the Greek pre-Socratic philosophers—and also in part of Plato—but also left permanently stamped on his mind the preciousness of the traditional Stoic qualities of character: "equanimity, complete and calm self-control, restraint in every aspect of emotion and feeling as well as in every action."

BISHOP, JONATHAN. *Emerson on the Soul.* Cambridge: Harvard University Press, 1964. A technical study of Emerson's conception of the soul in its several attributes or functions, with the aim of showing how the change in his belief, from an active soul to a passive soul, affected the quality of his prose, even to its texture and rhythm. The author prefers the earlier, active Emerson and makes a case for his value today.

CABOT, JAMES ELLIOT. *A Memoir of Ralph Waldo Emerson.* 2 vols., 809 pp. Boston and New York: Houghton Mifflin, 1887. One of the first biographies, by Emerson's literary executor, at once professor of philosophy and friend, still valuable and interesting, with substantial extracts from letters as well as addresses and a very useful Appendix which contains a chronological list of Emerson's lectures through his lifetime, many summarized by the biographer.

CAMERON, KENNETH WALTER, S.A. *Emerson the Essayist. An Outline of His Philosophical Development Through 1836 With Special Emphasis on the Sources and Interpretation of "Nature."* 2 vols. Raleigh, North Carolina: The Thistle Press, 1945. In these volumes Professor Cameron of Trinity College, Hartford, Connecticut, provides an invaluable service in making available texts of certain rare works of influence on Emerson in his period of intensive germination—for example, Sampson Reed's oration on "Genius" and his piece on the "Growth of the Mind"; compilations of relevant sentences and paragraphs from big works of various important writers (e.g., Coleridge) which had also left their mark on him; summaries of various unpublished Emerson works; and illuminating scholarly and critical observations of his own. The work has been supplemented through the years by other volumes, in which Professor Cameron aims to provide, apparently, as full a reproduction of the New England literary climate in which Transcendentalism flourished as is consistent with a thorough understanding of Emerson.

CARPENTER, FREDERIC IVES. *Emerson and Asia.* Cambridge: Harvard University Press, 1930. 282 pages. A very valuable book which traces the evolution of Emerson's knowledge of oriental poetry and wisdom, showing how his affinity for the Neoplatonic philosophers paved the way for his sympathetic exposure to thinkers of the Near East, China, and India and how, although he found them interesting, he never embraced the principal ethical doctrines of the other side of the globe but remained content simply to use them effectively in his work.

————. *An Emerson Handbook.* New York: Hendricks House, 1953. 268 pages. An admirable service volume covering Emerson's life, achievement in prose and poetry, thought, and relation to world literature, with valuable bibliographies.

CESTRE, CHARLES. "Emerson Poète," *Etudes Anglaises.* Libraire Didier, Paris, Vol. 4, pp. 1-14, 1940. (*PMLA* Bibliography, 1941, p. 1274). An appreciative appraisal of Emerson's performance as poet, with attention to, and quotations from, many individual poems. The author considers him the founder of philosophical poetry in America, notable in his ability to rise from esthetic perception to spiritual vision and supreme among all gnomic poets in the expression of the divinity of nature and the unity of the cosmos.

CHAPMAN, JOHN JAY. "Emerson" in *Emerson and Other Essays*. New York: Charles Scribner's Sons, 1898. 108 pages. A long essay, judicial and comprehensive, which, admitting the fact of his extraordinary influence as the "arch-radical of the world," aimed to assess the thought of Emerson, pro and con, in relation to the sterility of the contemporary American background, the Puritan past, the tradition of mysticism, and the new vein of Transcendental thought. With attention both to his prose and poetry, Chapman concluded that Emerson's art as well as his philosophy had suffered from being rooted in the priestly Puritan falsehood that human nature could subsist on conscience alone, with emotions and instincts ignored.

CONWAY, MONCURE DANIEL. *Emerson at Home and Abroad*. Boston: James R. Osgood and Company, 1882. 383 pages. An anecdotal volume of reminiscences by a younger man who revered Emerson and was a lifelong friend.

COWAN, MICHAEL H. *City of the West. Emerson, America, and Urban Metaphor*. New Haven: Yale University Press, 1967. An interesting book, exploring with emphasis a domain of Emerson's thought previously not much entered. The author shows how important the idea of the city—the new humane and healthful city of the new nation—was to Emerson's vision of the creative fulfillment of America, as the fact of the city, epitomized in his beloved Boston, was to his personal life.

DEWEY, JOHN. "Ralph Waldo Emerson" in *Characters and Events*. Vol. 1, pp. 68-77. New York: Henry Holt, 1929. The laudatory and perceptive address delivered on the occasion of the Emerson Centenary.

EMERSON, EDWARD WALDO. *Emerson in Concord* (A Memoir Written for the "Social Circle" in Concord, Massachusetts). Boston and New York: Houghton Mifflin, 1889. 266 pages. A volume by Emerson's son which, although marred by sentimentality, is useful for its recollections and its quotations from letters and the *Journals*.

FOERSTER, NORMAN. "Emerson" in *American Criticism*, pp. 52-111. Studies in Literary Theory from Poe to the Present. Boston and New York: Houghton Mifflin, 1928. One of the first efforts to reconstruct and appraise Emerson's esthetic, or theory of expression, with emphasis on his organicism, his doctrine of inspiration, and his debt to the Greeks, especially to Plato. The author finds his central deficiency, at once damaging to his creative work and his criticism, to be in his having had neither passions nor appetites. "He passed at one step from the life of the sense to the life of the spirit, virtually omitting that vast intervening realm of the human emotions which is the main content of ordinary life and literature."

GONNAUD, MAURICE. *Individu et Société dans l'Oeuvre de Ralph Waldo Emerson (Essai de biographie spirituelle)*. Paris: Didier, 1964. 539 pages. A long, detailed, and fully documented study to illustrate the thesis that in his early days Emerson was largely a conforming member of society, that from the time of his resignation of his pulpit until 1840 he was largely a nonconformist solitary from it, and that from 1840 on—most notably during the Civil War, although with effects that were regrettable—he was again in society, affirming its institutions. In his middle period he was an apostle of "spiritual egalitarianism" or "ideal democracy"; after his cyclical return he was an exponent of "natural aristocracy." The author has been much influenced by Whicher's *Freedom and Fate*.—With a long and admirable bibliography.

GREGG, EDITH W. (ed.). *Our First Love. The Letters of Ellen Louisa Tucker to Ralph Waldo Emerson*. Cambridge: Harvard University Press, 1962. A slight but poignant volume which reveals much about Emerson as a young man through the character of the girl who became his first wife and through the special quality of her affection for him.

HOLMES, OLIVER WENDELL. *Ralph Waldo Emerson* (American Men of Letters), Boston: Houghton-Mifflin, 1886. An eminently readable, often perceptive early biography in which Emerson's mature view of life is characterized as soft determinism and his nature as that of a gentle iconoclast, at whom it was impossible to take offense.

HOPKINS, VIVIAN C. *Spires of Form*. Cambridge: Harvard University Press, 1951. 276 pages. The most thorough study so far of Emerson's esthetic theory, considering in detail his ideas on the creative process, the work of art, and the esthetic experience of the work of art, and relating literature to the visual arts of architecture, painting, and sculpture. With an informative Introduction on the background of Emerson's theory and a final chapter on its significance for contemporary times.

IVES, CHARLES. *Essays Before a Sonata & Other Writings*. New York: W. W. Norton, 1961, 1962. Contains an essay in which the famous composer of the Concord Sonata emphasizes "the spiritual hopefulness in his humility" as the distinguishing trait in Emerson's character.

JAMES, HENRY. "Emerson" (33 pages) in *Partial Portraits*. London

and New York: Macmillan Co., 1888. A fine recollective study
of Emerson as concerned in one way or another with "the special
capacity for moral experience—always that and only that." In his
lectures, in which he made the esoteric audible and treated the
many as the few rather than the few as the many, Emerson never
achieved his form or his style, but in spite of that, because of the
beauty of his utterance seems destined to live.

JUGAKU, BUNSHO. *A Bibliography of Ralph Waldo Emerson in Japan
from 1878 to 1935.* Kyoto: Sunward Press, 1947. 70 pages. The
compiler of this informative volume was of the opinion that
Emerson was "more Oriental in his thinking than most of the
Orientals," yet praised him for demonstrating with his example
that although a thinker may again and again attack the chief
problems of life from widely divergent points of view, he need
not, in spite of contradictions, lose his own identity or sacrifice
his idiosyncratic point of view; Emerson was not really abstract but
concrete, and he loved life, not Nirvana.

KONVITZ, MILTON, AND WHICHER, STEPHEN (eds.). *Emerson.* Englewood Cliffs, N.J.: Prentice-Hall, Inc., 1962. 184 pages. A valuable
collection of essays which reflect the diversity of critical approaches to Emerson over the past seventy years, roughly since
the beginning of the century. An informative brief preface touches
on the salient features which distinguish the approaches from one
another; and a very good introduction discusses Emerson in
relation to today, as a humanist thinker who believed in man,
able to affirm his potential for nobility without blinking his
tendency toward weakness and evil.

MAETERLINCK, MAURICE. *On Emerson and Other Essays.* New York:
Dodd, Mead & Co., 1920. The first essay in this volume, originally
published in 1911 as the preface to a French edition of seven
essays of Emerson, discloses the singular attraction of an American
mystic to another of a different stamp, equally, however, a vene-
rator of intimation and intuition. "Emerson has come to affirm
simply this equal and silent grandeur of our life. He has encom-
passed us with silence and with wonder." "He is nearer than any
other to our common life," invaluable as "the sage of commonplace
days," which are the human lot.

MATTHIESSEN, F. O. *American Renaissance. Art and Expression in the
Age of Emerson and Whitman.* London, Toronto, and New York:
Oxford University Press, 1941. 678 pages. A splendid, epochal
work examining in rich detail and with admirable critical acumen
"the conceptions held by five of our major writers concerning the
function and nature of literature, and the degree to which their
practices bore out their theories," the theories, however, closely

related to the concern all five had for the destiny of our country. Emerson is considered as germinal; Thoreau and Whitman as positively deriving from him and extending his thought, Hawthorne and Melville as benefiting in negative reaction from exposure to his genius. Emerson's problem is defined as the same in art as in philosophy—"how to reconcile the individual with society, how to join sentences into a paragraph." With Henry James, Matthiessen believes he never succeeded in finding his form; his tendency to abstraction finally made of his prose hardly more than deliquescence.

————. *The James Family.* New York: Alfred A. Knopf, 1945. Fine and illuminating observations here and there about Emerson by the several Jameses, who knew and loved him.

MEAD, EDWIN D. *The Influence of Emerson.* Boston: American Unitarian Association, 1903. 304 pages. A preachily laudatory book which, in spite of its general lack of discrimination, contains informative chapters on Emerson and Theodore Parker, and Emerson and Carlyle.

METZGER, CHARLES R. *Emerson and Greenough. Transcendental Pioneers of an American Aesthetic.* Berkeley: University of California Press, 1954. Valuable book showing the kinship between Emerson's thought about art and that of the organicist Horatio Greenough, sculptor and architectural theorist, who had his own triad, of Beauty (the promise of function), Action (the presence of function), and Character (the record of function).

MICHAUD, RÉGIS. *Emerson the Enraptured Yankee.* Translated by George Boas. New York: Harper & Brothers, 1930. 444 pages. A spiritual biography, written in the impressionistic style in vogue forty-five years ago, but useful in showing the special way in which Emerson was a Romantic, intent on fusing the universe thought with the universe lived, and also in which he was a representative American, seeking to reconcile quality and quantity, individualism and democracy.

NICOLOFF, PHILIP L. *Emerson on Race and History. An Examination of English Traits.* New York: Columbia University Press, 1961. 315 pages. Revealing that after his second trip to England Emerson read and thought more about science and, as a consequence, turned "for spiritual insight from his somewhat static idealism to man's historical record," this work traces the growth of his cyclical view of human history and his deterministic idea of race. Without abandoning his earlier views, the author shows, Emerson moved from a belief "in individual liberty to an emphasis upon corporate destiny." A concluding chapter relates Emerson's evolutionary optimism to the teleological beliefs of some twentieth-century thinkers.

PARKER, THEODORE. "Emerson" in *The American Scholar* G. Willis Cooke ed., Boston: American Unitarian Association, 1907. pp. 54-125 (the essay which appeared originally in 1850 in *The Massachusetts Quarterly Review*). A fine appraisal by an admirer and colleague, unlike in mind, which emphasizes the singular originality which was the flower of Emerson's eclecticism and describes the essence of his mission as giving "man to mankind and mankind to the laws of God."

PAUL, SHERMAN. *Emerson's Angle of Vision (Man and Nature in American Experience)*. Cambridge: Harvard University Press, 1952. 268 pages. A work which subtly investigates the spiritual qualities of Emerson's view of the world. Rejecting the linear vision of the natural sciences, Emerson, through his need of seeing vertically, developed a circular vision, whose perpetually widening orbits more fully enveloped reality. Stressing Emerson's habit of seeing correspondentially, the author examines the relations between his thought and that of such figures as Plato, Swedenborg, Hume, and Coleridge.

PERRY, BLISS. *Emerson Today*. Princeton, N.J.: Princeton University Press: 1931. A humane, eminently readable little volume in which Emerson, the man as well as the thinker, is seen steadily and whole and especially recommended to the twentieth century for his embodiment of being.

RUSK, RALPH L. *The Life of Ralph Waldo Emerson*. New York: Charles Scribner's Sons, 1949. 592 pages. The definitive biography to date, with abundant information, sensitively chosen, to reveal Emerson as a human being—husband, father, and friend—as well as thinker and writer. Admirable in its coverage and its aim to let its subject speak for himself.

SANBORN, F. B. *The Personality of Emerson*. Boston: Charles E. Goodspeed, 1903. Interesting recollections by another who as a youth came under the influence of Emerson in his prime.

SOWDER, WILLIAM J. *Emerson's Impact on the British Isles and Canada*. Charlottesville, Virginia: The University Press of Virginia, 1966. 240 pages. A commendably comprehensive and explicit book on the consideration of Emerson between 1840 and 1903 by English periodicals, showing that in that time he received more attention by periodical writers than did any other American author. Emerson's poetry seems not at all to have been respected, because of its eccentric prosody, and in his prose he became stylistically acceptable only with the appearance of *English Traits*. Too often well regarded as a person rather than a thinker, in his philosophy he remained largely unintelligible and vexatious until the last two decades of the century, when some of the best critical minds addressed themselves admiringly to his work and revealed its substance to the public.

WHICHER, STEPHEN E. *Freedom and Fate. An Inner Life of Ralph Waldo Emerson.* Philadelphia: University of Pennsylvania Press, 1953. 203 pages. A volume which, exploring the alternating susceptibility of Emerson's mind to the ideas of determinism and freedom, shows that the decade of the 1830's, after a nadir of self-disparagement and acceptance of fate at its commencement, was marked by an ascendancy of jubilant belief in free will, which in turn was succeeded during the rest of his life by an extraordinary accommodation of the two contrary principles to one another. A germinal work, revealing the erroneousness of the notion that Emerson had no relation to a tragic sense of life, it may be said to have inaugurated a new era of Emerson criticism.

WOODBERRY, GEORGE EDWARD. *Ralph Waldo Emerson.* London and New York: Macmillan, 1907. A biographical volume written for the English Men of Letters Series, notable for its literary quality, its economy, and its dispassionate examination and assessment of its subject. Admirable in the fullness and coherence of its elucidation of Emerson's thought, divided for convenience's sake into Central Ideas, Primary Counsels, and Prudential Wisdom; the systematic reconstruction of Emerson's metaphysic is very valuable.

YOUNG, CHARLES LOWELL. *Emerson's Montaigne.* New York: Macmillan, 1941. 236 pages. A study of Emerson's interpretation of Montaigne which shows that central to his admiration was his discovery that the great Frenchman had believed in a "morality . . . not alien to human nature, not imposed upon it from without but consubstantial with it: natural, rational, and something more than either nature or reason."

Index

255

A5